D0765349

International Human Rights
and Authoritarian Rule
in Chile

Human Rights in International Perspective Volume 6

Series Editor

David P. Forsythe
University of
Nebraska-Lincoln

Advisory Editorial Board

Peter Baehr
University of Utrecht

Kevin Boyle
University of Essex

Jack Donnelly
University of Denver

Virginia Leary
State University of
New York-Buffalo

Laurie Wiseberg
University of Ottawa

DARREN G. HAWKINS

International Human Rights
and Authoritarian Rule
in Chile

University of Nebraska Press : Lincoln & London

Portions of chapter 3 have been previously published
as "Domestic Responses to International Pressures:
Human Rights in Authoritarian Chile," *European Journal
of International Relations* 3 (December 1997): 403–34.

Library of Congress Cataloging-in-Publication Data
Hawkins, Darren G., 1966–
International human rights and authoritarian rule in
Chile / Darren G. Hawkins.
p.   cm. – (Human rights in international perspective ; v.6)
Includes bibliographical references and index.
ISBN 0-8032-2404-4 (cloth : alkaline paper)
1. Human rights – Chile – History – 20th century.
2. Chile – Politics and government – 1973–1988.
3. Authoritarianism – Chile – History – 20th century.
4. Democratization – Chile – History – 20th
century. 5. Public opinion – Chile. I. Title. II. Series.
JC599.C5 H38 2002 323'.0983'09047–dc21 2001044597

"N"

To Ellen

Contents

Tables

Acknowledgments

Like many authors, I suppose, after having written and rewritten so much, I find myself strangely at a loss for words in thanking others for their help. It is not that their help is undeserving of my thanks; in fact, it is quite the opposite: my words are undeserving of their help. Yet words, and the meanings behind them, are all I have. In this book, I argue that words can change the world; I hope they can also convey my gratitude.

Some of my largest debts are to those who facilitated my research in Chile, in particular the many Chileans who each generously offered as much as seven hours of their time to discuss the military government with me. This research simply would not have been possible without them. Of equal importance, I gratefully acknowledge the help of the librarians at the Chilean Library of Congress and the National Library in Santiago; faculty and staff at the University of Chile, the Catholic University, and University Finis Terrae; and the archivists and staff at the Jaime Guzmán Foundation.

In the academic community, Kathryn Sikkink has often served as an intellectual guide and at times a personal mentor. Her ideas and arguments consistently stimulate my thinking and provide the intellectual framework for my efforts. My dissertation committee and other advisors at the University of Wisconsin played a crucial role in this project. Emanuel Adler, Leigh Payne, Michael Barnett, Rob McCalla, and Barbara Stallings deserve special thanks for the many hours they spent with me. Leigh and Michael in particular have been involved in this project from its beginnings in spring 1992 until its end and have always provided excellent and timely advice, encouragement, and constructive criticism. Among graduate student colleagues, two of them — Jutta Joachim and Michael Barletta — deserve particular mention for commenting on draft chapters and for providing constant encouragement. I also thank my peers in the MacArthur dissertator group and in our informal "constructivist group" at Wisconsin for offering valuable insights that never failed to hit the mark.

Since then, a wide variety of individuals have commented on previous versions of individual chapters and closely related work. They include Kathryn Sikkink, Jim Riker, Dan Thomas, Peter Liberman, Matt Marostica, Dan Nielson, Scott Cooper, Jay Goodliffe, Donna Lee Bowen, and Andrew Cortell. My work has also benefited from presentation to my classes, and I appreciate students who have provided comments and ideas. Additionally, I have received helpful research and editorial assistance on this project from Jon Theobald, Josh Lloyd, Jeremy Smith, Rachel Kirkland, Suvi Hynynen, and Steven Bitner. The reviewers for the University of Nebraska Press, including the series editor, David Forsythe, provided valuable feedback that undoubtedly improved the book.

Previous drafts of various chapters of this book have been presented at conferences sponsored by the American Political Science Association and the International Studies Association, and I thank the discussants and others who pushed me to sharpen the arguments and evidence. Nor should I neglect the many times I interviewed for a position at a university and presented a piece of this research. These presentations undoubtedly improved the quality of my work, to the extent that I was capable of learning.

The John D. and Catherine T. MacArthur Foundation through the Global Studies Research Program at the University of Wisconsin-Madison provided most of the research funding for this book. Once upon a time, the Latin American and Iberian Studies Program at Madison provided a predissertation grant that played a key role in launching this project. I also thank the graduate school at Wisconsin for a small but important travel grant to aid the research. Dartmouth College, Tulane University, the Danish Center for Human Rights and Brigham Young University have all provided hospitable institutional homes in which to update my research and write this book.

Finally, I would find it impossible to write a work of this scope without a network of personal support. Though all have touched my life in important ways, a few deserve special mention. While in Chile, Peter and Holly Prina and Christian and Vanessa Droguette consistently offered their friendship and aid. Mark and Judy Garff, my parents-in-law, always stood by my side. We were saddened at Mark's death during an earlier stage of the research, but I take comfort in his unshakable belief in me and my work. My own parents, Greg and Larene Hawkins, have given me never-failing love, the greatest gift possible. Their encouragement, support, aid, and guidance have always enabled me to push on. Most importantly, I depend deeply on my wife, Ellen, and my children, Adrienne, Samantha, Nathan, and Leah, to bring balance and perspective to my academic work. They provide unending diversions, constantly reminding me that my research is hardly my most important task in life. At the same time, they renew my energy, stimulate my curiosity, and provide the change of pace necessary to go back for another day of work.

International Human Rights
and Authoritarian Rule
in Chile

Introduction

Though once confined largely to the domestic realm, during the past thirty years the politics of human rights have become increasingly internationalized and transnationalized.[1] Since the early 1970s, states have signed and ratified an ever-growing number of human rights conventions, more carefully monitored a variety of abuses, and even intermittently penalized some of the worst violators. Intergovernmental organizations have adopted new methods of investigation and reporting and have expanded the array of abuses they track. Nongovernmental organizations dedicated to human rights have experienced explosive growth and have mobilized campaigns on behalf of the oppressed all over the world. As a result, domestic groups and individuals suffering repression now routinely seek political, moral, and financial support from international patrons and provide the international community with crucial information on the nature of repression.

These activities were not always commonplace, and, in fact, many were quite unthinkable before the 1970s. Progress, in the sense that more human rights norms exist and that more global actors promote those norms, seems undeniable.[2] Yet skeptics rightly ask whether it all matters. Do authoritarian governments respond positively to human rights pressures, or do they simply harden their stance and withdraw further into their repressive darkness? Do they care if they are condemned and sanctioned? Do all authoritarian governments respond in similar ways? Under what conditions do they respond, and how and why do they respond?

These questions get to the heart of theoretical debates in international relations about the relative importance of norms in shaping state behavior, the role of nonstate actors in world politics, and the origins of state preferences. If the accepted norms are essentially meaningless unless backed up by state power, then we should rarely expect authoritarian governments to respond to human rights pressures in a positive way.[3] There are few cases, save the celebrated ones like Kosovo, where important states have exerted substantial power to promote human rights in other countries. More often, human rights pressures center on intangible moral condemnation, backed up only occasionally by limited uses of economic and military power. However, if state preferences and practices change through social interaction – as constructivists argue – then we should expect authoritarian governments to alter their repressive practices as other states incorporate human rights concerns into their foreign policies.[4] Finally, liberal theorists in international relations adopt the position held by many comparativists when they argue that domestic politics shape state preferences.[5] If this is the case, then the extent of international pressure – whether tangible or intangible – matters less than the nature of the domestic social and political groups in the targeted state. In this view, different states react differently to human rights pressures in predictable ways related to domestic political and social structures.

Overview of Authoritarian Chile

I address the above-mentioned questions and debates by examining the case of human rights pressures on authoritarian Chile from 1973 to 1990. The Chilean military seized power in a 1973 coup and quickly gained a worldwide reputation for establishing a particularly brutal, bloodthirsty government. This notoriety was no small distinction in an age when authoritarian governments ruled Latin America and routinely terrorized their populations by murdering, torturing, exiling, and imprisoning tens of thousands of people. In many respects, the fame was well-deserved. Although the numbers are still disputed, most estimates put the death toll at three thousand or more during the years after the coup. Disappearances, in which the victim's body is never found and the victim's family lives in the endless terror of false hope, probably account for a third of this total. Several thousand Chileans were brutally tortured, while tens of thousands more were exiled or imprisoned for months and years without a trial. Additionally, the military government closed down all opposition media; disbanded political, labor, and social organizations; imposed a state of siege and a curfew; and tried civilian opponents under the harsh conditions of military courts. All of this took place in a country that proudly proclaimed a nearly century-old tradition of democracy and respect for human rights. The Chilean coup and subsequent terror were as unexpected and as shocking as they would be in almost any well-established democracy.

Given this early record, the government's later efforts to proclaim loyalty to human rights norms and to ease some forms of repression were equally unexpected and surprising. Chile's new military rulers rapidly found themselves forced to deal with human rights concerns, though few issues were further from their minds when they first seized power. Widespread international criticism surprised and angered them and at first motivated them only to launch international public relations blitzes. In late 1975, however, government officials began to adopt the discourse of human rights and claim that they, too, believed in these principles. How and why did this change occur?

Then, after four years of rule by terror, in August 1977, government officials rather suddenly reorganized the security apparatus that had carried out much of the most violent repression, thereby putting an end to most political murders and disappearances. Why?

In 1980 the government approved a constitution that set time limits on military rule and promised future democratic institutions. Previously, the government had insisted that it would never establish timetables for an end to its own power. Again, why did these changes occur?

In the 1980s, government officials created conditions that facilitated a basically fair presidential plebiscite, in sharp contrast with two previous plebiscites. President Augusto Pinochet unexpectedly lost the October 1988 vote and was thereby forced from office in 1990. Why did the government allow a fair plebiscite to occur for the first time in its fifteen-year history – an action that led directly to its demise? Taken together, these stop-and-go efforts to adopt the discourse of human rights and to ease some forms of repression constitute the central empirical puzzles to be examined in this book.

In global historical perspective, Chile marks a crucial case in the development of transnational human rights activities and state pressures on abusive governments. While international human rights norms were developed on paper from the 1940s to the 1960s, the 1973 Chilean military coup triggered one of the first and most extensive efforts to translate those norms into practice. International reaction to the Chilean coup and subsequent human rights abuses was unexpectedly swift, strong, and widespread from the outset. Rarely, if ever before, in world history had so many international actors reacted so strongly to human rights abuses. The reactions mushroomed into what was probably the largest international campaign against state repression in the

1970s, one that foreshadowed the massive effort against South Africa in the 1980s.

Before the early 1970s, the United Nations addressed repression in a country only when domestic human rights abuses threatened international peace and security.[6] In the 1950s, for example, the UN General Assembly justified its condemnations of apartheid in South Africa on the grounds that it posed a danger to regional peace. The Chilean case was the first instance in which this precedent was broken. UN General Assembly resolutions condemning the military government – which began in 1974 and continued for fourteen years – made no reference to threats to regional peace.[7] Chile was one of the first countries sanctioned by the United States for human rights abuses and one of the first countries to be targeted by newly formed transnational and domestic human rights groups in Western states. Along with South Africa, Israel, and Taiwan, Chile was one of the most politically isolated countries of the 1970s and 1980s.[8]

Throughout this period, states and human rights groups pioneered activities that are now standard practice, including monitoring, condemning and sanctioning authoritarian governments, and building transnational ties to domestic opposition groups. International efforts to prosecute Pinochet continued to set precedents for international human rights issues into the late 1990s and confirmed Chile's status as a historically crucial human rights case. For nearly thirty years, then, Chile has been an important case for the strength of human rights norms and actors who support them, and a detailed examination of the case promises important insights into the international politics of human rights.

A Sketch of the Theoretical Arguments

I make two key sets of arguments in this book. First, many, though decidedly not all, authoritarian governments have a stronger interest in legitimacy than most analysts realize. Such governments care about their legitimacy not only within domestic society – as some comparativist scholars have long argued – but also among their fellow states in the international arena. Strong human rights pressures threaten the legitimacy of authoritarian governments and are likely to prompt strategic government responses. Those responses can include, in order of increasing significance, discussing human rights issues as an agenda item, adopting the discourse of human rights, altering repressive policies, building new political institutions that blend liberal and authoritarian features, and facilitating widespread changes in the nature of the political system. These changes do not always improve the actual enjoyment of human rights, especially in the short term, because they may simply trade one form of repression for another or involve promises that the government never lives up to. Still, changes can alter the political landscape in important, and often unintended, ways and can contribute to the long-term enjoyment of human rights.

As is standard practice in many analyses, I use the concept of legitimacy to refer to widespread normative approval of a given set of political institutions. The most common approach in the literature is to theorize about the implications of high or low levels of legitimacy, to try to discern if a given government or institution has much legitimacy, and to draw causal connections between actual legitimacy and government behavior.[9] In contrast, I examine legitimacy from the perspective of government interests; that is, whether governments care about their legitimacy and whether they alter their discourse or behavior to improve their legitimacy. In this perspective, the government's actual legitimacy (to the extent that this is measurable) is less important than the strategic interaction between opponents attempting to undermine the government's normative support and the government's own efforts to improve its normative approval. I argue that human rights groups and their allies are capable of seriously threatening government legitimacy, that many authoritarian governments develop strong interests in protecting their legitimacy, and that governments seek legitimacy both within domestic society and among international peers.

Since the 1970s, human rights norms have become an important measure of government legitimacy. Human rights groups – often joined by other nonstate actors and sometimes joined by states – contest the legitimacy of authoritarian governments by demonstrating that they fail to conform to human rights norms. These transnational advocacy networks and their state allies employ a wide range of methods, from verbal condemnations and publicity campaigns to formal votes and economic sanctions.[10] Such efforts may be conceptualized broadly as human rights pressures. As a point of departure, then, I hypothesize that the stronger the human rights pressures on an authoritarian government, the more likely it will defend its legitimacy by altering its discourse and behavior in ways that appear to conform more closely with human rights norms. Although it is straightforward, this hypothesis is not obviously true and in fact is patently false in some cases; for example, Cuba and Iraq.

The second set of arguments therefore lays out the conditions within which the first hypothesis is likely to be true. I identify four domestic-level variables that influence government response to human rights pressures. The first variable, domestic structure, refers to the structure of the state and social institutions and the relationship between them. Following Risse-Kappen, the role of domestic structure can be conceptualized in two stages: access to policymakers and policy implementation.[11] To simplify the argument, I suggest that decentralized states with vibrant civil societies are more accessible to transnational networks, but the extent of policy change in such fractured polities is likely to be low. At the same time, transnational networks have a more difficult time accessing elites in authoritarian states, but if they do gain access the extent of change is likely to be higher. The second domestic variable is normative fit; that is, the congruence between international norms and widespread domestic beliefs and understandings.[12] Where international human rights norms resonate with domestic cultural understandings, states are more likely to respond to human rights pressures. The third factor is the presence of economic or security crisis. I argue that states facing relatively minor security and economic problems are more responsive to human rights pressures than those that face serious crises. This argument runs counter to the conventional wisdom in international relations, which holds that crises facilitate network influence and beneficial policy change.[13] Fourth, rule-oriented actors inside the targeted government increase the likelihood that human rights pressure will produce policy changes. This hypothesis offers a variation on traditional arguments about the importance of "softline" factions inside authoritarian regimes and suggests a theoretical logic explaining why some pro-authoritarian officials would be responsive to human rights pressures.[14]

The arguments advanced in this book draw eclectically on elements of various theoretical approaches to expand our understanding of how, why, and under what conditions international norms matter. For realists, norms matter when enforced by the actions of powerful states; for neoliberal institutionalists, they matter when they help resolve coordination problems. Constructivists argue that norms matter when promoted by international organizations and states through processes of social interaction. Finally, liberals argue that domestic groups with political clout must support international norms before they can influence state behavior.

I posit a fifth possibility: that norms matter when states and nonstate actors pressure noncompliant states to conform and certain domestic characteristics lead targeted states to become concerned about their legitimacy. This argument draws on the constructivist insight that states exist in normative environments, the liberal view that domestic politics shape state preferences, and the rationalist argument that states pursue strategic interests. I do not pretend that this argument represents a synthesis of these theoretical approaches or that it replaces them in any way. I do claim, however, that it represents one way of building bridges between them by drawing specific elements from each and combining them in ways that expand our understandings of the processes of change in international relations.

Rather than displacing realist and neoliberal-institutionalist hypotheses about the role of norms, my own analysis highlights their limitations and suggests alternative paths of influence that traditional approaches miss. It is fairly easy to think of examples where states adhere to international norms because of power differentials (for example, the spread of free trade policies to developing countries) or because they help resolve coordination problems (as in the spread of free trade among relative equals in the European Union). Yet many modern international norms are not consistently enforced by powerful states and do not clearly resolve coordination problems. These include not only human rights norms, but also many norms relating to women, children, environmental policies, some types of arms control, efforts to punish crimes against humanity, some rules of war, the holding of democratic national elections, and the structure and function of state bureaucracies. Questions about why some states adhere to unenforced, nonfunctional norms require alternative theories such as the one developed here.

8

Methodology

To establish causal links between human rights pressures and government responses, I utilize process-tracing methodology.[15] The Chilean case provides an ideal setting in which to probe the plausibility of arguments that human rights pressures affect authoritarian governments.[16] From the time they seized power in 1973, Chilean military officials were repeatedly forced to deal with human rights issues. Over time, they attempted a variety of responses, allowing analysts a valuable opportunity to trace the correlation between changing pressures and changing behavior. This variation over time increases the number of observations available to scholars searching for an understanding of the conditions within which human rights pressures matter.[17] I proceed by documenting human rights pressures and their limitations, by examining the details of government decision making and the motivations and perceptions of key government actors, and by analyzing government discourse and behavior. If human rights pressures matter, they should be systematically linked in internal government decision making to domestic policy decisions and, ultimately, to government discourse and behavior. The 1990 return of democratic rule in Chile allows an opportunity for scholars to employ process tracing by interviewing former government officials and by accessing some of the government's own records.

Evidence used in this book draws on four types of primary source data found in a variety of libraries and archives in Chile and the United States. First, U.S. and Chilean press reports and the reports of human rights groups, including intergovernmental organizations, were useful in chronicling the repressive behavior of the military government and the corresponding human rights pressures on Chile. Second, I used the public documents and pronouncements of the military government. These included published legislation and draft versions of the legislation; documents, books and memoirs published by the military government or its officials; and the public interviews and speeches of high-level officials.

Third, I conducted interviews with forty-one Chileans, which ranged in time from one hour to more than three hours each, and sometimes occurred in two or even three different sessions. My interview list included former junta members, cabinet ministers, top legal advisors, military officials who headed the security forces, lower-level government officials, political party leaders, journalists, human rights law-yers, and businesspeople, among others. To promote frank discussion and to discourage grandstanding, I promised anonymity to former government officials and their close associates. Although the authoritarian government is an increasingly distant memory, all officials preferred anonymity, in part because military norms of loyalty would otherwise prohibit frank discussion, especially to an outsider, and in part because human rights issues are still very much a politically sensitive topic – as the Pinochet case demonstrates. To more completely capture their responses and to supplement my written notes, I used a tape recorder. In several cases, interviewees requested I turn it off at sensitive points in the interview, and I, of course, obliged.

The final and perhaps most important type of evidence consists of formerly secret military government documents located in public libraries and private archives in Santiago. I carefully reviewed and analyzed the complete set of detailed, transcribed records from the junta's meetings during seventeen years of rule (1973-90). The junta served as the government's supreme legislative body and repeatedly made key decisions, enacted important legislation, and provided the setting for crucial political battles. Of an estimated twenty-five thousand pages of transcripts, I focused on roughly a thousand pages that dealt directly with the topics of human rights and repression. Other formerly secret documents analyzed in this study include the memos passed among the junta's legislative subcommittees, the transcribed minutes of other government bodies, including the Council of State and the Constitutional Commission, and the personal documents of Jaime Guzmán, a key civilian legal advisor to the Pinochet government during most of the 1970s and 1980s. Guzmán was gunned down by terrorists in 1991, leaving behind a number of memos, copies of draft speeches and legislation, and political analyses that he had prepared for the military government. Taken together, these documents provide the best possible source of evidence on the internal workings of the military government.

Overview of the Book

Although much of this book involves a detailed look at politics within Chile's authoritarian government, its point of departure is international relations theories about the ways in which international norms can influence states. It is an explicit attempt to bridge the divide between comparative politics and international relations by using methodologies more closely associated with comparative politics (interviews, archival work, and field research generally) to carefully trace the domestic impacts of international actions. The task is complicated by the diversity of audiences that are addressed, but current theoretical approaches require sustained efforts to build bridges to other methodologies and subfields. In chapter 1, I develop the theoretical arguments outlined above and discuss the type of evidence needed to show that states do or do not respond to human rights pressures to conform with international norms.

In chapters 2 through 5, I examine the evolution of authoritarian rule in Chile and the government's struggle for legitimacy. A vigorous human rights network formed quickly in the wake of the Chilean coup, as discussed in chapter 2. Network groups plus state pressures combined to place human rights issues on the new government's agenda. Chilean officials demonstrated a significant concern for the government's international legitimacy during this first stage, but refused to make any changes in their repressive practices or even to pay much lip service to human rights norms. Rather, they preferred to launch international publicity campaigns in which they tried to convince Western states that Chile had been nearly overrun by Marxism, that repression was a necessary response, and that the tales of extreme abuse were the fabrication of an international Marxist campaign. Chile's domestic situation during this period blunted human rights pressures, although moderate levels of normative fit ensured that repressive practices would gain an important place on the government's agenda.

Despite the government's best efforts, the human rights network continued to grow throughout 1976–77 and gained the strong support of the United States, which placed important diplomatic pressures and limited sanctions on Chile. In response, the government finally adopted the discourse of human rights, pledging its commitment, in words, to human rights norms – though with some important limitations. Then, in August 1977, the government rather suddenly disbanded its most important security apparatus, the Directorate of National Intelligence (Dirección Nacional de Inteligencia – DINA) and replaced it with the renamed and slightly restructured National Information Center (Central Nacional de Informaciones – CNI). While at first it appeared that military officials were practicing cosmetic surgery, it later became clear that the change in repressive strategy ran deeper. After 1977 the government ceased its systematic practice of disappearances and engaged in less open violence. Further, the DINA chiefs who had wielded enormous power from 1973 to 1977 were removed from office and then dropped quickly from sight. The government's adoption of human rights discourse and the limited but important changes in repressive practices form the subject matter of chapter 4.

To explain how human rights pressures caused a change in government words and in some deeds, I focus on the ways in which the rise of a rule-oriented faction, in conjunction with moderate levels of normative fit and decreasing economic and security threats, combined to produce a growing concern with the government's legitimacy. Civilian advisors and their allies utilized international opposition to convince Pinochet and the junta that the time had arrived to legitimize the government. At the same time, declining crisis levels suggested less "need" for repression and allowed the government more room to concern itself with legitimacy problems. As a result, government officials soon came to view high levels of repression as a liability rather than an asset. The combination of human rights pressures and a growing rule-oriented faction put an end to the DINA in mid-1977.

This argument lays the groundwork for an analysis of the government's institutionalization in chapter 4. After years of insisting that the government would maintain power indefinitely, in 1977 Pinochet announced a timetable for the end of military rule. Although the government later ignored this timeline, it also decided to finish work on a constitution that had been languishing in study committees virtually since the day of the coup. When finally approved in a flawed national plebiscite in 1980, the constitution contained a variety of human rights guarantees and promises of more democratic institutions, but delayed their implementation until at least 1989. Even these moderate bows to democracy were too strong for government hardliners, who argued it was too soon to set limits to military rule and who favored more authoritarian long-term political institutions. As it turned out, the constitution opened small opportunities for opposition groups, who eventually seized them in 1988 to usher in a transition to democracy.

Why did the military government develop a new constitution from

1978 to 1980, and what determined its content? Continuing challenges to the government's legitimacy required that Chile's leaders address human rights issues if they wished to ensure the government's long-term survival and to shape Chile's future political institutions. Rule-oriented actors utilized continuing human rights pressures to convince Pinochet and the junta to adopt a new constitution that would pay lip service to human rights in the short run and set up "protected" democratic political institutions in the long run. The domestic resonance of international human rights norms helped convince military officials that indefinite military rule and completely authoritarian political institutions would be rejected in Chile. Economic recovery and the receding memory of the coup increased the government's willingness to pay attention to its long-term legitimacy.

Finally, as the 1980s progressed, the government made a series of decisions ensuring that a comparatively fair plebiscite on Pinochet's rule would occur in October 1988. First, government-appointed officials on the Constitutional Tribunal unexpectedly reversed the government's decision not to have an independent electoral tribunal in place in time for the plebiscite. Second, the government rarely used state-of-siege provisions (as compared with Pinochet's desires to use them extensively) and lifted state-of-emergency provisions before the plebiscite. Likewise, government officials offered small concessions to opposition groups, such as limited television time for campaign ads to foster the appearance of free speech. Third, the government defied opposition expectations by failing to call the plebiscite on short notice or to hold it earlier than expected.

Chapter 5 offers an explanation for these events that focuses on the government's desire to legitimize its constitution and its political and economic program. Contrary to the hopes of the rule-oriented faction, the 1980 Constitution did not resolve the military government's problems with legitimacy. In fact, these problems became more severe and widespread in the 1980s. Human rights groups and many Western states (though not the United States from 1981 to 1984) continued to criticize the government's repression. More important, a variety of domestic opposition groups, which reemerged in the wake of the economic crash of 1982–83, took up the human rights cause. Although the economic crisis diverted the government's attention from normative human rights critiques, it ultimately increased the salience of domestic human rights norms. Once the economic crisis passed, intensive domestic and international criticisms of ongoing government repression in the mid-1980s led the government to prioritize its quest for legitimacy as a crucial interest. Thus, when the time came for a constitutionally mandated plebiscite in 1988, government officials grudgingly established and enforced fair electoral procedures. Although they did not intend it, the plebiscite put an end to Pinochet's rule. Government officials sought legitimacy to such an extent that they paradoxically sacrificed their control of the government to obtain it. They essentially gambled short-term government power for the long-term interest of laying down the political and economic rules that would govern Chile in the future. This decision was the result of strong human rights pressures, high levels of normative fit, and the absence of a serious crisis.

Chapter 6 provides the conclusion to this book and probes other cases of human rights pressures and government responses in South Africa and Cuba. The Cuban case demonstrates that strong human rights pressures matter little if domestic conditions block those pressures, while the South African case confirms that changing domestic factors determine the impact of human rights pressures. Additionally, I analyze the efforts of human rights groups to bring Pinochet to justice in Chile, Spain, and Britain, thereby applying some of the theoretical ideas about human rights pressures and domestic characteristics to democratic governments. I then draw out the policy issues of how international actors may seek to improve the human rights situation within authoritarian governments and summarize the implications of my arguments for broader theoretical debates.

In sum, changes in the Chilean military government's agenda, discourse, behavior, and institutions can be explained by strong human rights pressures, which were mostly normative and intangible, and Chile's shifting domestic characteristics. This analysis does not constitute a radical reinterpretation of Chilean history, but it differs in important ways from previous explanations of government behavior. Although many scholars highlight the government's concern with legitimacy, few emphasize the role of human rights groups or the international dimensions of the threat. Garretón and Varas, for example, view the government's legitimacy problems as a function of time and the result of natural attrition in power.[18] Valenzuela sees government actions as an effort to drape Pinochet's one-man rule in the robes of respectability.[19] Muñoz and Portales emphasize the limitations of international pressures in the government's decision making.[20] While these analyses offer crucial insights, it is impossible to explain the government's changing discourse and behavior without systematic reference to human rights pressures.

Furthermore, scholars have not satisfactorily explained why the Chilean government was so concerned about its legitimacy, while other authoritarian governments were not and are not. In this respect, an analysis of Chile's domestic political situation is crucial. Other scholars have explored the role of softliners, normative traditions, opposition social groups, and economic crisis in Chilean history. None of these factors is a new variable left unanalyzed by Chilean specialists. Yet to explain the influence of human rights pressures in Chile, I weave these old variables together in new ways. In doing so, I hope to achieve a holistic explanation of the government's historical evolution and to provide a theoretical basis for explaining why other governments may or may not be as responsive as Chile. I also seek to evaluate these variables side by side over time in an attempt to evaluate their relative importance. To offer a preview of the conclusions, I find that rule-oriented actors, crisis levels, and normative fit are jointly necessary and sufficient to explain the government's responses to human rights pressures. Domestic structures, on the other hand, add little to the explanation.

ONE

Human Rights Pressures, Legitimacy, and State Responses

International human rights norms and transnational human rights campaigns have been increasingly prominent features of world politics since the late 1960s. States first developed and codified international human rights norms in the two decades following World War II but allowed the norms to languish without monitoring or enforcement. Transnational and domestic nongovernmental organizations (NGOs) and some intergovernmental organizations (IGOs) began using these norms in the late 1960s to monitor state violations, to shame repressive governments, and to draw broad attention to human rights issues. Since the 1970s powerful Western states have intermittently joined transnational human rights campaigns against repressive governments. In the 1980s and 1990s, states expanded and strengthened human rights norms at the same time that human rights groups proliferated.

While scholars have documented the rise of human rights norms and organizations across the globe, we know little about their effects. Do human rights norms and campaigns have any effect on authoritarian governments? How, why, and under what conditions? Cynics might be tempted to dismiss these questions out of hand since human rights groups possess few material resources and authoritarian governments are not known for their attention to normative concerns like human rights. At the same time, the expansion of transnational human rights networks and international norms coincided in the 1980s and 1990s with the global trend away from authoritarian rule, and recent democratization research has drawn causal connections between the two.[1] In addition, theoretical developments in international relations suggest that persuasion and international social interaction – and not just tangible power resources – can alter state behavior in important ways.[2] Given these factors, it would be a mistake to dismiss human rights pressures too quickly.

Human rights norms belong to a broader set of international norms that serve no clear functional purpose and that are rarely enforced by third parties. Previous studies have shown that such norms can influence domestic politics in one of two basic ways: when they are promoted by powerful domestic groups, or when national leaders learn to accept those norms as appropriate behavior. In the first case, transnational or domestic groups utilize institutional access to key decision makers to promote international norms.[3] Human rights groups, for example, have used independent courts in European countries to promote changes in government policy in ways that are more consistent with international norms.[4] In the second case, international organizations "teach" governments how to behave appropriately by articulating new norms and demonstrating that other states abide by those norms.[5] In the absence of clear interests otherwise, government leaders accept these norms as appropriate procedure and alter their behavior accordingly. For example, Finnemore has argued that the International Committee of the Red Cross taught states that enemy wounded soldiers and medical personnel should appropriately be considered noncombatants.

While not denying the importance of these types of influence, I develop an alternative causal path in this chapter. International norms and the actors who support them influence domestic politics by threatening the legitimacy of the government. This causal pathway differs from the first form of influence because transnational and domestic actors promoting the norms never gain meaningful access to decision makers or to influential political institutions. It differs from the second form of influence because government leaders never accept the relevant norms as appropriate. Rather, governments realize that *others* accept them as appropriate and alter their behavior strategically in an attempt to appear to conform with widespread standards. Governments that care about their legitimacy, in other words, respond by altering their agenda, discourse, behavior, and even institutions in ways that better comply (or seem to) with prevailing norms. In this process, small steps toward compliance set precedents and create opportunities for more significant steps later on.

Yet not all governments are equally concerned about their own legitimacy, especially in the international arena. As a result, I develop four domestic-level factors that identify the conditions within which this form of influence is likely to operate. Domestic structure determines the access of human rights activists to policymakers and the extent to which policy changes can be implemented. Normative fit determines whether policymakers will be concerned about an international norm because it resonates among domestic social groups. Crisis, in contrast to the conventional wisdom, blocks positive policy change in human rights issues and instead contributes to escalating abuses. Elite coalitions determine whether policy proposals that are more consistent with international norms will be considered by top decision makers.

This argument shares much in common with recent work on the socialization of international human rights norms into domestic politics. Risse and Sikkink argue that transnational networks trigger changes in domestic policies by pressuring governments to make tactical concessions, by persuading them that civilized states respect human rights, and by implanting human rights norms in domestic institutions in ways that ensure their habitual respect.[6] While not disagreeing that these causal forces are at work, two problems exist with these arguments. First, it is not clear why states care enough about human rights pressures to make tactical concessions. Such pressures are usually relatively feeble, and invoking the language of human rights can be a risky business for governments seeking to hold on to power, as Mikhail Gorbachev and others have discovered. Second, it is evident that not all states are equally open to change, and that change occurs at very different rates in different countries. As I elaborate below, these problems can be resolved by focusing on the politics of legitimacy and on the domestic conditions within which international norms are influential.

Questions about the effects of human rights pressures raise two key theoretical issues in international relations. The first concerns the role of norms and nonstate actors in the international system. Realists, who focus on international anarchy and state power, do not expect human rights norms or nonstate actors to have much of an impact unless enforced by powerful states.[7] Neoliberal institutionalists argue that norms influence behavior when they help states advance their interests by resolving coordination problems with other states.[8] Human rights norms would not be expected to have much impact from this perspective because they do not resolve coordination problems or advance the common interests of states, especially those who rule by repression. Constructivists, in contrast, suggest that both norms and IGOs form part of the social environment in which states interact.[9] Utilizing this logic, states should comply gradually with international human rights norms through learning or socialization processes character-ized by state and nonstate social interaction in the international arena. Finally, domestic liberal theorists suggest that "societal ideas, interests, and institutions influence state behavior by shaping state preferences, that is, the fundamental social purposes underlying the strategic cal-culations of governments."[10] In this view, international human rights norms and transnational human rights groups can influence states, but they first have to be activated in domestic politics before they shape state preferences.[11]

The second theoretical issue has to do with the ways in which states make decisions, a debate characterized as the "rationalist-constructivist divide."[12] The rationalist approach focuses on the "logic of conse-quences," in which states adopt policies and practices that offer the most benefits with the fewest costs to help them achieve their goals. Constructivist approaches champion the "logic of appropriateness," in which states make choices based on the context in which they find themselves by adopting the correct rules of behavior governing that situation. If repressive states follow the logic of consequences, we should expect them to comply with human rights norms only when pressures raise the costs of repression higher than the benefits. If they follow the logic of appropriateness, we should expect repressive states to comply with human rights norms once they become persuaded that the political context requires such behavior. Otherwise, they are likely to abide by more traditional norms, such as respect for sovereignty, to justify and validate repression.

Human Rights Pressures

Global, comprehensive human rights norms first developed in the years following World War II, in response to the atrocities of that war and to the petitions of concerned individuals, groups, and less powerful states.[13] At first, these norms were relatively weak, enumerated only in a United Nations General Assembly resolution rather than in treaty form and simply declared as broad principles without any mention of moni-toring or enforcement. Over time, however, they became stronger, more specific, and more closely tied to efforts at monitoring and enforcement. Two broad human rights covenants – one for civil and political rights and another for social and economic rights – marked the first significant step forward when they were opened for ratification in 1966 and went into force in 1976. Most of the world's states have ratified both treaties, and nearly all states have ratified at least one of them. These treaties were followed in the 1980s and 1990s with a proliferation of issue-specific global and regional conventions focusing on topics such as children's rights, women's equality, torture, and domestic violence. As a result, an increasingly well-defined set of principles exists detailing state responsibilities with respect to individual human dignity.

These norms would mean little, however, if not for the efforts of human rights groups to monitor violations and to shame states into compliance. Both IGOs and NGOs have played instrumental roles in this respect. Intergovernmental human rights bodies like the UN Human Rights Commission and the Inter-American Commission on Human Rights (IACHR) began to monitor and report on violations in the early 1970s.[14] Although these groups function under serious constraints, over time they have expanded the issues of concern and the ways in which they operate. Modern international nongovernmental human rights groups first formed in the years after World War II, achieved wider recognition in the 1970s, and experienced a rapid increase in numbers in the 1980s and 1990s.[15] Many of them have become well-respected, unbiased sources of information and serve as prominent pressure groups in a variety of countries. Finally, domestic NGOs dedicated to human rights issues multiplied quickly in the 1980s, especially in Latin America.[16]

These groups routinely create linkages with their international counterparts, churches and other concerned social groups, philanthropic foundations, and even parts of foreign states to create transnational advocacy networks.[17] Transnational advocacy networks consist of "those relevant actors working internationally on an issue, who are bound together by shared values, a common discourse, and dense exchanges of information and services." The hallmark of these networks is their ability to move information rapidly across the globe in an effort to shame governments into policy changes.

Because networks lack both economic resources and statehood, they attempt to persuade sympathetic states to penalize norm-violating governments. From the 1940s to the 1960s states were quite content to create human rights norms and then ignore violations, often invoking nonintervention and domestic jurisdiction as the primary reason not to become involved. Beginning in the late 1960s, however, some Western European states began to incorporate human rights concerns into their foreign policies.[18] In the 1970s, the U.S. Congress passed a series of laws tying foreign aid and U.S. votes in multilateral banks to human rights in the receiving country.[19] Additionally, Congress required the U.S. State Department to track and report violations in other countries, a process that has produced widely used information and placed important pressures on other states. Even though their efforts are riddled with contradictions and hypocrisy, Western states have become more willing to verbally condemn abusive governments, impose sanctions on them, and fund social groups seeking democratic change abroad.

Human rights pressures, then, may be defined broadly as nonviolent activities carried out by transnational networks and states with the primary purpose of improving individual rights by creating economic and political costs for a repressive government. These activities employ both tangible and intangible resources. Tangibly, human rights pressures usually consist of state-sponsored economic sanctions and the threat of more sanctions. Intangible human rights pressures consist of efforts to shame repressive governments by gathering and distributing information on the nature of repression, and to persuade repressive governments to alter their behavior by pointing out their hypocrisy.[20]

I operationalize human rights pressures by examining the strength and scope of international sanctions, by looking at the efforts of intergovernmental organizations and foreign states to verbally condemn and investigate abusive governments, and by detailing the efforts of domestic and international nongovernmental organizations to publicize abuses and motivate state action. For each of these components, detailed quantitative indicators that can be compared across countries and time are generally unavailable. The only partial exception concerns the strength of sanctions, which has been measured as a percent of gross domestic product in the targeted country in a variety of cases during the twentieth century.[21] Even this measure fails to distinguish the strength of sanctions across time within a single country. As a result, I generally construct ordinal and qualitative measures based on a variety of sources that track the behavior of states and NGOs on human rights issues. Such sources include IGO documents, government documents from different states, newspaper and newsmagazine articles, and secondary sources that have made incomplete inventories of these pressures.

It is important to note that human rights norms play a crucial role in constituting and facilitating the social activities that produce these pressures.[22] Most obviously, norms provide widely accepted standards by which state behavior can be measured and condemned. Where norms already exist, human rights groups do not have to first build a consensus that the behavior is reprehensible – as, for example, the antislavery advocates did. Additionally, human rights norms have moved issues of state repression into the international arena, making it more appropriate and acceptable for foreign actors to bypass objections about sovereignty in order to investigate and sanction abuses in other states. As a result, these norms have altered the pattern of interaction between states. They have forced repressive governments to consider the international costs of domestic repression when just a few decades earlier, the international costs were negligible. Human rights norms also help endow a variety of nonstate international actors with identities and roles. By way of example, norms identify the IACHR as a legitimate judge of government human rights violations. Norms are constitutive here in the sense that there would be no Human Rights Commission without the international norms to assign it an identity and a role. As a result, authoritarian governments in Latin America have often disputed the findings of the IACHR, but have only rarely questioned the ability of the commission to issue findings.[23]

Do human rights pressures have any effect on abusive governments? Admittedly, assessing their impact is fraught with difficulties and is probably best done with historical hindsight. To begin, it is difficult to determine what constitutes a change in government behavior as opposed to mere "window dressing." Authoritarian elites delight in playing games of cat and mouse in which they announce positive changes that subsequently fall far short of expectations. Additionally, the centralized decision making and veil of secrecy surrounding authoritarian governments make it difficult to assess the reasons why they change their discourse and strategies, if changes in fact occur. Finally, the question of the impact of human rights groups falls victim to politically prejudiced responses. Western governments seeking to maintain friendly relations with authoritarian governments are likely to overemphasize the degree of positive change, while government opponents tend to dismiss any changes as so many irrelevant charades.

However, scholars should not simply ignore the potential influence of human rights norms and pressures because of these difficulties. The issue engages central theoretical questions about the relative importance of international norms and power in shaping state behavior and about the nature of international-domestic connections. If only power – defined in terms of tangible military and economic resources – matters, then we should not expect human rights groups to have much of an impact. Most human rights-related pressures are simply not strong enough to make much of a difference to authoritarian governments. But if, on the other hand, governments are also susceptible to challenges to their legitimacy, then we would expect more changes to occur. From a practical perspective, knowledge of how authoritarian governments respond to pressure could enable human rights activists to conduct better campaigns and allow foreign policy experts to make better policy.

Two arguments are commonly advanced against the effectiveness of transnational efforts to improve human rights. First, human rights pressures imposed on authoritarian governments are too feeble to have any impact.[24] Human rights groups within authoritarian states tend to be small, subject to severe repression, and short on resources. Human rights groups in democracies often have access to more resources and can lobby Western states to pressure repressive governments. In many cases, however, states respond with low-profile diplomatic pressures and threats of sanctions that are never implemented. Despite U.S. legislation mandating that economic and military aid be tied to human rights, for example, studies have consistently shown that the regulations have been largely ignored.[25] Even when sanctions from Western states are imposed on notorious violators, they tend to be limited to foreign aid, excluding areas that might have more impact such as international trade and loans. As a result, many human rights campaigns rely more on the discourse of shame than on material penalties, and their rhetoric is quickly dismissed by critics as ineffective, empty rhetoric.

Second, even in cases where human rights groups gain multilateral support and generate material sanctions, authoritarian governments are likely to react negatively to human rights pressure. Rather than buckling to transnational demands, authoritarian elites rally nationalistic domestic support in the face of these pressures. In fact, transnational action can hurt rather than help because authoritarian governments may increase or extend repression simply to demonstrate that they are not susceptible to transnational pressure. As a result, many analysts dismiss the potential impact of human rights activities. As Falk put it, "The maximum impact of human rights pressures, absent enforcement mechanisms, is to isolate a target government, perhaps denying it some of the benefits of trade and aid. There are no positive examples where such pressure has led to abandonment of the pattern of violation or to a collapse of the governing process responsible for such abuses of human rights."[26]

There are three problems with these arguments against the effectiveness of international human rights norms and networks. First, they fail to consider the possibility that international pressures can amplify and strengthen domestic processes that favor human rights.[27] A number of case studies have provided evidence supporting this possibility. Schoultz points to a correlation between a decline in murder, torture, disappearances and similar abuses in Latin America in the late 1970s and strong U.S. pressures from the Carter administration.[28] He concludes that many improvements in human rights would not have occurred, at least not as quickly as they did, without U.S. prodding. Martin and Sikkink have found that international pressures combined with a softline government faction contributed to the decline of disappearances in Argentina in the late 1970s.[29] Strong international pressures and transnational movements arguably contributed to the demise of apartheid in South Africa and political liberalization in the Soviet Union and Eastern Europe.[30] Transnational and domestic groups combined to delegitimize the authoritarian government in Argentina and to institutionalize human rights norms in the new democratic government.[31] While human rights pressures failed to end repression in timely fashion in these cases, they reinforced domestic processes and contributed to changes in government behavior.

Second, arguments against international action rely on a narrow conception of influence by focusing on large-scale domestic change. Scholars should also consider the possibility that international pressures yield more limited yet important changes in an authoritarian government's discourse and behavior. These include: (1) placing human rights on the government's agenda; (2) government adoption of a human rights discourse; (3) changes in repressive policies; (4) changes in political institutions, such as the creation of a limited legislature or government-sponsored opposition parties.[32] While these changes do not constitute "success" in the sense of ending human rights abuse, they lay out a more realistic array of government responses.

Third, prima facie evidence suggests that the influence of human rights groups and norms may be profound and widespread. The expansion of human rights pressures from the mid-1970s to the mid-1990s partially preceded and largely coincided with the "third wave" of transitions to democracy in the 1980s and 1990s.[33] Of course, it is possible that this causal pathway in fact worked in the opposite direction. In other words, it is possible that as countries democratized, they became more supportive of international human rights norms and that their newly independent civil societies formed more human rights groups. It is also possible that the linkage is spurious and that human rights pressures had little to do with the liberalization of authoritarian rule in a wide variety of countries. At the least, this intriguing connection makes questions about human rights pressure worthy of more investigation.

Domestic Political Change: Repressive Strategies

I focus on the repressive strategies of authoritarian governments as the dependent variable. A repressive strategy is defined as the bundle of coercive and ideological activities promoted by a government that restrict individual civil and political rights and are designed to engender the obedience or acquiescence of citizens to authoritarian rule. I use the term *repressive strategies* in part because it is awkward to refer to changes in state-sponsored terror as *human rights strategies*. The term is intentionally broad, as it is intended to capture not only the quantity of violations of political and civil liberties but also the general political context within which these violations take place and the institutional background that facilitates and authorizes the violations. The use of the word *strategy* reflects the assumption that authoritarian governments consciously and deliberately carry out repression to achieve certain purposes and that they alter their actions to suit new circumstances.

By focusing on the repressive strategies of authoritarian governments, this study casts a wider net than many other works on human rights, which tend to focus narrowly on particular issues such as torture, disappearance, or free speech.[34] While narrow approaches are useful, they fail to capture the fact that human rights violations form part of a government's strategy to keep itself in power and to reshape society. In authoritarian governments, the politics of human rights is not only about individual well-being but also about appropriate systems of government and proper political institutions. Changes in a government's repressive strategies can have profound implications for the strength of the opposition and for the nature of fundamental political institutions like the constitution or the judicial system.

Repressive strategies vary widely from one government to another and change considerably even within the same government over time. For example, repressive strategies range from widespread state terrorism backed by a particular reading of Marxism – as in Cambodia under the Khmer Rouge – to less violent efforts to squelch political participation by using nationalist and developmentalist ideologies – as in much of twentieth-century Mexico. Repressive strategies pass through phases of more and less violence, adopt different ideological interpretations, and require building new government institutions or destroying old ones.

Drawing on Keck and Sikkink's groundbreaking work, changes in a government's repressive strategies may be divided into four types. The first is a change of agenda, in which human rights issues are either placed on the government's agenda or taken off it. Many scholars unfortunately continue to underplay the importance of agenda setting. Forty years ago, authoritarian governments did not need to bother with human rights questions in their international relations. Most now are forced to do so. That this change is important is evidenced by the fact that most states try desperately to keep human rights issues off their agendas and out of the public eye, both domestically and internationally. Although it is theoretically possible, few authoritarian governments have succeeded in removing human rights issues permanently from the agenda once they have been placed there.

Second, states change their discourse by incorporating or dropping the language of human rights, by strengthening or weakening their rhetorical commitments to human rights norms, by changing what they mean by human rights, or by changing their positions on whether and why violations occur. Human rights networks and interested states pressure abusive governments to declare their allegiance to human rights norms, often by signing international conventions or by incorporating human rights guarantees into domestic legislation. Strong pressures also exist for authoritarian governments to clarify what they mean by human rights, to adopt Western interpretations of those rights, and to admit that human rights abuse is sometimes a problem. At one level, rhetorical changes are meaningless because they do not improve anybody's lives. At another level, accepting the discourse of human rights is a dangerous bridge for governments to cross. It opens them to charges of hypocrisy in addition to the previous charges of repression. It may raise hopes among government opponents or lead to a redoubling of their efforts against the government.

The third type is a change in practices. Liberalization refers to a sustained program of easing government repression by allowing greater civil liberties. More limited forms of changing government practices are often overlooked, but include:

Decreasing the most visible and most hated practices, such as murder or disappearances;

Dismissing government officials associated with notorious abuses;

Ending punitive measures such as exile; and

Releasing political prisoners.

Changes in practices, of course, could be neutral or negative as well as positive. Ron shows how human rights pressures on Israel led to the decline of physical torture and a rise in psychological violence that leaves few visible scars.[35] Although human rights advocates did not intend this outcome or think it wholly desirable, it was the product of human rights pressures and domestic politics in Israel.

Fourth, abusive governments may alter governing institutions in an attempt to find new formulas that somehow respond to human rights pressures while maintaining government power. Because institutions set the parameters for future behavior, institutional change has the potential for the largest impact on the human rights situation. Normatively desirable institutional changes include:

Setting up a government office for human rights;

Establishing intermediate institutions that channel the concerns of labor unions, human rights groups, or political parties;

Drafting a new constitution that includes human rights guarantees;

Giving more independence to the judiciary; and

Professionalizing the security or intelligence organizations.

Of course, institutional change can easily be negative or neutral, as when authoritarian elites set up institutional Potemkin villages as a facade to consolidate their own power.

Most changes in government institutions and practices, even when superficially positive, are the result of hypocritical efforts to put on a good face or to increase a government's power. Few make any immediate or important improvements in human rights conditions. It would be a mistake, however, to dismiss these changes as meaningless. Changes in government discourse can launch authoritarian elites down the slippery slope of living up to liberal promises. Changes in government practices can create small breathing spaces for the opposition which can eventually place important constraints on authoritarian rule.[36] Many institutions intended originally as cardboard facades can eventually be brought to life by determined opposition forces or dissenters within the government. Examples include authoritarian Brazil's national congress in the early 1980s, which struck an increasingly oppositional stance, and national human rights offices in Guatemala and Mexico in the 1990s, which became increasingly autonomous of executive control and critical of government abuses.

Legitimacy

In this section I wish to defend the proposition that most governments respond to human rights pressures because they care about their legitimacy in both the domestic and international arenas. For one set of comparative politics scholars, with roots reaching back to Max Weber, this proposition is commonsensical, even if its extension to the international arena is unfamiliar. For most international relations scholars, the proposition is problematic or, at best, worthy of sustained skepticism. I hope to build some bridges among the two subfields by showing how the concept of legitimacy can be usefully applied to the international arena and by making plausible the claim that a government's concern for its own legitimacy can motivate changes in its behavior. Although many scholars dismiss international norms and the NGOs that support them as weak and irrelevant, an analytical focus on legitimacy suggests just the opposite.

Domestic Dimensions of Legitimacy

In the Weberian tradition, legitimacy refers to a widespread belief that a given government was established in appropriate ways and that it continues to behave appropriately. In Linz's influential definition, "legitimacy is the belief that in spite of shortcomings and failures, the existing political institutions are better than any others that might be established, and that they therefore can demand obedience."[37] Although this definition is useful, it includes unnecessarily one of the potential effects of legitimacy – obedience – within the definition. Further, it restricts the concept of legitimacy to a comparison between the existing political institutions and realistic alternatives. It thus excludes the common political phenomenon wherein people judge political institutions by abstract standards rather than by real-world alternatives.

Stripping away these limitations, legitimacy may be defined as "a generalized perception or assumption that the actions of an entity are desirable, proper, or appropriate within some socially constructed system of norms, values, beliefs, and definitions."[38] A government has low levels of legitimacy when the majority of its citizens believes that it consistently fails to meet expectations of correct behavior and high levels of legitimacy when most think that it conforms with those standards. In the Weberian view, legitimacy constitutes one method of governance, among many. In other words, governments can maintain power and gain obedience from their citizens by fostering legitimacy. Other governance methods include direct coercion (gaining obedience through the use of force), meeting the narrow self-interests of individual citizens (gaining obedience by providing a tolerable quality of life), or habit and apathy (gaining obedience by building on traditions of consent and ensuring that people have no motive to rebel).

Conventional wisdom suggests that most governments routinely rely on legitimacy to govern their citizens effectively. As Weber put it, "Custom, personal advantage, purely affectual or ideal motives of solidarity, do not form a sufficiently reliable basis for a given domination. In addition there is normally a further element, the belief in legitimacy."[39] Although some governments dispense with legitimacy and govern through terror or apathy, most governments realize that gaining legitimacy is a low-cost strategy for generating obedience and political stability.[40] Further, declining legitimacy can have disastrous consequences for governments.[41] As legitimacy declines, governments find themselves forced to rely more heavily on economic performance, naked coercion, apathy, fear, or other mechanisms to generate obedience. The lack of legitimacy thus creates a fragile government that is likely to break down during times of economic or social difficulty.

A government's legitimacy, of course, is subject to intense political contestation. At the most basic level, the government and its supporters wish to strengthen the belief that the government is acting appropriately, while opposition groups seek to spread the idea that the government is behaving contrary to appropriate social values. This political struggle to shape people's beliefs about their government occurs in two parts. One part involves contests to identify and articulate the appropriate standards (norms and values) by which governments are measured. The second part consists of efforts among competing groups to demonstrate that the government either does or does not meet those standards. Although a variety of standards can be used in the political contest over government legitimacy, human rights have become increasingly important in most countries.[42]

A focus on legitimacy suggests that even resource-poor actors like human rights groups can play significant political roles in authoritarian states. Activists and groups must first articulate human rights norms and persuade others to believe in them. In most countries, the spread of human rights standards is a long-term process that requires persistence, communication, education, and gradual social change as younger generations are socialized into new ways of thinking about the individual's relationship to the state.[43] Such efforts began as early as the 1700s in European and Western Hemisphere countries, but are just getting underway elsewhere. The standard-setting process is often marked by reversals and ongoing efforts rather than easy, linear progress. Authoritarian governments and their supporters routinely propose alternative standards – such as national unity, economic progress, tradition, or religion – and use their control of education systems and the media to perpetuate those values.[44]

At the same time that human rights groups seek to articulate human rights norms as appropriate standards, they must also mobilize information to demonstrate a state's noncompliance with those norms. Even when governments themselves endorse human rights norms, they often deny violating those standards, or else justify those violations in the name of other values, such as national unity. Human rights groups routinely respond by collecting clear and systematic evidence that violations are far worse than the government asserts and by using details that evoke strong emotions in order to persuade others that nothing can justify the government's actions. In these ways, human rights groups can erode a government's legitimacy as more and more people come to believe the government is behaving inappropriately.

International Dimensions of Legitimacy

Thus far, I have focused on domestic politics; yet these arguments about legitimacy also apply to the international arena, in two ways. First, international actors focused on human rights can erode a government's legitimacy in the domestic arena. Human rights NGOs operating within authoritarian states face immense difficulties collecting and distributing information. Although torture, death, and violence are often widespread, people living under a repressive government do not necessarily realize how systematic, far-reaching, or brutal the abuses are. Even the families of victims are often surprised to see how many others have suffered a similar fate. People are prevented from communicating with one another owing to the government's control of the media and to social taboos against discussing repression.

As a result, domestic human rights groups routinely turn to international NGOs, IGOs, and foreign states for help. International actors have the resources to compile isolated stories of abuse into more systematic information and then to feed that information back into the country through informal channels. Further, IGOs and states can conduct investigations, issue official statements, and take dramatic steps that may be reported in the domestic media. Diplomatic slaps from other states constitute reportable news in authoritarian countries, as do international efforts to condemn the country by either sanctions or votes in multilateral organizations. Domestic opposition groups take heart from such reports and redouble their efforts to inform others of the extent of the problem. International reports can carry credibility among individuals who were previously agnostic about the scope of the abuses. Over time, systematic information compiled and reported by international actors can erode a government's legitimacy as more and more domestic actors become willing to speak out.

Second, governments are also concerned about their legitimacy among other states in the international arena. Internationally, governments interact in a social environment in addition to the more well-known material contexts of trade and war.[45] This social environment is replete with formal and informal understandings among states about appropriate behavior. In the modern world, human rights have become widely accepted standards of behavior, making it difficult for authoritarian governments to legitimize themselves.[46] Governments interact socially in part by monitoring and passing judgment on the appropriateness of the behavior of other governments, a form of influence sometimes labeled "soft power."[47] As Barkin and Cronin summarized this argument:

> States also relate to each other in terms of common practices, norms, and rules where such rules provide the basis for making judgments of just and unjust international conduct, for advancing claims of rights, and for seeking redress when rules are violated. States are concerned with their social as well as their physical well-being, in particular the legitimation of their own authority and of the system as a whole. As Claude argues, legitimation requires that "power be converted into authority, competence be supported by jurisdiction, and possession be validated as ownership." The maintenance of legitimacy requires that states conform with the international community's conception of justice.[48]

If some governments fail to live up to their commitments – whether in peace, trade, diplomacy, financial obligations, or something else – then other governments call attention to these lapses and express normative disapproval.

Even though realist and liberal scholars do not emphasize the importance of this social environment, they have long utilized concepts such as reputation and prestige that assume the existence of an international society. Constructivist scholars, however, emphasize the importance of international society, but have used the concept of legitimacy in ways that differ from the approach adopted here. As a result, conceptual confusion reigns. A brief review of the various concepts should illuminate the distinctions between them.

Reputation is a highly elastic term referring to judgments about an individual's character or disposition.[49] Virtually any characteristic may fall within the domain of a reputation. Although game theorists and deterrence theorists have focused on reputations for resolve, governments can also gain reputations as open- or narrow-minded, as even-handed or unfair, as hard bargainers or easily influenced, as committed to their agreements or as backsliders. Prestige, in contrast, is a reputation for power.[50] The purpose of the policy of prestige is "to impress upon the other nations the power one's own nation actually possesses or which it believes, or wants the other nations to believe, it possesses."[51] Reputation and prestige, in short, both refer to widespread beliefs about a given government, but these beliefs are oriented toward the nature or power of a government rather than a judgment about its appropriateness. They therefore differ from the concept of legitimacy in important ways.

In constructivist and legal approaches, studies of legitimacy tend to equate the term with a normative obligation to obey. Franck, for example, defines legitimacy as a property of a rule or an institution "which itself exerts a pull toward compliance," while Hurd suggests it is "the normative belief by an actor that a rule or institution ought to be obeyed."[52] This conceptualization is unduly restrictive, however, because it fails to capture social relationships that have little to do with obedience. In international affairs, governments routinely pass moral judgments on other governments, yet their relationship is not one of rule and obedience. It makes more sense to say that a government lacks legitimacy in the international arena when other governments believe that it is not conforming to widespread international norms.

Governments desire international legitimacy among their fellow governments for three reasons. First, it validates their claims to rule a given territory. New governments that have just seized power are in particular need of normative approval from other governments; otherwise, opponents will view them as transitory and vulnerable. Governments essentially accept obligations to comply with international norms in return for a recognition from other governments of their right to rule and of their identity as the appropriate authority within that territory.[53] Second, governments are fundamentally social organizations. Like all organizations, they maintain their autonomy and respectability by conforming – or at least appearing to conform – to acceptable procedures.[54] As organizations, they even learn appropriate behavior from other governments and from both IGOs and NGOs. Third, being perceived as an illegitimate government can create important tangible costs. Illegitimate governments can fall into isolation and become marginalized from important cooperative efforts and decision-making processes in regional and global IGOs. Other governments sometimes impose economic sanctions and in extreme cases even employ force against the illegitimate government. Even if sanctions are light, the pall of illegitimacy emboldens a government's international and domestic enemies and limits the places a government can turn for help.

In short, most governments want not only to receive the normative approval of their citizens but also of their fellow governments, fearing the loss of their legitimacy in both domestic and international arenas. In this way, domestic and international human rights NGOs and their supporters threaten authoritarian governments, even when they do not enjoy large economic resources or large grassroots memberships.

Government Responses to Challenges to their Legitimacy

Of course, governments do not simply respond by reshaping their behavior to conform completely and instantly with human rights standards. Rather, they begin to change in small and gradual ways that can become self-reinforcing and lead to larger changes over time. Risse and Sikkink describe this process as a "spiral model" of change that occurs in stages.[55] I adopt and build on their model by employing the types of change laid out above. Although each change creates favorable conditions for further changes, the various steps in the process are not inevitable or irreversible. Unfortunately, Risse and Sikkink fail to theorize and systematically examine the conditions in which countries are likely to make changes in their repressive strategies. As a result, I first lay out the steps in the process of change and in the following section discuss the conditions under which change is likely.

In the first stage, governments argue that human rights standards do not apply to them or to the country's circumstances, and they suggest other standards of measurement. Any number of authoritarian governments routinely adopt this response when they cite security threats or cultural traditions as reasons why human rights standards are inappropriate measuring rods. Over time, these denials lose credibility as increasing numbers of people and groups endorse human rights standards as appropriate measures of government behavior or as circumstances change so that denial is no longer a plausible strategy.

In the second stage, governments change their discourse, accepting human rights standards as an appropriate goal and admitting some abusive "excesses." As with all changes in a repressive strategy, a change in discourse benefits the government, but also benefits the opposition and thus opens the government to greater long-term risk. By making such changes, governments hope to gain some credibility and legitimacy. Yet they also open themselves to charges of hypocrisy, and they offer opposition groups a way to validate their efforts by wrapping themselves in the government's own rhetoric.

In the third stage, governments make "tactical concessions" by changing their policies in ways intended to conform (or appear to conform) more closely with human rights norms without actually yielding significant political power.[56] As with changes in discourse, these concessions are intended to ease the amount of pressure on the government and to earn the government some legitimacy. At the same time, by easing repression a bit, they open up small political spaces for the opposition to grow and gain strength.

Finally, some tactical concessions can become institutionalized in legislation or constitutions. As with other changes, governments intend such a step to bestow greater legitimacy on themselves. Yet, this step also offers opposition groups a chance to use the government's own institutions to promote human rights. Institutionalized commitments to human rights allow opposition groups to engage in new kinds of tactics, including appeals in the legal system and greater access to the media. Further, it strengthens the persuasive power of their claims by increasing the level of government hypocrisy. Although an end to the authoritarian government is far from a foregone conclusion, these changes strengthen opposition forces to the point where regime transition is more likely.

How can scholars tell if changes in a government's repressive strategies are caused by human rights pressures and related concerns about legitimacy? Although the process takes place at the level of beliefs, a few important evaluative methods are available. Signs that a government is concerned about its legitimacy include:

> Changes in discourse, behavior, or institutions in ways that are more consistent with widely held norms in domestic or international society;

Process-tracing evidence that government officials discussed their concerns with legitimacy, prestige, image, status, or related concepts, and feared the consequences of losing legitimacy; and

Evidence that government officials consistently framed arguments for or against policy changes on the basis of winning widespread acceptance for those changes.

In sum, human rights pressures challenge the legitimacy of repressive governments; that is, they undermine the belief that a government is acting appropriately. The stronger the pressures, the greater the threat to the government's legitimacy and the more likely a government will respond by altering its repressive strategies. A change in repressive strategies does not necessarily lead to an improvement in the human rights situation, especially in the short term. Changes in agenda and discourse, however, can open authoritarian governments to even more pressures, and changes in practices and institutions can open new spaces for opposition actors.

Conditions of Influence

Although governments exist in social-normative environments both domestically and internationally, not all governments care equally about their legitimacy. All governments violate norms some of the time, and some governments seem to violate a wide range of norms most of the time – even in the face of fierce pressures. Why do some governments ignore human rights pressures while others respond? Even within the same government, why do legitimacy concerns sometimes rise to the top but remain in the background at other times? In this section, I develop and operationalize four variables that are likely to influence government response to human rights pressures.

Domestic Structure

A variety of scholars have argued that the influence of international norms and transnational actors depends on a state's domestic structure.[57] For these scholars, domestic structure consists of three components: the key political institutions of the state, the nature of civil society, and the ways in which state and society are linked by intermediary organizations. In Risse-Kappen's influential conceptualization, each of these components varies along a central dimension.[58] Political institutions are either centralized or fragmented. Centralized states concentrate executive power in the hands of the few and tolerate very little input from either legislatures or local decision makers. Societies are conceptualized as either strong or weak. Strong societies have few ideological or class cleavages, can be mobilized for political action rather easily, and are endowed with relatively vibrant and centralized social organizations. Policy networks can be either consensual or polarized. Consensual state-society ties are characterized by strong intermediate associations, like political parties, which can articulate and aggregate societal demands and by decision-making rules that stress compromise rather than dissent.

Using this operationalization, six types of domestic structures emerge.[59]

Corporatist – centralized political institutions, strong society, consensual policy networks

Stalemate – centralized political institutions, strong society, polarized policy networks

State-Dominated – centralized political institutions, weak society, consensual policy networks

State-Controlled – centralized political institutions, weak society, polarized policy networks

Society-Dominated – fragmented political institutions, strong society

Fragile – fragmented political institutions, weak society

Transnational networks can gain relatively easy access to the political arena in states with fragmented political institutions and can find important domestic support in states with strong societies.[60] In contrast, networks have the most difficulty accessing state-dominated and state-controlled polities. Yet, as Risse-Kappen points out, access does not necessarily translate into influence. Proponents of norm-centered change must first build "winning coalitions" allowing them to influence domestic policy. Such coalitions are nearly impossible to build in fragile and stalemated polities, for obvious reasons. In society-dominated polities, access is easy, but building a winning coalition requires sustained time and effort because of the fragmented nature of decision making. It is somewhat easier to build winning coalitions in corporatist polities, but access is more difficult. Finally, in state-dominated and state-controlled polities, the policy impact of norms and networks can be profound owing to the state's domination of society, yet gaining access to key decision makers is especially difficult.

To summarize the argument as it applies to most authoritarian states, international norms should have either no influence or else a profound influence on state-dominated and state-controlled countries. Whether the influence is negligible or profound depends on the ability of transnational norm proponents and their domestic allies to gain access to top decision makers and persuade them that the norm constitutes appropriate behavior. Although this process of elite learning is perhaps relatively rare, constructivists have found evidence that it has occurred in crucial cases.[61] Most notably, transnational networks promoting new conceptions of security, including new ideas about disarmament and arms control, influenced Soviet leader Mikhail Gorbachev in the middle to late 1980s and thus helped produce an end to the Cold War.[62] For this process to work, it is essential that persuasive and politically influential norm proponents gain access to a national leader willing to listen to and learn from new ideas.

Some authoritarian states may take the form of corporatist (Mexico, pre-2000), stalemated (Hungary, pre-1989), or fragile (Kenya) polities. International norms are expected to have little influence in stalemated or fragile polities because of the extreme polarization in domestic society and weak decision-making structures. Under these conditions, norm proponents have little chance of building "winning coalitions." Corporatist regimes are the most open to the influence of international norms, according to this logic, because norm activists can gain access to powerful societal actors who have institutionalized methods of influence within the polity.

Normative Fit

Normative fit refers to the extent to which well-ingrained domestic cultural beliefs are compatible with international norms and with the discourse and activities of transnational groups. International norms and transnational actors are unlikely to have much impact if they promote ideas, beliefs, and values that fit poorly with preexisting, domestic social understandings.[63] The failures of the transnational campaign against female genital mutilation in many parts of the world illustrate the problem of applying international norms to deeply ingrained cultural practices.[64] New international norms are much more likely to have an impact if they resonate with established cultural understandings and historical experience. Although the relevant domestic norms are usually diffused throughout society, they may also be concentrated in particular state organizations. Legro has shown, for example, that military organizational culture determines whether states adhere to international norms proscribing different forms of combat.[65]

The question of fit with pre-existing cultural understandings is partly the result of political struggle between norm proponents and opponents. Transnational and domestic groups can sometimes find ways to package or "frame" international events in ways that make them meaningful to civil society and state actors and spur them to action.[66] Anti-apartheid activists in the United States, for example, framed the issue in terms of human rights and justice by conjuring up images of slavery and inhumanity through their innovative use of mock shantytowns. By moving the debate away from norms of nonintervention, activists reframed the apartheid issue and successfully changed U.S. policy. In this respect, it is often easier to repackage an international norm than to change well-ingrained domestic-level understandings. Antislavery crusaders, for example, did not eradicate beliefs in racial superiority in the United States, but they did succeed in linking antislavery ideas with religious beliefs about the importance of individual choice and responsibility.[67]

The importance of normative fit can be illustrated by reference to the difference between Asian and Latin American countries on the issue of human rights. Where domestic human rights norms are relatively well-developed – as in the Southern Cone of South America – repressive governments have greater difficulty justifying their rule in terms unrelated to human rights and are thus vulnerable to the politics of "shaming." In these cases, the normative environment offers transnational networks a greater opportunity to expand within the country's civil society and to gain media attention. Where domestic human rights norms are weak, as in many Asian countries, governments can more easily justify repression by appealing to other cultural norms, such as community responsibility, and networks face a steep uphill battle expanding through domestic civil society.

The normative fit within a given country may be classified as high, medium, or low, reflecting the degree to which widespread social norms are compatible with international norms. I operationalize this variable by examining the degree to which social groups publicly articulate those norms. The normative fit is low when only a few brave individuals endorse human rights norms (for example, the Soviet Union in the 1970s). Medium levels are observed when some prominent social groups articulate the importance of human rights norms, but a variety of other social groups actively support repression and authoritarian rule (for example, Poland in the 1980s). Finally, high levels occur when social groups representing a broad range of society (lower, middle, and upper classes, women's groups, churches, leftist and rightist parties) endorse human rights norms (for example, Western European countries).

Crisis

Transnational actors, international norms, and states do not interact in a vacuum. Even if they succeed in establishing numerous connections to domestic groups and in gaining access to state officials, transnational actors must compete with other actors and problems for the state's attention and meaningful responses. The political and economic context within which the state operates helps determine whether transnational actors and norms will have any influence.

The conventional wisdom suggests that crisis situations open windows of opportunity in which decision makers are willing to consider new ideas espoused by transnational actors and others and to make the relevant policy changes.[68] Crises create political climates that are ripe for change by discrediting old policies that helped produce the crisis (or at least failed to stop it), by forcing overly routinized organizations to consider new facts and circumstances, and by creating a fear that if no new action is taken, the crisis will deepen. In fact, Checkel goes so far as to call it a "truism" that "politics opens up, becomes more fluid, under conditions of crisis and uncertainty."[69]

This line of reasoning fails to recognize, however, that this "opening up" and "fluidity" does not benefit all ideas and actors equally and that policy change may actually involve an abandonment of a reform process and a return to a status quo ante. The emphasis on "new" ideas obscures the fact that the nature of the crisis may actually discredit some new ideas while favoring others and that rather "old" ideas, discarded a few years previously, may in fact begin to look more attractive. O'Donnell and Schmitter, in their discussion of the opening of authoritarian regimes, refer precisely to this problem when they theorize the problem of authoritarian regression.[70] Authoritarian governments, having started tentatively down a reformist path, often reach a crisis point in which threats to the government's power increase dramatically. "In such situations, the longer-term benefits of an eventual liberalization (not to mention democratization) will seem to [government officials] much less appealing than the shorter-term security of an immediate return to authoritarian rule."[71] In short, crises can easily end reformist experiments and produce a sort of change that simply returns the state to its previous condition.

Rather than arguing that crises make way for new ideas and actors, it would be more accurate to argue that crises create opportunities for ideas and actors *not tied to the crisis or its causes*. Although previous literature has focused on the winners, crises create clear losers as well. Actors and ideas associated with the crisis are discredited, even if those actors have not previously held any influence and even if those ideas are untried. For example, an impending war would certainly discredit disarmament activists, even if the ideas of those activists were new and had never been tried before. In authoritarian states, government officials always affiliate human rights norms and their supporters with the losers in a crisis situation. By definition, crises threaten the power and stability of a government. When crisis breaks, authoritarian governments invariably associate human rights activists with the causes of the crisis or believe they have the ability to exacerbate the crisis. In situations of war, these governments view human rights protesters as enemies who wish to tie the government's hands. In economic crisis, human rights activists are seen as agitators capable of mobilizing mass protests. In either case, government officials believe that the adoption of human rights norms would demonstrate weakness and further erode the government's power.

As a result, I hypothesize that crises produce a hardening of authoritarian rule rather than a positive change toward greater human rights guarantees. Change occurs, but it is change in favor of rather "old" ideas about the need for more repression and in favor of time-tested actors like security forces that are capable of dealing with the threat. Human rights norms and actors are marginalized as the government retreats within itself and turns its attention to matters of sheer survival. Government officials change their policies and open themselves to new ideas, but they simultaneously close themselves off to rights-oriented actors and policy proposals. In terms of operationalization, I associate crises with international war, violent domestic rebellion, or economic depression.

States enjoying periods of relative prosperity and peace (the absence of crisis), on the other hand, are more open to gradual positive change in their repressive strategies. They have more time and resources available to improve their legitimacy, and problems related to their social interactions with others seem relatively more important. They are therefore more sensitive to the judgments of others and to the differences between their normative commitments and reality. In addition, they enjoy more strategic space to implement changes without exacerbating existing problems. Elites in peaceful and prosperous times are more willing to consider changes in their repressive strategies because they do not risk losing power. They have little reason to fear human rights groups, who cannot take advantage of a poor economy or an unpopular war to press their cause. Finally, states not in crisis situations do not need to stand defiant in the face of human rights pressures as a way to rally nationalistic support for their policies.

Elite Coalitions

Liberal approaches to international relations emphasize that states are made up of competing factions and groups all seeking to graft their particular ideology and interests onto the state as a whole.[72] As scholars of comparative politics have long realized, this observation is true even in relatively centralized authoritarian governments. Domestic groups with different ideologies and interests compete for influence with key decision makers and capture key decision-making posts. Although this competition is obviously constrained to many fewer ideas and interests than in a democratic polity, the struggle for influence can nevertheless be intense.

One of the most important divisions within authoritarian governments occurs between rule-oriented and force-oriented actors. Rule-oriented actors emphasize the importance of governing by consent rather than by coercion, especially in the long term. Rule orientation does not imply a preference for democracy and even-handed rules over authoritarianism and biased rules. Quite the contrary, rule-oriented elites in authoritarian governments seek to lay down legal principles that justify and legitimize authoritarian decision making and that are capable of winning the consent of the governed without freeing them from subordination. Rule-oriented actors often take a long-term view of politics and emphasize the importance of creating a self-sustaining system that does not rely on any one person for stable governance. With respect to the international arena, rule-oriented actors are cognizant of the costs of violating international norms, even if those costs are intangible. They value rule conformance not because they believe the rules are morally good but because they realize that political gain can be made by conforming to rules.

Force-oriented actors, on the other hand, stress short-term security threats to the survival of the state and the need to fight fire with fire. They fear that rule making will simply tie the hands of the government, which needs flexibility in responding to threats in forceful ways. They also fear that rules will demonstrate weakness to opposition forces and open up loopholes that can be used against the government. Force-oriented actors emphasize the importance of authority and centralized decision making without artificial constraints. They prefer a "strong hand," which is often a euphemism for the coercive action of security agencies. With respect to the international arena, force-oriented actors do not see benefits accruing from norm compliance, largely because they discount intangible costs and benefits. They pay attention to international rules only if violating those rules will create large-scale economic or military costs for the government – a rare occurrence.

These categories are obviously ideal types rather than careful descriptions of the positions of particular groups. In reality, most supporters of authoritarian governments recognize the need for both rules and force. Yet most individuals and groups emphasize one over the other, especially in the long-term, and many governments experience important factional splits along these lines. To some extent, these categories correspond with the distinctions between softliners and hardliners that are often made in the democratization literature and mass media. Yet there are important differences. The term *softliners* often refers to those who want to make substantive reforms in state policies, whereas rule-oriented actors do not necessarily endorse substantive reform. Rule-oriented actors are concerned mostly with gaining the consent of others, which does not necessarily lead to substantive reform, though it may. Above all, they prefer the creation of rules and policies that justify their use of power without actually changing the nature of that power. Further, the term *soft* is not the best descriptor of actors who, after all, loyally support authoritarian rule and its "necessary" brutalities.

The trick for rule-oriented actors in authoritarian governments is to reconcile and balance form and substance. That is, rule-oriented actors must discover ways to justify coercive practices in ways that are acceptable to a wide audience. They must appear to conform to international norms while in fact hiding violations of those norms. Achieving such balance is a difficult process. At times, appearance and reality are so widely divergent and so readily apparent that no amount of rule making or misleading discourse will bridge the gap. In such cases, rule-oriented actors are likely to endorse some small substantive reforms in order to narrow the gap between discourse and practice and to regain the appearance of rule conformance.

This reasoning leads to the following hypothesis: The larger the presence of rule-oriented actors within an authoritarian government, the greater the influence of international norms. Although this reasoning is straightforward, it is not tautological or obviously true, and it faces important competing explanations. The presence of a set of actors who share a given preference within any government does not guarantee that policy outcomes will reflect those preferences. A powerful decision maker may simply overrule his advisors, circumstances may induce government officials to set aside their preferences, or decision-making processes and institutions may produce outcomes different from the preferences of the participants. To cite one example, conventional wisdom holds that pressures on behalf of an international norm often backfire by creating a nationalistic reaction in the targeted state. I argue, in contrast, that international pressures can find an echo within a targeted government if rule-oriented individuals hold important political positions. This argument constitutes a clear alternative to arguments focusing on domestic structure, normative fit, or crisis – none of which rely on rule-oriented actors in order for international norms to influence states.

Measures of the strength of rule-oriented actors must be separated from measures of the policy outcomes. One cannot infer the presence and influence of rule-oriented actors from policy outcomes that correspond with international norms. Rather, operationalization requires a careful three-step process. The first step involves documenting the position that different individuals took in policy debates within the government. Useful sources include public speeches and media interviews of top government officials, publications from state entities (military branches, government think tanks), investigative journalism reports, archived government documents, and legislative records. These are supplemented by memoirs and interviews with the key participants and with journalists who covered the government at the time. The various statements are carefully scrutinized to classify an individual as either rule-oriented or force-oriented, depending on the consistency of their claims with the two ideal types as defined above.

The second step involves an assessment of the strength of the two groups. Their strength can be measured by the extent to which they articulated their views publicly and the number of key political offices they held within the government. Rule-oriented individuals can be said to have a small presence if major media outlets publish few of their views and if they hold a minority of the key offices. They have a moderate presence if major media sources publish and endorse their views about the same amount as they publish and endorse force-oriented views and if rule-oriented individuals hold about half of the key offices. Finally, they have a large presence when they dominate public media discussions and hold a substantial majority of key government offices.

Third, process tracing is used to determine whether these groups have actually influenced policy. To demonstrate their influence, individuals who held rule-oriented views must be shown to have first articulated those views well before policy decisions were made, had contacts with key decision makers, endorsed rule-oriented claims during policy debates, and contributed specific arguments and ideas to the final policy. Such assessments are made possible by examining internal government documents and interviewing the key participants.

Norms and Power

I have argued that, given the right conditions, states act strategically to protect their legitimacy in the face of human rights pressures. This argument draws eclectically from rationalist, constructivist, and liberal theoretical approaches in international relations and highlights blind spots in each of them. From rationalist approaches, I adopt the idea that states are strategic actors that calculate costs and benefits in the pursuit of basic goals. At the same time, I accept the constructivist insight that states interact in an environment that is fundamentally social and ideational as well as material. Norms and nonstate actors are important features of this social world and, along with states, play key roles in identifying appropriate standards and pressuring states to conform. From liberalism, I draw the idea that domestic politics is directly responsible for shaping state preferences and behavior. States and nonstate actors can use human rights norms to pressure authoritarian governments, but whether government elites see any need to respond depends primarily on the (largely) domestic conditions laid out above. Identifying these three features does not represent a synthesis between theoretical approaches nor does it simply buy into every possible assumption that they each make. Rather, it represents an attempt to build bridges and find productive ways to combine some of their assumptions while rejecting others.

Although realist approaches conceptualize states as strategic actors, they have neglected the normative side of state struggles for power in favor of material forces like military and economic might. Some realist scholars have recognized that beliefs are an important source of state power, but these insights have remained undeveloped and have rarely included beliefs about legitimacy. Carr, for example, wrote that states need not only power but also moral authority. He included power over public opinion as one of three sources of power.[73] At the same time, he argued that military and economic power are required to change public opinion, thereby dismissing the importance of small states and nonstate actors. Further, he viewed public opinion as a tool of states rather than as an independent influence on their behavior. As noted above, Morgenthau wrote of states' desire for prestige, but defined the term narrowly as a "reputation for power."[74] In other words, Morgenthau viewed prestige as a belief that a given state has military-economic power and is willing to use it; he was not at all interested in judgments about the appropriateness of state behavior. More recent realist analyses generally follow this pattern of emphasizing military and economic power while neglecting the ways in which states pursue strategies to improve their normative standing.[75]

Neoliberal institutionalists, in contrast, argue that norms influence state behavior when they help resolve problems of "collective action, high transaction costs, and information deficits or asymmetries."[76] Yet recent research demonstrates that many international norms do not serve clear functional purposes. Rather than finding norms useful for serving functional needs, many states in fact resist many international norms. Such "nonfunctional" or unwanted norms include some that impinge on state sovereignty (for example, environmental norms and human rights norms), some that limit state options in the face of threats (for example, norms limiting weapons developments and rules of war), some that embody "foreign" values (for example, norms on birth control and women's rights), and some that inform states which functions they should take on (for example, coordinating science and fighting poverty).[77] It makes little sense, for example, to argue that authoritarian states have a functional need to cooperate with others to respect human rights in the same way that they have needs to coordinate economic interactions.

Constructivist approaches suggest that states adopt norms through a process of social interaction and learning. Yet these conceptualizations create a view of states that is too apolitical and nonstrategic. They do not adequately capture the sense of threat posed by human rights pressures and the struggle for power implicit in state responses. To argue that states interact socially is not to deny that they interact strategically for political power within a broader social environment, although constructivists have been slow to realize this point. States do not simply learn what is appropriate behavior and become socialized into it through gradual interactive processes. They also think strategically about how to improve their social standing and normative approval, and they adopt new behaviors intended to achieve those goals. In other words, "the utilities of actors could be specified as social or ideational as easily as they can be material."[78]

Finally, liberal and transnational approaches correctly emphasize the importance of domestic politics in shaping state preferences, but have neglected theorizing about some of the important ways in which this happens. Moravcsik argues that an independent civil society and robust domestic legal institutions can take advantage of international human rights norms to pressure governments from within.[79] In a similar vein, Cortell and Davis argue that international norms matter when influential state or societal actors appeal to those norms in policy debates or when they are incorporated into national legislation.[80] Both analyses assume that at least some powerful decision makers accept the validity of the relevant international norms and are open to persuasive arguments or legal rulings that rely on those norms.

Yet even when government officials reject the validity of international norms, they realize that other powerful actors accept the norms and sometimes back them up with sanctions. As a result, governments sometimes strategically modify their discourse and behavior to correspond more closely to these norms. Complying (or claiming to comply) more closely with norms allows the government to shore up its authority and legitimacy and to deflect human rights pressures. This avenue of international influence does not require a strong autonomous civil society, nor does it require that government elites accept the international norm. At the same time, it does require certain domestic conditions in order to operate. This argument recognizes that domestic responses are often slow and incremental. Small and seemingly insignificant government concessions to human rights pressures, however, often open up demands for more change and expand expectations that such changes will occur.

Liberal approaches also help scholars understand why different states respond differently to human rights pressures. Rationalist and state-centric constructivist approaches fail to appreciate the domestic differences between states that make some more likely to comply with norms than others. From a neoliberal perspective, it is difficult to understand why some states have a functional need to comply with generally unwanted international norms like human rights. From a state-centric constructivist approach, it is hard to understand why international organizations are better able to teach some states rather than others. In contrast, a liberal approach that examines domestic characteristics and transnational pressures helps answer questions about the conditions under which international norms are effective. This study suggests that states respond to international norms in complex ways that relate to domestic structure, dominant domestic norms, the extent of crisis, and the role of government factions.

By arguing that states act strategically within a social environment, I am attempting to build one bridge across the rationalist-constructivist divide. This argument accepts both the logic of consequences and the logic of appropriateness. In reality, states use both types of logic, and scholars who focus on one rather than another "slight the multiple roles norms play in social life."[81] It would be foolish to deny that states act strategically by asking themselves which means will help them achieve their ends (logic of consequences). Likewise, it seems unlikely that states will ignore questions about which behavior is the most appropriate in a given situation (logic of appropriateness). In fact, the two forms of logic often interact to produce the same outcome, and it becomes difficult or impossible for scholars to separate out their effects. States pursue appropriate behavior in part because it helps them achieve their goals of peaceful, stable interaction with other states. On the flip side, when calculating the costs and benefits of different actions, states favor some means over others precisely because they are widely accepted as appropriate behaviors.

More broadly, this book highlights the importance of the normative bases of a state's authority. Even authoritarian governments frequently rely on some form of legitimacy in order to rule. In the modern era, human rights norms have become important standards of legitimacy in many countries. International action that challenges the government's human rights record therefore challenges the government's legitimacy and its long-term political stability. International relations scholars focused exclusively on the material bases of power – economic and military – are likely to miss this potentially important avenue of international influence in domestic politics. International and transnational actors routinely use both norms and power to pressure authoritarian governments to improve their human rights records, and an analysis of both is necessary to understand how governments respond.

TWO

Placing Human Rights on the Government's Agenda, 1973–1975

When they seized power on September 11, 1973, Chilean military officials identified a relatively narrow agenda. It consisted of re-establishing order, eliminating the Marxist strongholds within state and society, restoring the rule of law, and returning to "economic and social normality."[1] Some officials even spoke of simply reforming the 1925 Constitution and returning power to civilians within two to three years.[2] Human rights issues and ideas were not even on the radar screen.

Over the next few months, however, human rights issues occupied an increasingly prominent place on the government's agenda. By mid-1974, it was clear that the human rights issue would not simply vanish but would continue to grow in importance. Government officials desperately wished to rid themselves of the issue, spending significant amounts of time and resources in attempts to deflect human rights criticisms. They were unsuccessful.

Over time, human rights became the setting and backdrop for innumerable political battles, both within the government and between the government and its domestic and international opposition. The issue led, directly or indirectly, to the fall of junta members, intelligence chiefs, and cabinet officials. It became perhaps the most important factor in Chile's international relations and the source of constant concern and embarrassment for Foreign Ministry officials. It has continued to plague former military government officials – as the stunning arrest and ongoing prosecution of former president Augusto Pinochet demonstrated – and it will assuredly hang about their necks in the annals of history.

How and why did human rights come to occupy such a central and persistent spot on the agenda of a government that had set other tasks for itself and that poured some of its best resources into attempting to rid itself of the issue?[3] I will argue that an emerging transnational human rights network, with significant help from state allies, pushed human rights issues onto the military government's agenda within a few weeks of the coup and applied continuing pressure to ensure they would stay there. The military government became concerned about its international legitimacy and thus routinely discussed international human rights pressures and appropriate responses. The human rights network and Western states successfully activated government concerns for its legitimacy owing to moderate levels of normative fit; that is, the strength of Chile's pre-existing domestic norms of human rights and democracy.

At the same time, Chile made scarcely any changes to its human rights policies in the first years of military rule, refusing even to adopt a discourse of human rights until late 1975. Rather, the government focused on propaganda and diplomatic efforts intended to convince others that human rights abuses were either unimportant or justified. This minimalist response can be explained by the combination of economic and political crisis, the absence of rule-oriented factions, and the government's closed, state-dominated structure. Two possible alternative explanations fall short in explaining the emergence of human rights on the government's agenda: (1) the rise of a softline faction within the government; and (2) costly economic sanctions from powerful states, analyzed in isolation from the transnational network and intangible normative pressures.

This chapter is organized as follows. I first offer an overview of the new authoritarian government in Chile, including its structure and decision-making processes, its repressive mission, and its violent, militaristic, anti-Communist view of the world. I then show how a transnational human rights network supported by foreign states formed quickly in the wake of the coup and began pressuring Chile on its human rights record. Chilean military officials originally thought the effort would die out in the face of an international public relations blitz, but as time passed the campaign picked up strength. Within six months of the coup, it was clear that human rights issues would remain on the government's agenda despite the government's best efforts to ignore or dilute the issue. Before concluding with a discussion of the importance of "framing," I analyze the reasons why the government addressed human rights issues and demonstrate the problems with alternative explanations.

A New Government and Its Mission

The military coup on September 11, 1973, marked a radical turning point in Chile's tradition of human rights and democracy.[4] A weak, disintegrating state unable to retain order was transformed virtually overnight into a strong, predatory state seeking to destroy basic social institutions and then rebuild them in its own image. Although nearly everyone in Chile expected a military coup and many pleaded for it, few had envisioned the brutality and long years of terror that would follow. The new government was characterized by highly centralized authority, a worldview that emphasized the military's total war on Marxism, and wide-ranging, violent repression. It seemed a particularly poor candidate for influence from human rights pressures.

The Chilean military not only seized power but also set out to eradicate all traces of Marxism from Chile. In the weeks following the coup, military officials rounded up tens of thousands of prisoners and detained them for questioning. Military personnel executed more than a thousand victims – sometimes acting after brief military court proceedings but other times simply murdering them – and tortured thousands more.[5] After this initial frenzy had subsided, the military government embarked on a systematic campaign of terror that included disappearances, widespread detention and torture, exile, curfew, state-of-siege restrictions on free speech and assembly, and a general climate of fear.[6] The final toll of seventeen years of military rule is sobering: estimates suggest at least three thousand dead, tens of thousands tortured, hundreds of thousands arrested, tens of thousands exiled, and untold numbers scarred emotionally or psychologically by government terror.

Virtually every social and political institution that could resist this campaign – with the exception of a few churches, including parts of the Roman Catholic Church – was destroyed within a few weeks of the coup or quietly acquiesced to the climate of fear.[7] Arguing that they were afflicted with decay from Marxist infiltration and required complete rebuilding, the new military rulers disbanded Congress, censored the media, and repressed political parties, labor organizations, student groups, and neighborhood organizations. State agencies designed to check and balance the executive power, such as the judiciary and the comptroller general's office, generally failed to take an independent stand.

Chile's new government consisted of a four-man military junta made up of the commanders in chief of each of the three branches of the armed forces – Pinochet for the army, José Merino for the navy, and Gustavo Leigh for the air force – and the commander of the militarized police known as the Carabineros, César Mendoza. In theory, junta members collectively held legislative and executive authority and made all the key decisions, but in practice Pinochet increasingly dominated the others.[8] During the first year, Pinochet gradually took on all the trappings of executive power and made many decisions in consultation with his cabinet rather than the junta. By December 1974, Pinochet had gained enough influence within the junta to be formally named president of Chile. Subsequently, the junta played a legislative role that imperfectly balanced the growing power of the executive.

After seizing power, the new government turned its attention to three related tasks: eliminating Marxism, rebuilding the economy, and constructing a new political system.[9] Officials conceptualized this ambitious agenda as a "foundational" effort. That is, the military government decided to completely wipe away the vices of the past and the institutions that housed them and to create – virtually *ex nihilo* – a new mentality among Chileans, a radically restructured economy, and a completely new socio-political system.[10] Military officials were well-trained and well-equipped to complete the first task. They quickly embarked on a violent and effective all-out war against Marxists. After a six-month period of uncertainty, they also began vigorously reconstructing the economy by implementing neoliberal economic principles. They placed their third task – which they labeled the "new institutionality" – on the back burner. They were less certain about how to construct a new political system and saw no immediate need to proceed rapidly. As a result, they created a constitutional study commission dominated by civilian jurists and then largely ignored its proceedings. Human rights issues could not have been farther from the agenda.

The war on Marxism easily dominated the government's agenda during its first few months and remained one of the government's central tasks until it handed over power in March 1990. In the military's worldview, Marxists were responsible for the near-destruction of the Chilean state. The only solution, according to military officials, was to excise Marxists from Chile by force (death, exile, or endless imprisonment). Chilean military officials shared a visceral anti-Marxism that traveled to Chile with Europeans in the early twentieth century in response to the Russian revolution.[11] In the military mind, Marxists were dehumanized creatures who betrayed their country and God to insidiously spread Soviet imperialism to all corners of the earth. Marxism, in this view, corrupted the moral cornerstones of Western society such as the family, Christianity, and patriotism. Worst of all was the Marxists' intent to capture the Chilean state and society and turn them into tools to be used by the Soviet Union – thereby surrendering Chile's national heritage and even its very sovereignty. This anti-Marxism became deeply ingrained into military life and provided a touchstone of loyalty to the military and to Chile. "I am anti-Marxist," imperiously declared one of the junta members shortly after the coup, "because I am a living being, created in the image and semblance of God, who has a superior creative spirit, and Marxism throws out all fundamental principles."[12]

Chilean military officials conceptualized war as a never-ending series of battles against their Marxist enemies that took place in a variety of settings – social organizations, churches, state institutions, poor urban neighborhoods, and so forth. They were heavily influenced by Prussian and German conceptions of war as "absolute." As Arriagada put it, "Absolute wars are wars of annihilation. They are fought not to obtain something from the defeated but rather to sweep them from the face of the earth. Peace is conceived only as a world where the enemy does not exist. The enemy is defined in the worst terms possible, as a total and imminent threat for all the values of those who combat it."[13] This conceptualization of war suggested that military officials must utilize a variety of methods to combat Marxism, including antiterrorist activities, broad police powers, economic development (to take away Marxism's base among the poor), education, and instilling nationalist values in the population. The anti-insurgency efforts of France and the United States in northern Africa and southeast Asia in the 1950s and 1960s provided important lessons for Chilean officials on how to turn war doctrines into practice by battling Marxists among their own people.[14]

A centralized intelligence and security agency, known as the Directorate of National Intelligence (DINA), emerged in the aftermath of the coup and quickly consolidated extensive power.[15] The DINA, headed by Col. Manuel Contreras, actually carried out most of the campaign of terror unleashed inside Chile. DINA agents were responsible for a significant portion of the disappearances, murders, torture cases, arrests, and cases of harassment that occurred in Chile from 1973 until the organization was disbanded in 1977.[16] During those years, the DINA was directly responsible only to Pinochet – not the junta. Contreras, though only a colonel in the army, answered to no one else in the military or in the government. Despite the DINA's dominance, other government institutions were also responsible for carrying out repression. These included the Carabineros, the civilian police, other intelligence agencies in the armed forces, and officials in the Interior Ministry.

While military conceptualizations of war and Marxism were quite clear and well-defined, military ideas on the nature of government and appropriate political institutions were much more muddled and less developed.[17] Military officials did not devote much time to thinking about these issues and had not been trained to govern nor to design political institutions. Pinochet admired Franco's corporatist state in Spain, built with the armed forces as the backbone, but offered few ideas on how to adapt it to Chile. For the foreseeable future, Pinochet believed that the military could govern Chile directly through states of emergency. In the long term, he thought military officials should serve as tutors for a few elected officials and participate actively in the formulation of policy.[18]

Although vague on specifics, military officials universally agreed that Chile's political system should be dominated by the armed forces for an indefinite period. From the Allende experience, they drew the lesson that democracy and constitutional rule could not withstand the assaults of Marxism. In the face of permanent Marxist aggression, the armed forces would need to retain power indefinitely to ensure that Marxism would never again corrupt Chile's true character. Many of the government's early declarations suggested that the military would serve as Chile's political guide far into the future. This was best summarized by the popular phrase indicating that the military government had set goals for itself, not deadlines ("metas, no plazos"). Further, military officials claimed that the armed forces were uniquely positioned to act on Chile's true national interests, thereby preserving the essence of Chilean nationalism.[19]

Human Rights on the Agenda

The violent coup and subsequent terror stimulated vigorous responses from human rights advocates, both within Chile and across the globe.[20] While international human rights norms were developed on paper from the 1940s to the 1960s, the Chilean coup triggered one of the first and most extensive efforts to translate those norms into practice.[21] International and domestic human rights groups formed transnational linkages that set precedents for later human rights networks. The transnational network organized around Chile pioneered activities that are now standard practice, including extensive monitoring, efforts to achieve international condemnation, funding domestic opposition groups and research centers, the use of special rapporteurs, and lobbying powerful Western states to take action. In a break with traditional policies of nonintervention, many states set important precedents by actively and publicly condemning the human rights situation in Chile and imposing sanctions on the new government. Taken together, these activities constituted one of the first and most important international campaigns against gross and systematic human rights abuses in a single country.

The Emergence of the Transnational Network and the Government's Response

From the very beginning, responses to the coup had a strong transnational character. Two transnational NGOs – Amnesty International and the International Commission of Jurists – were among the first groups to react. They cabled the Inter-American Commission on Human Rights (IACHR) just three days after the coup, urging action in Chile to make sure that refugees would be allowed to request asylum and to leave the country and that the newly installed government would respect human rights.[22] Within a month of the coup, the IACHR had responded to these cables by sending an observer to Chile to gather information on the human rights situation there. After a six-day visit, the observer returned with reports of torture, disappearances, illegal arrests, and murders and recommended further action in Chile.

At the same time, Chilean churches began to set up human rights organizations that became the core of the transnational network. From their inception, church-sponsored Chilean human rights groups enjoyed important transnational ties. The United Nations High Commissioner for Refugees (UNHCR) sent a representative to Chile soon after the coup to facilitate the safe exit of foreigners.[23] In late September, a variety of Chilean religious groups cooperated with the UNHCR and the UN's International Committee for Migration to establish the National Committee for Aid to Refugees (Comité Nacional de Ayuda a los Refugiados – CONAR). With the assistance of the World Council of Churches, CONAR helped a few thousand foreigners to leave the country safely within the next several months.[24]

Concerned about the fate of not only foreigners but also Chileans, a variety of Chilean churches set up the Committee of Cooperation for Peace (Comité Cooperación para la Paz en Chile – COPACHI) on October 6, 1973, for the purpose of aiding "those Chileans who, as a result of recent political events, are in serious financial and personal need."[25] Although headed by Chileans, the establishment and funding of COPACHI was a transnational endeavor facilitated by personal contacts between the World Council of Churches' representative in Chile, Presbyterian pastor Charles Harper, the head of the Chilean Lutheran Church, Bishop Helmut Frenz, and Santiago Archbishop Raúl Silva. Harper expressed concerns to Frenz about the need to help Chileans, and Frenz – who shared his concerns – passed them on to Silva through a mutual contact. Then at the first committee coordinating meeting, Bishop Frenz presented a check for fifteen thousand German marks from the World Council of Churches to be used for the committee's work.

During the next two years, COPACHI continued to build its ties to a variety of foreign and international groups. This effort came naturally to COPACHI activists because of their training, beliefs, and values – many of which they shared in common with human rights activists in other countries. "The conception that we lawyers had was that we formed part of an international community," said Rosemarie Bornand, a lawyer associated with COPACHI from its earliest days.[26] "In the teachings and the culture of the country we believed that we were part of an international community founded on law. So it was something very natural that we would look to the international arena for help."

One of COPACHI's most important activities was to investigate carefully the circumstances surrounding alleged human rights abuse and to compile detailed reports. Those reports were then used in legal proceedings in Chilean courts – which rarely provided any real solution

– and were also distributed to an expanding circle of international actors.[27] Over time, COPACHI circulated its reports to the Red Cross, Amnesty International, Americas Watch, the International Commission of Jurists, the United Nations, the Organization of American States (OAS), and others.[28] Between 1974 and 1979, COPACHI and its successor organization, the Vicariate of Solidarity, sent an estimated 1,720 petitions to international organizations on behalf of 1,928 individuals.[29]

While COPACHI, and later other Chilean human rights groups, provided crucial information to the international community, international actors offered important funding, moral support, international visibility, and some small measure of protection to Chilean human rights groups.[30] For example, about 86 percent of COPACHI's funding from 1973 to 1975 (when it was disbanded) came from foreign sources, with the remainder provided by the Catholic Church's Caritas Chile.[31] One activist who worked in a variety of human rights organizations throughout the seventeen years of military rule observed that international support was "perhaps the very fountain" of the existence of human rights groups in Chile and explained "why the military dictatorship did not destroy" those organizations.[32]

In Washington, newly formed human rights organizations adopted Chile as one of their first campaigns and tried to shame the United States into action by highlighting U.S. support for the military government. The Chilean coup served as a key catalyst to energize U.S. humanitarian groups and to move their focus away from Vietnam and toward U.S. support for other abusive governments throughout the world.[33] Amnesty International issued two reports on torture in Chile in 1974, providing some of the first systematic evidence on abuses to reach a widespread audience. A new NGO, the Washington Office on Latin America, appointed a director in 1974 who had worked until October 1973 as a Methodist missionary in Chile. Horrified and shocked by his experiences there, he helped lead the charge on Capitol Hill against Chile.[34]

The presence of foreign journalists in Chile also served as an important early source of information about human rights abuses and placed pressures on Western states to respond. A sensationalistic article in Newsweek titled "Slaughterhouse in Santiago" offered a first-hand report of mass graves, dozens of rotting bodies littering a morgue, mass arrests, extrajudicial executions, and so forth.[35] Senator Edward Kennedy placed the story in the *Congressional Record* and used it to support his initially unsuccessful efforts to cut off U.S. aid to Chile. In a more cautious story a few days later, the *New York Times* also reported credible evidence of mass executions and other atrocities, and reported the death toll at about two thousand.[36] Other media sources reported thousands dead and tens of thousands illegally imprisoned. In response to the highly visible brutality and the urging of human rights activists, some Western European countries suspended economic and military aid, and many lodged strong diplomatic protests.[37]

Given the enormity of the rebuilding tasks facing Chile and the military mindset in which violence against Marxist enemies was fully justified, Chile's new rulers might have been expected to simply ignore these developments. Instead, military officials routinely discussed the threat posed by human rights advocates and Western states and expressed a surprisingly high level of concern about the government's international legitimacy.

During the junta's second recorded meeting, in the afternoon of September 13, 1973, members discussed three items relating to the international arena (of thirty-one total items discussed during this session).[38] First, they discussed the need to defend themselves in the United Nations against accusations that they expected Cuba to make at any moment. Second, they discussed how to get aid from the United States, with Pinochet reporting that the U.S. ambassador had offered all the help that might be needed. Finally, naval commander in chief José Merino suggested that a secret Marxist shadow government had been set up to feed damaging and deceitful information about Chile to international actors, noting that much of this information had already turned up in the foreign press.

By the time the junta met for its fourth recorded session on September 17, 1973, it was ready to take action to defend the government's legitimacy on the international stage.[39] The junta instructed the foreign affairs minister to prepare a list of distinguished Chileans who would visit countries in the Americas and Europe and let others know what was really happening in Chile so they could correct "the distorted image of Chile abroad."[40] Junta members were convinced that Chile's problems abroad were caused by misinformation generated by an international Marxist campaign against Chile.[41] In fact, the interior minister suggested on September 21, 1973, that important international actors

should be brought to Chile in order to see Chilean reality for themselves.[42] Junta members agreed with this idea and allowed a variety of
international observers to visit Chile until the junta formally decided
to restrict such visits on November 5, 1973, because of the variety of
negative reports that resulted.[43]

The junta continued to demonstrate a strong concern for Chile's
international legitimacy during the following months. In most of its
sessions, the junta considered at least one agenda item on how to
change the beliefs that other states and international actors held about
the government. Junta officials commonly identified two methods:
(1) more and better information (propaganda) about Chile's situation;
and (2) better legal arguments to deal with the petitions emanating
from intergovernmental bodies.

A few examples may serve to demonstrate the general pattern. On
September 27, 1973, the foreign minister told the junta that the large
number of refugees in foreign embassies was "damaging Chile's foreign
image" and needed to be resolved.[44] In the same meeting, the junta decided to send media representatives to a variety of embassies in Europe
"so that they [could] work with maximum speed to try to change the
distorted opinion" about Chile. On October 3, the junta met with the
foreign minister to discuss his upcoming talk in the United Nations
and recommended that he show photos demonstrating the arms, forti-
fications, and secret plans of the Communists in Chile.[45] On October 8,
the junta debated whether the death penalty was being applied to too
many minor crimes, which was "increasing the distortion of the country's image abroad."[46] In January 1974, junta members discussed the
"human rights problem," by which they meant the international petitions to investigate human rights in Chile.[47] They asked their legal advisors how to respond to these ongoing international petitions, especially
from the IACHR, and discussed ways to change legal descriptions about
the prisoners' status so that they might avoid the petitions altogether.
Throughout these months, the junta continually received a stream of
prominent Chileans who had traveled to Europe with the mission of
improving the country's image. They consistently reported mixed results; one summed up the sentiment when he lamented that Chile was
being turned into a "public relations Vietnam."[48]

It is remarkable that junta members worried so much about this issue when they were dealing with concerns such as re-establishing order, rooting out Marxists, reconstructing a failed economy, creating a new institutional apparatus to govern Chile, and coordinating a never-ending series of administrative tasks. If the order of items on the official agenda is an indication of their importance, then economic and internal security concerns certainly took priority for the junta. In a consistent fashion, however, questions about how to improve the government's international legitimacy routinely came up after dealing with these issues.

Junta officials and many government supporters seemed genuinely baffled by the wide scope of the international condemnations and especially by the participation of Western countries. Junta officials ascribed Chile's bad international press to a successful Marxist propaganda machine. They believed they had triggered such a backlash because Chile was the only country that had successfully thrown off Communist rule, thereby creating a turning point in the West's global struggle with Marxism.[49] They attributed the negative international reaction to Marxist influence within those countries and were reassured by contacts with high-level U.S. officials (especially Henry Kissinger), businessmen, and bankers that the United States would support Chile.[50] Military officials believed that if Western states only understood the extent of the Marxist threat in Chile, then the criticism would die down. To that end, they invited a special commission from the Organization of American States to study the problem of Marxist infiltration in Chile and launched new public relations campaigns in the United States and Europe.[51]

Official Chilean documents and speeches addressed to international audiences during these early months rarely even bothered to dignify Chile's critics by denying human rights abuses. Rather, the government attempted to achieve international legitimacy by making four key points.[52] First, the new government claimed to enjoy broad popular support because it had seized power from an undemocratic government that was in gross violation of Chile's constitution. Second, Chile was fighting an internal conflict that bordered on civil war, and some violence was unavoidable. Third, the transnational human rights network itself was devoid of moral authority because it was sponsored by Marxist countries and formed part of a vast international Marxist conspiracy against Chile. Fourth, Chile would some day return to some form of democracy, but only after society had been purged of its vices.

Expanding Network Activities and Ongoing Chilean Resistance

The government's hope that its efforts would alter opinions and improve Chile's image were not entirely groundless. At the time, it seemed reasonable to expect that the initial shock of the coup would gradually fade and that the human rights pressures on Chile would eventually die out. Before 1973, very few countries had experienced sustained and intense scrutiny for their human rights violations. International human rights norms were relatively new and untested, and any number of third world countries were under authoritarian rule that was just as violent and repressive – if not more so – as the Chilean variety.

Human rights issues, however, did not simply fade away. Within a few months of the coup, the transnational human rights network actually expanded its size and its activities, and Western states placed even greater pressures on the military government. For intergovernmental human rights organizations such as the IACHR and the Human Rights Commission of the United Nations, consideration of the Chilean case represented a sharp break from their traditional practice and established crucial precedents for later cases of widespread abuse. Western States, especially the United States, also plowed new ground in the Chilean case by making human rights issues a more prominent part of their bilateral relations. All of this ensured that human rights issues would retain a place on the military government's agenda.

Intergovernmental organizations played a key role in keeping the spotlight on Chile. The IACHR followed up its initial observation with a team of investigators in mid-1974 and issued a report later that year that was highly critical of the military government.[53] Meanwhile, the UN Human Rights Commission began considering the Chilean case in March 1974. In a test of procedures recently authorized by member states, the commission sent an ad hoc investigative team to Chile in July 1975, and – though the team was denied entry – issued a report that accused the government of systematic human rights abuses in late 1975.[54] In June 1975, the International Labor Organization issued a report accusing the military government of unlawfully executing labor leaders or torturing them to death.[55]

The first UN General Assembly condemnation of Chile in December 1974 especially created a stir. The General Assembly had previously condemned South Africa and Israel for human rights abuses, but repression in these cases was tied to international conflicts, more easily justifying UN involvement.[56] By placing Chile in the same category with South Africa and Israel and by condemning human rights violations without tying them to concerns about regional security, the United Nations set an important precedent.[57] Because the vote passed by such a wide margin, ninety to eight with twenty-six abstentions, it was clear that the condemnation could not be dismissed as simple opposition from Communist states. The Chilean media widely reported the results of the voting, though also carefully repeating the junta's arguments that it was part of a Marxist conspiracy. Still, the vote placed Chile in the same category as other international pariahs and garnered widespread attention among Chileans proud of their traditional respect for human rights and democracy. It ensured that discussions of human rights abuses were raised, albeit briefly, on the public's agenda for the first time.

In part because of urging from domestic human rights groups, Western states increased the pressure on Chile. In April 1974, Great Britain's Labor government announced a halt in arms sales to Chile and even blocked the delivery of a frigate and two submarines then under construction.[58] Other European governments, including France and Germany, tied Chilean loans in this period to the release of specific political prisoners. Once Chile released the prisoners, the governments granted the loans. Italy, the Netherlands, and Norway all cut most economic aid and voted against World Bank loans to Chile.[59] Then in September 1974 Senator Kennedy and others succeeded in passing legislation in the U.S. Congress that would limit economic aid to Chile to $25 million in fiscal year (FY) 1975, far less than the Ford administration's request. The legislation also mandated an end to military aid, though not U.S. arms sales. In early 1975 several West European countries in the Paris Club refused to renegotiate their portions of Chile's massive foreign debt because of human rights concerns.[60] Nonmilitary-ruled Latin American countries also pressured Chile: Mexico broke diplomatic relations in November 1974, while Colombia and Venezuela reduced the level of diplomatic contact.[61]

As I argue later, these various pressures did not fundamentally threaten Chile's economy or security, but they did manage to catch the attention of government officials. As a result, human rights issues continued to occupy a place on the government's agenda in a variety of ways. Chile's Foreign Ministry, in particular, constantly listened to accusations, fielded (and usually turned down) requests for information or permission for fact-finding visits, responded verbally or in writing to international condemnations, and defended Chile in speeches, documents, and private conversations.[62] Even though they avoided using the term *human rights*, other Chilean officials also found themselves forced to deal with the transnational network. In their meetings, junta members regularly discussed how to deal with Chile's critics and in their public speeches and interviews often took the opportunity to denounce the so-called Marxist campaign. After the General Assembly voted against Chile in November 1974, the pro-government mass media even began discussing human rights issues. One newsmagazine, *Ercilla*, went so far as to argue that "Our country . . . should take concrete steps to demonstrate that human rights are not trampled underfoot and that, in a dynamic and progressive way, the situation is being normalized."[63] In the context of the times, the statement could be read as a carefully worded criticism of the government's repressive policies.

Throughout this period, Chilean officials demonstrated concern for the government's international legitimacy and the potentially corrosive effects of the transnational campaign. Evidence of this concern can be found in government documents, speeches, and interviews published during the government's first two years, as well as in the minutes of the junta meetings and in interviews with government officials that occurred after they left power. Two types of evidence may be found: (1) Expressions of concern about the damaging effects of the transnational campaign and efforts to halt the network's activities; and (2) Discourse and actions intended to change the beliefs held by foreign states and by actors in the transnational network.

Throughout 1974–75, the junta continued to discuss the international community's poor opinion of the military government and how to improve it. For example, on May 13, 1974, the Chilean ambassador to the United States reported to the junta that the international Marxist campaign was exercising a lot of influence in the United States through human rights groups.[64] According to the ambassador, these groups wrote letters to the U.S. Congress, to the press, to the Chilean Junta, and others, and thereby gave Chile an unfavorable international image. He complained that he needed better information on the state of affairs in Chile and required some publicists to distribute the information. In response, the junta ordered a renewed public relations offensive in the United States.[65] Then on May 27, the minister of defense argued before the junta that Chile's international situation was very grave because of problems with human rights and the unresolved situation of some asylum seekers in foreign embassies.[66] The junta assured him the problem was being studied.

In public interviews and speeches, top officials repeated these concerns about Chile's international legitimacy. In an August 1975 interview, Pinochet said that the problem that bothered him most was the foreign journalists and international commissions who would come to Chile to investigate the situation, and then report only the information provided by Chile's adversaries.[67] He stated that Chile's main foreign policy goal was "to recover the place that it deserves and that it has held in the international community." It is difficult to see a domestic political motive for Pinochet to make these statements, making it more likely they were an honest reflection of his thought. Chilean officials tried hard to distinguish their government from other military governments in the Third World. Many military men were descended from European ancestry and loathed comparisons between Chile and other military-ruled countries in the developing world. Such a mindset seems evident in Government Secretary General Pedro Ewing's curt response to a question during a 1974 interview: "Yes we're a legal government. We are not a dictatorship of the tropical variety."[68]

The government's strong-arm tactics against relatively small and weak human rights groups also provides evidence of the government's concern for its international legitimacy. Although human rights groups had no mass membership, no media outlets, and little money, Chilean officials correctly understood that they were funneling information about Chile to the outside world. As a result, security agents routinely harassed, imprisoned, and exiled human rights activists.[69] Pinochet placed especially strong pressure on Archbishop Silva and the Catholic Church to disband COPACHI. Although the archbishop ultimately complied, he quickly created a new, stronger human rights organization under his direct control.[70] Officials also tried desperately to undermine the credibility of human rights groups through propaganda. In one incident, they planted media stories – later discredited – about disappeared citizens being killed in guerrilla violence outside of Chile. In another, they produced death certificates to show that disappeared people had actually died of natural causes—a claim that was true only in some of the cases.[71]

The pro-government media echoed official concerns and sometimes went even further in identifying the human rights campaign as a serious threat. In the wake of the negative UN General Assembly vote, the two most important Chilean news magazines, Qué Pasa and Ercilla, noted in prominent stories that Chile had never before been the subject of such international scorn.[72] After dutifully reporting Pinochet's prediction that Chile would ably confront the international conspiracy, Qué Pasa argued that it would nevertheless be an error to underestimate the threat facing Chile—even while it simultaneously dismissed the possibility of an international boycott. Even government supporters openly faulted the Foreign Ministry for its inability to protect Chile from a "dangerous isolation."[73]

Yet still government officials resisted making any serious changes to their discourse and policies in the first two years. The closest they came was to downgrade Chile's internal juridical status from a state of war to a state of siege—a meaningless policy change. On August 29, 1974, Chile's ambassador to the United Nations met with the junta to express concern that the country's repressive policies were weakening Chile's international position.[74] As if revealing a remarkable strategy, Pinochet then told the ambassador of a plan to change the legal status to a state of siege rather than a state of war in an effort to improve Chile's international image. He noted, of course, that this name change would not result in any actual decrease in government powers. In a junta meeting a few days later, Pinochet expressed hope that this maneuver would ease international criticism somewhat because a state of siege did not sound as harsh as a state of war.[75] Jaime Guzmán, a trusted civilian advisor, explained to the junta that "Chile would begin living under a state of siege ... which gives you all the powers that you want, and at the same time, the name is very presentable, because, for example, Colombia lived twenty years in state of siege and Argentina fourteen years. Any country can live in a state of siege and no one becomes alarmed." Pinochet then announced this change with great fanfare on the one-year anniversary of the coup.

One might surmise from these comments that the junta and its advisors demonstrated significant naiveté. Chile's critics would not stop complaining simply because of a decree changing the legal name of the state of emergency operating in Chile. However, the debate over this legislation shows not only naiveté, but also the high-level concern for the government's legitimacy and the ambiguous status of human rights abuses in Chile. International actors had succeeded in putting this issue on the military government's agenda and in creating concern about Chile's possible isolation, but government officials hardly knew how to respond because they all agreed that repression was justified. Thus, the junta debated at length and with fervor name changes that were insignificant, both to the people suffering repression and to the international observers monitoring it.

One of the simplest responses to the government's critics would have been to proclaim Chile's loyalty to human rights norms, yet top government officials avoided human rights discourse in the first two years and did not even spend much time denying the abuses. It is striking that the Chilean foreign minister's first address to the UN General Assembly failed to deny human rights abuses, save only a brief denial that foreigners in Chile were being forcefully repatriated.[76] It is equally striking that prominent military officials, especially Pinochet, scarcely ever used the term *human rights* in their speeches and interviews during the first two years of military rule, even though they frequently referred to democracy and democratic governance.

The only prominent reference to individual rights in the government's first two years is remarkable for its exceptional nature. Six months after the coup, the junta released its most important ideological statement, the *Declaración de Principios del Gobierno de Chile*. Authored largely by the civilian legal advisor Jaime Guzmán, the declaration revealed a deep tension between the government's desire to defend its legitimacy to a Western liberal international community and the military's war on Marxism. While declaring that people have natural rights superior to the state and that the state should be at the service of individuals, the declaration also argued that the most important end of the state is to achieve the common good. Likewise, the declaration endorsed human rights yet argued that important restrictions needed to be placed on those rights: "The right to disagree should be maintained, but the experience of recent years indicates the necessity of placing admissible limits on that disagreement." Even this limited concept of human rights did not find any important echo in other government documents or speeches in the first two years of military rule.

Explaining Chile's Response

Why didn't the military government ignore the human rights pressures or at least assign them a lower priority? Why spend the valuable time of the four junta members in repeated meetings in the first two years of rule discussing international criticisms and how to respond? Why launch so many public relations campaigns, send abroad some of the best and brightest government supporters, and work so hard to assure Chile's good name in the international arena? Not all authoritarian governments appear to be so concerned about the beliefs of other international actors. Why Chile?

The answer may be found in the moderate extent to which international human rights norms resonated inside Chile. Unlike other Latin American countries, Chile had considerable historical experience with the rule of law, democratic politics, and respect for human rights. In fact, in the 143 years before 1973, "Chile experienced only thirteen months of unconstitutional rule under some form of Junta and only four months under a Junta dominated exclusively by the military."[77] Chileans generally expected the state to respect civil and political liberties, and many initially believed (or hoped) that the military would hand over power after restoring order.[78] The stance of the centrist Christian Democratic Party in the early years of military rule illustrates this point. Party leaders welcomed the coup as a necessary antidote to the excesses of the Allende government, but then rejected the authoritarian discourse and practices of the military government, calling instead for a return to civilian, democratic rule.[79] Bishops in the Catholic Church, in turn, carefully articulated their concerns about state terror and rights violations in April 1974.[80] Despite heavy repression, labor unions also continued to function and to call for better respect for labor rights.[81] These efforts in the face of severe repression demonstrate that human rights norms did not simply disappear from Chilean society with the advent of military rule.

At the same time, the social and economic turmoil preceding the coup and the systematic terror after the coup reduced the saliency of human rights norms in Chile. Conservatives supported the coup and ignored human rights abuse, while many centrists failed to strongly condemn the government, and repression prevented leftists from speaking out.[82] Many Chileans undoubtedly supported human rights in the abstract, but cared little about ensuring that human rights were respected in reality. This sentiment is reflected in the recollections of one civilian who later became an advisor to the military government:

> Well then, the military is the military. They implemented a state of siege and shot a few people, but were also shot at a little. What happened at first did not receive much attention. It was seen as a type of war. There were also a lot of people who committed excesses. People to whom morals were not important. After that, the security services began their abuses, let's call them. People said that there were tortures, but no one knew for certain. I believe that after about one and a half years, people came to see this as a real problem. There was at least a year or more in which there were very few who knew anything or who even realized that human rights was an issue.[83]

While Chile's moderate levels of normative fit ensured some sensitivity to human rights pressures, other domestic factors worked in the opposite direction. A closed domestic structure, a crisis atmosphere, and the dominance of force-oriented elites prevented greater changes from occurring despite a vigorous transnational effort. Most noticeable, of course, was Chile's state-dominated political structure. State power was centralized in the hands of the junta, which subjected all other actors to its authority. Before the coup, Chile had enjoyed one of the most vibrant and politically active civil societies in Latin America.[84] Although violence and repression did not completely crush all social organizations, they enjoyed very little room to maneuver. As Garretón summarized it: "During the first years of the military government, there was no opposition, strictly speaking, but rather a resistance by the parties and social sectors that had supported the Popular Unity government. These groups sought to assure the survival of their members and leaders (many of whom were killed, imprisoned, or exiled) and to maintain what they could of their organizational apparatus."[85]

With respect to elite coalitions, no government supporters questioned the need for forceful, violent repression, nor did any suggest a pressing need for new rules to regulate and legitimize government power. The military's tradition of subordination to hierarchy, Pinochet's skillful manipulation of military promotion and his complete control over the feared secret police ensured absolute loyalty within the military.[86] Government officials and their conservative supporters had been united by their undying opposition to Salvador Allende's ill-fated government (1970–73), and they remained unified during these first years of rule.

Finally, a sense of crisis and the need for forceful action pervaded the new government. The last two years of the Allende administration had witnessed rapid economic deterioration that continued and even worsened in the first years of the military government.[87] Inflation shot from 20 percent in 1971 to 78 percent in 1972, to 353 percent the year of the coup, then to 505 percent in 1974.[88] Economic growth declined in 1972, dropped sharply in 1973, barely pulled back into the black in 1974, and collapsed in 1975. At the same time, unemployment mounted from 9.2 percent in 1974 to 14.5 percent in 1975, while real salaries in 1975 stood at only 62.9 percent of their 1970 level.[89] Although the state faced no serious security threat, military forces carried out their war on Marxism by hunting down and exterminating the remaining leftist groups and by cracking down on labor leaders, human rights activists, and centrist politicians. As a result, the slings and arrows of transnational groups and foreign states paled in comparison to the tasks of rebuilding a broken economy and carrying out this "war" on Marxism.[90]

Alternative Explanations

Is there an alternative explanation for human rights gaining a place on the government's agenda? Two possibilities need to be examined. First, O'Donnell and Schmitter argue that softliners are responsible for initiating changes in authoritarian governments.[91] The best available evidence, however, suggests that a softline faction did not yet exist in Chile in 1973–75. No government officials called for liberalization in those early years, nor did they raise concerns about government repression and human rights.[92] In the late 1980s and early 1990s, prominent government supporters claimed that they had raised human rights issues during the early days of the government and had in fact moderated government practices in some cases.[93] Little – if any – independent evidence of these claims exists, and they deserve to be treated with skepticism. To be sure, prominent government officials, including Pinochet himself, repeatedly promised that Chile would one day return to the path of democracy. The concept of democracy, however, was rarely defined and rarely associated with human rights. As Pinochet put it, "It must be understood that there cannot now be a liberal democratic government. That there has to be a government with democratic characteristics, but very authoritarian."[94]

The government's Constitutional Commission – created within a week of the coup and charged with drafting a new constitution for Chile – discussed a future governmental system in which human rights would be respected.[95] Commission members did not yet constitute an important political faction, however, because they played the role of philosophical wise men engaged in abstract debates rather than active proponents of changes in government policy. During its sessions, the commission discussed the broad outlines of a future constitution and heard expert testimony on the topic. In a memo drafted to guide its work on November 26, 1973, the commission argued that all of Chile's history had been characterized by the development of human rights, that the new constitution would broaden and perfect human rights guarantees, and that Chile would be in harmony with international human rights declarations and treaties.[96] The commission, however, labored in relative obscurity at a very slow pace without any effort to actually promote human rights. Its members supported the official position that a new constitution must be indefinitely delayed.[97]

Rather than raise concerns with the violation of human rights, civilian advisors schooled in Western liberalism worked out elaborate justifications of repression by positing a hierarchy of human rights. They argued that it was at times necessary to violate some of the less important rights in order to protect the most important ones. One argument articulated by Constitutional Commission President Enrique Ortúzar became quite common: "When the social body gets sick – which happens when states of emergency are imposed – it is necessary to restrict some rights so that citizens may enjoy the more important ones."[98] Specifically, government officials argued that they must restrict free speech and free assembly in order to better combat Marxist terrorism and thus protect the more important rights to life, property, and peaceful living. Likewise, government officials often argued that those who promoted totalitarian ideologies forfeited some of their rights. Because Marxism seeks an end to democracy and because democracy is inherently superior to Marxism, they argued, democracy must be protected by restricting the ability of Marxists to circulate their ideas or to organize. Many ordinary Chileans agreed with the sentiments expressed by one Chilean lawyer to a foreign reporter a month after the coup: "I don't believe the stories you tell me, but after the things the supporters of Salvador Allende have done to Chile, they deserve whatever happens to them."[99]

Even if we accept the possibility that some civilians with access to the junta expressed concerns about torture and murder, there is little evidence that junta officials treated these concerns seriously. One instructive example is offered by the junta meeting on April 15, 1974. At this meeting, the justice minister told the junta that military courts could make mistakes while trying and sentencing people, and noted that the Supreme Court was incapable of reviewing military court decisions under current law and practice.[100] He repeatedly suggested that history would likely blame the mistakes of the military courts on the military institutions more broadly (and by implication, the junta), and so the government should study the possibility of Supreme Court review of military court decisions. The junta responded superficially by setting up a study commission.

The second possible explanation concerns the realist argument that states make cost-benefit calculations based on national interests defined in terms of military and economic power – not social issues like legitimacy. In this perspective, it is powerful states that coerce changes in others through sanctions and military force. For realists, the mobilization of the transnational network and concerns about government legitimacy would play only a secondary explanatory role, at best. For this explanation to make sense, we should find evidence that the sanctions enacted by Western powers posed a clear and serious threat to Chile's economic growth or national security.

Viewed in the proper context, however, economic penalties imposed by foreign states were not very damaging to Chile's economy or to its military capabilities. The sanctions were significant because they were among the first to be tied to domestic human rights abuses and because they demonstrated the influence of new human rights groups in Western countries. At the same time, a variety of powerful states and financial institutions actively supported the military government, thereby undermining the limited sanctions. In the United States, the Nixon-Ford administration, which had drastically reduced loans and economic

Table 1: International Aid for Chile, 1962–76 (by fiscal year, in millions of U.S. dollars)

	1962–70 yearly average	1971–73 yearly average	1974	1975	1976
U.S. economic aid: Loans and grants	80.0	6.0	8.5	93.7	82.3
U.S. military aid: Loans and grants	12.1	11.0	15.9	0.7	0.0
World Bank and Inter-American Development Bank	42.2	3.9	110.8	65.5	58.2
Private bank funding of Chilean government	NA	NA	304.7	216.6	245.0

Sources: Rows 1 and 2 from Agency for International Development (AID), *U.S. Overseas Loans and Grants and Assistance from International Organizations* (Washington DC: U.S. Government, various years). Row 1 includes all loans and grants from AID and the Food for Peace program, the two major sources of aid. Row 2 includes all forms of loans and grants tracked by AID. Row 3 from Schoultz, *Human Rights and United States Policy*, 283. Row 4 from Brian H. Smith, *Church and Politics in Chile*, 326. Row 4 includes private banks in the United States and Western Europe.

aid to Allende's government, took the lead in helping the new military rulers. Within three weeks of the coup, administration officials were arguing on Capitol Hill that economic and military aid should be sent to Chile despite the widespread human rights problems.[101] Although Senator Kennedy succeeded in passing legislation limiting U.S. economic aid to $25 million in FY 1975, economic aid actually increased, as noted in table 1. The Ford administration circumvented the congressional cap by redefining aid categories, by drawing on discretionary funds, and by increasing forms of assistance that arguably fell outside the mandated limits.[102]

Intergovernmental financial institutions and commercial banks poured capital into Chile's new government that more than offset any small losses in economic aid from Western countries.[103] At the urging of the United States, the Inter-American Development Bank approved two loans for Chile in April 1974 – over the objections of Mexico, Venezuela, and others – while it had previously failed to approve a single new loan for Chile during Allende's three-year presidency.[104] In fact, intergovernmental lending agencies like the World Bank had restricted loans during the Allende period to an average of about $4 million per year, but then poured an average of $78 million per year into Chile from 1974 to 1976.[105] Even some Western European countries that cut off economic and military aid continued to authorize loans and arms sales for the military government.[106]

With respect to military security, Chile faced no serious threat from a rival state until 1978, when long-standing disputes with Bolivia and Argentina threatened to escalate into war. Interestingly, the Nixon-Ford administration respected congressional sanctions on military aid, which fell sharply to less than a million dollars in 1975 – perhaps because discretionary funds were less available or perhaps because the region was now relatively secure from Communist threats. Still, the British and U.S. military sanctions did not seriously damage Chile's military or threaten its ability to defend itself. From 1970 to 1974, Chile accounted for 17 percent of South American military imports, and from 1975 to 1979 Chile bought 14 percent of the military hardware shipped into the region.[107] Great Britain, the major Chilean arms supplier from 1970 to 1974, was replaced by France in the latter part of the decade. The United States remained a major weapons supplier, despite the cutoff of concessional loans and grants, thanks to commercial arms sales and deliveries of previously ordered goods. Brazil and Israel, among others, became major weapons suppliers in the mid-1970s, and Chile even began manufacturing some of its own weapons. Generally speaking, Chilean arms imports fluctuated widely, but did not fall below 1972 levels and in fact rose sharply in 1976, as illustrated by table 2. The dramatic dip in arms imports in 1975 could be explained by the deep economic recession in Chile that year as well as by the initial impact of British and U.S. sanctions. Further, overall Chilean military spending was consistently and substantially higher, in real dollars, in the first three years of military rule, as compared with the Allende period.

Given Chile's ability to find new sources of capital and arms, it is difficult to argue that sanctions alone forced the military government to discuss human rights issues. Of course, sanctions were not entirely cost-free for Chile. They certainly gave some teeth to the documents, reports, and verbal condemnations issued by states and network actors.

Table 2: Chilean Military Expenses, 1972–76 (in millions of U.S. dollars)

	1972	1973	1974	1975	1976
Military expenditures	225	360	627	489	487
Arms imports	16	108	99	25	160
U.S. commercial arms deliveries	0.5	0.5	1.8	0.6	1.4

Sources: Row 1 from Stockholm International Peace Research Institute, World Armaments and Disarmament, in constant 1979 prices and exchange rates. Row 2 from Arms Control and Disarmament Agency, World Military Expenditures and Arms Transfers (Washington DC: U.S. Government, various years). Row 3 from Schoultz, Human Rights and United States Policy, 321–22.

Chilean officials worried about the government's declining international legitimacy in part because it could generate even harsher sanctions. At the same time, government officials demonstrated concern for Chile's social acceptance among other states in ways that cannot be explained solely by reference to the economic and military penalties that social exclusion implies.

Similar political events can often take on very different meanings, depending on how they are framed. State-sponsored summary executions may be viewed as either justifiable violence in the name of self-defense during warlike conditions or as an egregious and irreversible abuse of a human being's fundamental right to life. Which one of these meanings is adopted depends on pre-existing cultural understandings and strategic efforts by political groups to endow the events with particular meanings. In this respect, framing may be defined as "the conscious strategic efforts by groups of people to fashion shared understandings of the world and of themselves that legitimate and motivate collective action."[108]

The early conflict between the military government and human rights groups was at root a contest to frame events in Chile in a way that would fashion shared understandings about their meaning. Both sought principally to influence the understandings of Western states. The government-sponsored executions, torture, and illegal detention did not automatically occur within a human rights frame. In fact, in 1973, the prevailing frame among states was that of sovereignty and nonintervention in domestic affairs. This frame was supplemented by an anti-Communist frame which divided the world into black and white, East and West, and tyranny and freedom. It would have been natural for Western states to view Chile's activities as first, none of their business, and second, quite justified in any case. Chilean military officials certainly expected this reaction.

Yet human rights groups moved very rapidly to marshal evidence in ways that persuaded most Western states that the government's activities should be viewed as intolerable human rights abuses. The sheer violence of the coup in a country that had experienced decades of democratic governance worked to the advantage of human rights groups. Many Western European states and social groups admired Allende's progressive policies and viewed Chile as one of their own. As a result, most Western states interpreted Chile's actions within a human rights frame. Constant efforts by domestic, transnational, and intergovernmental human rights groups reinforced and strengthened this view.

Having lost the framing battle, the military government found itself at a distinct disadvantage. Chile was in danger of being a pariah nation. Domestic human rights groups funneled crucial information about repression to international actors. These actors, in turn, used the information to challenge the legitimacy of the military government and to encourage states to impose sanctions. To complete the virtuous circle (from the perspective of the human rights network), military and economic sanctions undoubtedly strengthened the network's efforts to shame and to isolate Chile. The sanctions did not substantially alter the flow of military and economic resources into Chile, but they did suggest the potential that tangible costs would result from Chile's troubles with legitimacy.

Military officials did not accept the human rights frame and generally refused to see their activities as violations of human rights. Yet they understood that other states interpreted their behavior in this way. The government could have ignored these pressures – especially because they included few tangible sanctions – and could have refused to discuss the issue by invoking norms of nonintervention. Yet officials repeatedly expressed concern about the implications of human rights pressures for Chile's legitimacy among Western states. They were sensitive to these pressures in part because of the cultural resonance of human rights norms in Chile; that is, the widespread domestic understandings that Chile was fundamentally a democratic country and would one day return to the democratic path. At the same time, the absence of other domestic characteristics capable of amplifying human rights pressure ensured that the government would continue to discuss the problem without taking much action. As a result, government officials simply fought the framing battle without enacting changes in domestic policies.

THREE

Changing Discourse
and Security Practices,
1976–1977

After two years of resistance, government officials began adopting the discourse of human rights in late 1975. Two years later they made the first substantive, though limited, changes in their repressive practices. The government first explicitly endorsed a wide range of human rights standards on September 11, 1976, when it introduced Constitutional Act Three, a detailed list of human rights guarantees. Unfortunately, other legal measures nullified these rights by authorizing the junta to suspend them under the states of emergency that were constantly in force in Chile. In practice, the government continued to systematically violate all types of human rights. Then on August 6, 1977, the government unexpectedly disbanded the Directorate of National Intelligence (DINA)–a pillar of government power and the central agent of state terrorism–and replaced it on August 12 with a new security agency known as the National Information Center (CNI). The demise of the DINA altered the face of repression in Chile. Rather than actively seeking out and destroying all opposition, the government switched tactics and began to contain the opposition, employing the most brutal repression only when opposition was openly manifested.[1] Further, government officials enshrined repression in a legal framework of new laws rather than relying strictly on the politically costly logic of war.[2]

Why did the government adopt a discourse of human rights in 1976 and then change its repressive strategy in 1977? Human rights pressures on Chile increased substantially in 1976. The transnational human rights network expanded and strengthened when the Catholic Church created a new human rights organization, the Vicariate of Solidarity, in January 1976. Other Chilean rights groups either formed or expanded their activities in the mid-1970s, greatly enlarging the network. After Jimmy Carter's election, the United States joined multilateral votes to condemn Chile's human rights abuses and imposed new economic and military sanctions, which were actually implemented. At the same time, declining economic and security threats, the rise of a rule-oriented faction, and moderate levels of normative fit created favorable conditions for human rights pressures. As Chilean officials interacted with international actors and with each other, they constructed a stronger government interest in legitimacy. As this interest grew, top officials first adopted a discourse of human rights and then began to view the DINA as more of a liability than an asset and disbanded it. Consideration of Chile's domestic structure adds little to the explanation.

This analysis complements rather than replaces previous arguments. Valenzuela argues that two factors explain the demise of the DINA.[3] First, softliners became more powerful, especially after finding anti-DINA allies among military generals who feared the power of the security apparatus. Second, the United States placed tremendous pressure on Chile in connection with the car-bomb murder of prominent Chilean human rights activist Orlando Letelier in Washington DC, in which the DINA was implicated. These two factors are crucial, but should be understood in the context of broader human rights pressures and the government's growing interest in legitimacy. On their own, U.S. sanctions on Chile did not substantially threaten Chile's economic growth or military preparedness. Without a focus on legitimacy, it is difficult to explain why human rights pressures – even when backed up by a powerful state like the United States – would produce important domestic changes in Chile or why a new rule-oriented faction was able to make such headway against a well-established and powerful security apparatus.

In this chapter, I first set the context by describing the rise of network activities and state pressures. I then trace the domestic conditions that were changing during this period, namely, the rise of a rule-oriented faction and the decline in threat levels because of economic recovery and the end of violent opposition. The following sections document changes in the government's strategy, including the important rhetorical changes in 1976 and the end of the DINA in 1977. I then assess alternative explanations, discuss the importance of the changes, and offer a conclusion.

Network Activities and State Pressure

Government officials hoped that the dissolution of the Committee of Cooperation for Peace (COPACHI) in late 1975 would strike a serious blow to the transnational network and the flow of information out of Chile. Quite the opposite occurred. In January 1976, Santiago Archbishop Raúl Silva created what would become one of Latin America's best-known human rights organizations, the Vicariate of Solidarity.[4] Almost immediately, the Vicariate began playing a central role in gathering and disseminating information about human rights abuses and quickly built a well-developed network of transnational ties to other human rights and religious groups. Over the next fourteen years, the Vicariate tracked thousands of cases of disappearance, arbitrary arrest, torture, harassment, and imprisonment for political views and furnished that information to a wide variety of domestic and international organizations and foreign states. The Vicariate's primary publication, the bimonthly bulletin Solidarity, circulated thirty thousand copies in Chile and abroad and became well-known among human rights activists in the West.[5] At the same time, the Vicariate presented thousands of writs of habeus corpus in the courts, offered legal assistance, food, medical assistance, and other financial help to hundreds of thousands of people, and organized a large number of social and community groups.

A variety of international donors funded these activities and became an essential part of the transnational network.[6] Although the Catholic Church paid most of the Vicariate's expenses, especially in the early years, foreign donors provided the bulk of the church's funds. As Smith has noted, "None of the new projects begun under the auspices of the Chilean Church since 1973 could have been inaugurated or sustained over time without very considerable outside support."[7] International actors donated an estimated $100 million to the Chilean Church from 1974 to 1979, dwarfing the total of $4 million the church received during the same period from its domestic tithing campaigns.[8] In addition, a number of churches, government agencies, and large foundations in Germany, Belgium, France, Austria, Switzerland, the Netherlands, Canada, Sweden, the United States, and elsewhere, directly funded the Vicariate's work.[9] Over time, these direct funders became more important than money funneled through the Catholic Church.

Other Chilean human rights groups sprang up or expanded their activities in the mid to late 1970s and enjoyed important links with the Vicariate and with international human rights groups.[10] After COPACHI was disbanded, evangelical churches focused their support on the Social Help Foundation of the Christian Churches (Fundación de Ayuda Social de las Iglesias Cristianas – FASIC). With active church support, FASIC expanded its activities by working with refugees and exiled families, by offering psychological help and counseling to the government's victims and their families, and by circulating reports and statistics on human rights abuses, especially the problems of political prisoners.[11] The Service for Peace and Justice, a Latin American human rights NGO that won the Nobel Peace Prize in 1980, established a Chilean chapter in 1977. Chilean human rights victims and their families established other human rights organizations that favored dramatic public protests and personal denunciations.[12] They included the Association of Families of the Detained-Disappeared, founded in 1974, the Association of Families of Political Prisoners, founded in 1976, and the Association of Families of Executed Political Activists, founded in 1978.[13] These groups generally lacked international funding and recognition, but still enjoyed personal contact and moral support from the Vicariate and other human rights groups.[14] The Vicariate helped organize and fund the relatives of the disappeared and gave them office space, but victims' groups chose their own strategies and activities.[15]

The large number of Chileans living in exile facilitated the formation of new human rights groups in Europe, the United States, and Latin America with strong ties to each other and to dissidents who remained in Chile.[16] Exiles formed solidarity committees in more than fifty countries, helping to ensure that Chile's abuses would remain an important international issue.[17] In 1974, four prominent government opponents exiled in Rome founded the magazine Chile América, which served as a platform for a variety of exiled Chileans to critique the government for its human rights abuses and other problems.[18] The Institute for the New Chile, in Amsterdam, served as a meeting place for the opposition, as a place to share information and produce new critiques of the Chilean government, and as a launching pad for lobbying campaigns seeking support from Western governments and agencies. Exile also facilitated ties between existing Western human rights groups and their counterparts in Chile. Pepe Zalaquette, a Chilean lawyer, became active in human rights work soon after the 1973 coup, later joined the

Vicariate, was imprisoned and expelled from Chile, and then joined the board of directors for Amnesty International USA, later becoming chair of the international executive committee of AI.[19]

Influenced by the reports coming out of Chile and personal contacts with exiled Chileans, Western intergovernmental and nongovernmental human rights organizations stepped up their pressures on the government. In June 1976, the Inter-American Commission on Human Rights presented its second report on the human rights situation in Chile, unveiling it in Santiago itself at an annual meeting of the Organization of American States (OAS).[20] The report accused the military government of systematically violating fundamental rights and was accompanied by a letter signed by five prominent Chilean lawyers confirming the essence of the report. A third report followed, in March 1977, documenting little change. In 1976, the UN Commission on Human Rights first voted (twenty-six in favor and two against, with four abstentions) to formally accuse Chile of human rights violations and to call for improvements.[21] In the United States, a variety of organizations, including the Washington Office on Latin America, Americans for Democratic Action, and the Center for International Policy documented U.S. support for human rights abuses in Chile and attempted to change U.S. policy. [22] A new coalition of U.S. organizations formed the Human Rights Working Group in January 1976 and focused their first efforts on changing U.S. Congressional legislation toward Chile. Some groups, such as the Chilean Commission of Human Rights, focused exclusively on Chile and generally enjoyed more media attention and longer institutional lives than other country-specific human rights lobbies.

Under pressure from U.S.-based network groups and from Congress, the Ford administration began to make cosmetic changes in its policy toward Chile in late 1975. In December, the United States first joined ninety-four other states in a UN General Assembly vote imploring Chile to improve its human rights situation. Then in June 1976, U.S. Secretary of State Henry Kissinger visited Santiago in conjunction with the annual Organization of American States meetings and publicly stated that human rights violations were impairing U.S. relations with Chile. At the time, and for years afterwards, analysts interpreted this statement as an important policy change for the Ford administration.[23] Yet recently declassified documents demonstrate that the Ford administration was making rhetorical concessions designed to head off pressures from domestic human rights groups while maintaining the closest possible ties with the military government.[24] During a private meeting, Kissinger reassured Pinochet that Chile was the "victim of left-wing groups all around the world" and that its "greatest sin" was the overthrow of a "government which was going communist." Kissinger explained that the U.S. human rights campaign would force him to refer publicly to Chile's human rights situation in an attempt to head off congressional sanctions, but that the administration remained quite sympathetic with the government.

Kissinger's ploy failed to work on a U.S. Congress eager to curtail a weakened executive even further and happy to please domestic human rights groups in an election year. Human rights groups found an especially receptive atmosphere in Congress owing to the continuing political fallout over Vietnam and widespread public sentiment favoring an injection of morality into U.S. foreign policy. The Human Rights Working Group convinced Rep. Donald Fraser to introduce legislation in the House that would permanently and effectively restrict economic aid to Chile.[25] Fraser used data from another human rights–oriented interest group, the Center for International Policy, to persuade the House Committee on International Relations to adopt the measure, which was later approved by the full House. With strong support from human rights activists, Senator Edward Kennedy introduced an amendment to the International Security Assistance and Arms Export Control Act of 1976 in the Senate that would tighten up the economic sanctions and significantly expand the military sanctions on Chile.[26] As combined by House-Senate conference committee, and adopted by Congress in June, the legislation entirely ended all U.S. military aid and sales to Chile, both public and private, and reduced all forms of government economic aid to $27.5 million per year.

The most important event of 1976, however, was the September car bomb murder in Washington DC of Orlando Letelier, a former minister in Salvador Allende's government and fervent international opponent of the Chilean military government. In the ensuing investigation, U.S. officials slowly came to the conclusion that Chilean security forces had masterminded the crime.[27] In May and June 1977, the United States began using diplomatic channels to ask the military government for more information on any links between Chilean security officials and the Cubans who had been indicted for the murder. Although Chile denied that it possessed evidence of any such connections, the United States used the Letelier case to maintain heavy pressure on the Pinochet government until an initial resolution (detailed below) was achieved in early 1978. U.S. pressures were especially strong because the state-sponsored terrorism had occurred on U.S. soil, rendering invalid the normal protests that U.S. human rights activities constituted intervention in Chile's internal affairs.

Changing Domestic Conditions

Beginning in 1976, the Chilean political landscape changed in two ways that made the government more sensitive to these human rights pressures. First, several splits developed in the authoritarian government, most importantly between rule-oriented actors who worried about legitimizing the government and force-oriented ones who did not. Second, crisis levels decreased as an economic recovery took hold and it became apparent that security forces had completed their task of exterminating Marxists. At the same time, Chile's domestic structure and level of normative fit remained unchanged.

The Rise of Rule-Oriented Actors

Although Pinochet retained his considerable power and remained the final decision maker, factions began to develop among his advisors in the mid-1970s as they competed for influence.[28] The DINA and its supporters comprised the dominant force-oriented faction until 1977. Military officials formed its core, but this faction also included civilian lawyers, conservative politicians, journalists, and other professionals who admired corporatist principles. Influenced principally by military-style nationalist thought, faction leaders stressed first and foremost the principle of national unity, treating everyone as an enemy who did not trumpet the need for military guidance of the state.[29] They openly defended extreme repression, arguing that Marxists were not Chileans (and scarcely human beings) and must be excised like cancer from the body. Force-oriented actors favored corporatist economic arrangements in which the state would lead industrial and agricultural interests to create a strong economy that would nurture a strong state. They paid little attention to human rights pressures, dismissing them as irrelevant or utilizing them to drum up nationalist support.

A rule-oriented faction first began to emerge in 1976, centered around a prominent group of civilian legal advisors who held key advisory posts to Pinochet and the junta.[30] These individuals emphasized the importance of long-term government survival and believed that ongoing extreme repression was counter-productive for long-term political stability. They viewed human rights pressures as a serious threat because they could undermine the legitimacy of the government and could embolden the domestic opposition. Rule-oriented actors proposed that military rulers build new political institutions centered around the concept of "protected democracy." This form of democracy would restrict any political participation from Marxists, would depoliticize labor unions, student organizations, and other social groups and would be overseen by the armed forces whose mission was to ensure that politics remained within certain bounds.[31]

The chief policy preference of rule-oriented actors was to create a new constitution that would institutionalize the principles of "protected democracy."[32] The proposed constitution would extend military rule for several years, but at the same time would promise democratic institutions and human rights guarantees at some future date. The promised democratic institutions included an elected congress, political parties, free and fair elections, and an independent judiciary. The institutions would be "protected" from possible Marxist influence (read broadly) by active military participation in politics and by rules excluding Marxist parties and individuals from participation.

In 1976, the battle between government factions heated up. The principal points of contention included whether and how to legitimize the government. Force-oriented actors opposed any attempt to legitimize the government through a constitution – especially one that appealed to human rights and democratic norms – because they feared it would tie their hands in the war on Marxism. Rule-oriented actors, led by the well-known lawyer and political analyst Jaime Guzmán, argued that a new constitution would help consolidate military rule in the short run while simultaneously offering a blueprint for new political institutions enabling the military to control politics in the long run. Guzmán and other civilian advisors lacked a popular political following or the economic clout of big business and so had to rely on personal access and persuasion to convince Pinochet and the junta of the importance of their proposed constitution. Though he held no cabinet position, Guzmán enjoyed virtually unrestricted access to Pinochet, other junta members, and many of Pinochet's top cabinet officials. Rule-oriented actors also dominated university posts, media outlets, and many government legal-study commissions. They used these institutional positions and access to top decision makers to formulate and spread their ideas.

Rule-oriented advisors found allies among both military officials and the powerful economists known as the "Chicago Boys." Presidential Chief of Staff Sergio Covarrubias, an army general who wielded significant influence within the junta, was the most important of the military officers. He quietly formed a friendship with Guzmán and helped persuade junta members of the need to counter human rights pressure and to legitimize the military government.[33] Odlanier Mena was another significant military ally. As chief of army intelligence in 1974–75, he had many disagreements and turf battles with the DINA. When it was clear that Pinochet backed the DINA without reservation, Mena resigned his army commission and served in diplomatic posts abroad. He continued, however, to work with rule-oriented individuals and in fact returned to Chile in 1977 as Pinochet's choice to head a reorganized intelligence agency after the DINA was disbanded.[34] A number of top economists – many of whom held key cabinet posts – also tacitly supported institutional plans "in order to secure the continuity of authoritarianism and the neo-liberal model."[35] By 1978, many economists were openly endorsing the rule-oriented political agenda.

Economic and Military Success

In 1976, the economy began to pull out of a deep recession and embarked on a six-year economic growth spurt. Foxley has argued persuasively that this economic recovery was not nearly the "miracle" that the government claimed because it still failed to pull Chile up to the economic levels it had achieved in 1970.[36] Nevertheless, the growth cycle represented a remarkable recovery from the harsh economic conditions of 1972–75. The economy grew at a healthy rate of 8 to 9 percent per year while unemployment began a gradual decline and real wages embarked on a long recovery. International capital fueled the recovery as

Chile piled up petrodollar debt and investors flocked to Chile to take advantage of its newly implemented neoliberal economic model.[37]

At the same time, the military successfully completed the first phase of its war on Marxism by wiping out all remnants of organized Marxist groups and leftist guerrillas. Three leftist groups – the Revolutionary Leftist Movement (Movimiento de Izquierda Revolucionaria – MIR), the Communist Party, and the Socialist Party – had reorganized underground after the 1973 coup, and the MIR attempted some assaults on military and government targets. In the face of the overwhelming force imposed by the military, however, these groups were quite ineffective. Leftist gunmen successfully killed thirty people in the relatively chaotic weeks following the coup, but then gunned down only six more victims during the next four years, from 1974 to 1977.[38] Extremist groups were neutralized (unable to carry out violent attacks) by early 1974 and were completely decimated in the ensuing months.[39] By late 1975, the DINA had systematically murdered, disappeared, tortured, jailed or exiled all underground opposition leaders. As the Rettig Commission put it, "during this period the regime's security services enjoyed complete mastery over the political movements that had supported the previous regime and had some capacity for violent response. This was the period when the MIR, the Communist Party, and the Socialist Party were under the harshest repression. Their structures fell apart and their members fled the country or were under continual pursuit."[40]

Economic recovery and the decimation of leftist party organizations substantially decreased the level of crisis. At the same time, military officials continued to operate with a mindset focused on all-out war against Marxism and continued to believe in the need for harsh repression. Nevertheless, with its economic survival no longer at stake and with its major military task accomplished, the government was free to focus attention on other concerns. Pressures from the international community, especially the United States, quickly grabbed the government's attention.

The Discourse of Human Rights

In the first two years of military rule, the government generally avoided any commitments to human rights norms, even in the abstract. In fact, government officials rarely even used the phrase *human rights* in major documents, speeches, and interviews.

Change came slowly. On the second anniversary of the coup, September 11, 1975, Pinochet first discussed human rights in a major speech to a domestic audience.[41] Although he did not explicitly endorse human rights norms, he implicitly accepted their validity by rendering a lengthy defense of Chile's restrictions on those norms. In a sentence notable for its contradictions and lack of clarity, Pinochet declared, "Human rights, as long as they are truly such, are universal and inviolable; but not without restrictions, nor of equal hierarchy." He then justified Chile's "restrictions" on human rights by arguing that it was required for the common good, that Chile was sick and needed to be cured, that Chile was in an appropriate legal state of emergency, that the majority of Chileans approved of the restrictions, that the restrictions brought order and safety to Chile, and that without the restrictions, Marxists would destroy not only all individual liberties, but also Chilean traditions and Chilean sovereignty.

The following year, Pinochet demonstrated far more willingness to claim adherence to human rights norms – even if it was completely insincere and hollow – without all of the exceptions and justifications for violations. During this third anniversary speech, Pinochet introduced three new pieces of legislation, officially known as Constitutional Acts Two, Three, and Four, that purported to provide an institutional basis for governing Chile.[42] Act Two served as a general statement of principles and aspirations, Act Three laid out human rights guarantees, and Act Four defined government powers under legal states of exception.[43] Pinochet boasted that Act Three actually improved on Chile's previously existing constitutional guarantees of human rights (in the 1925 Constitution) by explicitly recognizing the right to life, the right to physical and mental integrity, and equal rights for women. Given his long tirade against Marxism in the same speech, it was peculiar that he also highlighted the act's commitment to "social rights" like education, health, a clean environment, work, labor organizations, and social security. Rather than exhaustively defending innumerable violations of human rights, he briefly placed one broad restriction on the enjoyment of these rights: they would not sanction activities against basic Chilean values such as national security, sovereignty, and national unity. Act Four, restricting rights, was not mentioned at all; in fact, for unexplained reasons, it never took legal effect. At the same time, the government continued to cloak its repression in the robes of similar legislation that established states of emergency nullifying the claimed human rights guarantees.

The acts, intended as a piecemeal approach to a new set of governing institutions, never took on a life of their own and were soon forgotten. It is nevertheless useful to analyze their language to get an idea of the claims concerning the discourse of human rights that the government was making in late 1976. Further, the junta intended the acts to become important and fought intense political battles over their wording that offer valuable insights into military government politics. Act Three laid out an impressive array of human rights guarantees that would rival those of any fully democratic country. In addition to the rights outlined in Pinochet's speech, the act established rights to a legal defense (including a state-paid defense if necessary), to travel, to personal liberty, to freedom from illegal arrest or detention, to meet and assemble, to present petitions, to associate, to privacy, to free expression, and many others. These were only occasionally limited, as in the case of free speech where the act established that courts could prohibit the publication or dissemination of information and opinions that would affect public morals, public order, national security, or private lives.

Act Four identified four different types of threats that could face the government (external war, internal war, latent subversion, and public disaster) and carefully codified which rights could be restricted in each different legal state of exception. Even this act implicitly accepted the validity of human rights norms by noting that the restrictions were exceptional and should only be imposed for six months at a time. In the context of Latin American history and current practice, these claims were not entirely unusual.[44] Chile's 1925 Constitution, in force at the time of the coup, gave the president a number of extraordinary powers to restrict rights in a state of emergency and had been supplemented by numerous grants of power in national security legislation in the ensuing years.[45] Other Latin American constitutions contained similar provisions granting executive branch powers to suspend citizens' rights in times of emergency. Even the U.S. Constitution stipulates that the right of habeas corpus may be suspended when required by the need to protect public safety (Article 1, section 8). Of course, Act Four went much further than most other constitutions in granting repressive powers to the government. Yet laying out the constitutional bases of government authority in legal states of exception should itself be viewed as part of the effort to bring Chile into greater normative conformity with its own constitutional history and with other constitutions in the region.

A desire to establish the government's legitimacy motivated the new-found commitment to discourse concerning constitutionally enshrined human rights norms and constitutionally sanctioned violations. Rule-oriented civilian advisors in particular emphasized the importance of establishing a normative basis for the government's power even though they agreed with military officials that it was still too soon to introduce a new constitution.[46] Thus, civilian advisors on the Constitutional Commission – in particular, Guzmán, Enrique Ortúzar, and Jorge Ovalle – produced the Constitutional Acts as a way to buy legitimacy without committing to an entirely new constitution.[47]

Pressures from Chile's human rights critics prompted the government's increasing concern with its legitimacy.[48] On the second anniversary of the coup, Pinochet devoted the first portion of his most important speech of the year to Chile's diplomatic isolation, declaring that in order for Chile to achieve its foreign policy goals, the country must "fully recover the position that belongs to Chile in the international community, projecting its true image." He then detailed a long list of diplomatic initiatives and successes and strongly criticized international organizations for their hypocrisy. The following year, Pinochet again devoted the first section of his speech to international pressures, claiming that Chile's international position was improving, despite growing international criticism. These speeches were undoubtedly intended to rally support for the government in the face of foreign criticism. At the same time, the prominence that Pinochet assigned human rights pressures in his speeches, and the frequency with which he raised this theme, suggest that government officials viewed it as a serious threat.

An examination of private junta debates confirms that government officials seriously worried about the government's legitimacy in the international arena, even though it also used international human rights critics as a way to rally public support. The junta met twice to discuss the Constitutional Acts in detail, on September 3, 1976, in a marathon fifteen-hour session, and then on September 9, in a shorter four-hour session, producing some three hundred pages of typewritten, double-spaced minutes.[49] The two most prominent commission members, Ortúzar and Guzmán, presented and defended the acts to the junta and actively debated junta members about the appropriate phrasing and meaning of the acts during these sessions.

During these sessions, junta officials and their military and civilian advisors repeatedly discussed how to phrase the acts so that they would be well-received internationally. Although those present often disagreed with each other about the appropriate language, they never quarreled about the fundamental purpose of using the acts to improve Chile's international legitimacy. They understood that the acts would establish the legal bases of the government's legitimacy, sometimes even using the word *legitimacy*, though more often using the language of *image* or *prestige*. Not all of those present at the debates emphasized the importance of Chile's international legitimacy to the same extent, yet none opposed the notion of endorsing human rights norms to meet this goal. Generally, junta members clearly hoped the acts would deflect some of the international pressure because the government was adopting the discourse of human rights and providing constitutional-legal justifications for restrictions on those rights.

Naval commander José Merino laid concerns about the government's international legitimacy squarely on the table soon after the first discussion session began:

Well now, we're going to sign this. We are, legitimately, from September 11, the holders of power in Chile. [With this document] we are legitimizing a situation that in some way is going to have repercussion in the United Nations; because we must remember that what comes out at this moment, in the United Nations it will be analyzed with a magnifying glass, word by word. And if before they attacked us, now they will continue doing it and saying things. This worries me. . . . For this reason, I would like it if you [representatives of the Constitutional Commission] told us why or how you consider your judgment to be better than the criticism, not ours, but rather international, that will try to destroy everything we've written.[50]

Ortúzar, president of the Constitutional Commission charged with drafting the acts, responded by explaining how the particular phrase in question was written to avoid just such criticism. Guzmán then lectured the junta on the origins of its legitimacy, claiming that all revolutionary or innovative movements create their own legitimacy by virtue of their wide-ranging acts that reshape socio-political systems. Further, he argued that the people of Chile had called the junta into existence, thereby giving it legitimacy, and that both these sources of legitimacy were written into the acts for schoolchildren and others to read and understand.

Later, junta members discussed at length whether they should repeal a reference in the 1925 Constitution to the right to join political parties.[51] On one hand, Pinochet and his legal advisor wished to abolish parties entirely because they believed them susceptible to Marxist influence and responsible for the near destruction of Chile. On the other hand, many others feared that simply abolishing political parties would seriously damage the government's legitimacy. Naval officers repeatedly argued that the government had never banned political parties, only suspended their operations, and that a ban would contradict other rights, such as the right to association. The minister of justice argued that abolishing parties would be viewed as totalitarian, and Ortúzar suggested that the time for banning parties was not right. Air force general Gustavo Leigh argued that party activities had already been suspended and that if the junta went any further, it would appear to the world like the junta was "striking a totalitarian blow."[52] Ultimately, Pinochet agreed that it would sound better to merely *suspend* party activities than to *suppress* them entirely, and the junta approved language to that effect.

At another point in the debate, Merino listened to a civilian advisor explain how a human rights provision of Act Three had been approved by prominent Chilean jurists. Given the usual tenor of the junta debates, Merino's response was explosive: "Very well, but it turns out that the opinion of Mr. Silva and Mr. Evans does not interest me in the very least for Chile's international prestige. It does not interest me in the least when compared to the boycott that could buffet us tomorrow. It does not interest me in the very least compared with what may happen in the International Labor Organization. What is needed is something that will give the image that, whatever is happening, Chile has the most legal character possible, and is the easiest to govern."[53] Leigh often agreed with this sentiment, though he broadened it to include the government's domestic legitimacy as well: "These Acts have enormous transcendence, because they are awaited within the country as well as outside the country. If they come out with any weak points, they will attack us very strongly, and we would have to do what we've done before, modify the acts within a week, as has happened with some decree laws."[54]

Act Four, granting the government special powers to restrict human rights in states of exception, created the most concern in a junta torn between its desire to improve Chile's international legitimacy and its desire to wield a firm hand domestically. Significantly, Merino opposed the entire act because of concerns about international reaction.[55] "As we said last time, Act Number Four is the one of greatest importance for international politics, because it creates governments of emergency that impinge directly on human rights and all the rest, and they are new [governmental powers] with different characteristics. In the current [1925] constitution, there were three powers: forced movement, arrest, and expulsion. But now no." In other words, Merino was concerned that the government was restricting a wide variety of rights under various states of exception, an action that did not conform with Chilean tradition and that would be rejected internationally.

In addition, Merino objected strongly to a proposed legal state of exception based on "latent subversion," on the grounds that all countries always had "latent subversion," and it would thus be viewed internationally as an illegitimate attempt to routinely give the government more power. Guzmán responded by arguing that the state of latent subversion would actually improve the government's international image because it "corresponds to [Chilean] reality and is less rigorous than a state of siege and will thus be restricting fewer guarantees and liberties" while still granting the government the authority it felt it needed to fight Marxism. Others agreed, arguing that "no one in this world is going to dispute [the fact] that if we are at war we have a right to suspend or restrict all the rights that Act Three establishes, save those of life and honor."

Leigh, in turn, wanted to know if the state-of-siege provisions would be similar to those in other countries like Argentina, Peru, and other Latin American states. When assured that they were even less harsh, he supported the Fourth Act. Merino, however, was not so easily satisfied, especially with the state of "latent subversion." In one of the most biting remarks recorded in junta debates, he argued:

> In other words we can assume that the world will accept, by the work of the Holy Ghost and your brilliant minds, a new system that is neither the state of siege, nor that of war, nor that of commotion, but one of internal subversion [sic]; that they will accept that for the purpose of preserving the lives of citizens, liberties are curtailed, that

this is admissible, and that in regards to human rights it is not scandalous. And I repeat the word "scandalous" because it has been said to me in the United States and Brazil in reference to certain norms and ways that we have been operating.[56]

In short, junta debates are replete with evidence that human rights norms activated by the international community strongly influenced the strategic thinking of the military government. In 1976, the government was unwilling to make substantive changes in its human rights policy, but for the first time was willing to substantially alter its discourse to conform more closely with international, regional, and domestic norms. Although the acts made little difference in the way Chile was governed, they established an important precedent. For the first time, concerns about human rights pressure and long-term government legitimacy affected important domestic policy debates and produced a new form of discourse within the government.

The Demise of the DINA

As 1976 dawned, the DINA was at the height of its power.[57] During 1975 it had completed its task of annihilating leftist organizations that had organized underground after the coup. Col. Manuel Contreras presided over a network of informants and security officials that kept most Chileans locked into a perpetual state of fear and insecurity. Not one to rest on his laurels, Contreras turned his attention to the international arena and planned to join with like-minded security organizations in Latin America and elsewhere to fight the international Marxist network.[58] Even within the military government, few dared speak against the DINA. Contreras' forces enjoyed the full support of Pinochet, whose power and authority the security agency helped maintain.

Human rights pressures convinced the junta of the need to legitimize the government, but the DINA posed a major obstacle to this process — and to the political ambitions of civilian advisors. Contreras despised Guzmán and his friends and believed they were selling Chile out to foreign influences. Until early 1977, the DINA's power was virtually unassailable. Contreras met daily with Pinochet and enjoyed his complete confidence and support. A few top military officials who protested DINA actions in 1974–75 were sharply rebuffed, removed from their posts, and in some cases wound up dead from mysterious causes.[59]

By 1977, however, two factors significantly weakened the DINA. First, opposition to the DINA grew within other sectors of the government. Despite the fact that most of the DINA's personnel were drawn from military ranks, the relationship between the DINA and the Chilean armed forces was filled with friction and jealousies from the start, and it only worsened as the years progressed. Each branch of the armed forces had its own intelligence unit, and these frequently engaged in turf battles with the DINA.[60] Civilian police officials joined in the rivalry and complained bitterly to Pinochet when DINA agents would feign police identities.[61] Military intelligence experts detested Contreras' methods and ideas, labeling them crude and unprofessional – an attitude exacerbated by the fact that Contreras had been trained as an engineer and knew little about intelligence operations as a military discipline. Additionally, some military officers feared Contreras' power within the government. As only a colonel, Contreras held much more power than most generals; further, he was always defended by Pinochet and seemed completely immune to criticism.[62] Some military officers even worried he might gain enough power to challenge Pinochet or to split the armed forces.

Top-level economists and the DINA also came into more open conflict in 1976 when Contreras used his security forces to spy on the activities of the Chicago Boys, convinced they were ruining Chile's economy and getting rich in the process.[63] While undoubtedly benefiting from repression in order to more fully implement their economic plan, the economists had a strong distaste for Contreras-style repression in the long run and completely opposed military-style corporatist economic ideas.[64] As a result, the economists generally opposed the power of the DINA, though they preferred to ignore, rather than to fight, it.

Second, U.S. pressure associated with Jimmy Carter's presidency generally, and specifically with the Letelier bombing in Washington DC, intensified in 1977–78 and came to focus on the DINA. The Carter administration actively supported UN condemnations of the military government, abided by congressional restrictions on military and economic aid, and voted against multilateral development bank loans to Chile.[65] Administration officials constantly pressed the government in public and in private to free political prisoners, disband the DINA, clarify the fate of the disappeared, lift the state of siege, and adopt other measures to protect human rights.[66] In addition, the Carter administration attempted to humiliate the military government by inviting prominent Chilean opposition figures to Washington, while turning a cold shoulder to Pinochet and his top officials. Obviously, the United States had a strong self-interest in pressuring Chile because of the terrorist attack on U.S. soil. At the same time, U.S. pressure went far beyond an effort to resolve the Letelier case and to ensure punishment of the perpetrators. More than simply seeking an end to Chile's international terrorism, the United States pressured Chile to halt domestic repression and to begin a democratic transition.

In August 1977 Pinochet attempted to ease this pressure by dismantling the DINA and replacing it with the CNI and by removing Contreras as its head. At the same time, Pinochet retained Contreras as a close advisor and elevated him to the rank of general. The ploy did not deter U.S. pressure, however. In early March 1978, U.S. investigators finally made a crucial breakthrough that unquestionably linked two former DINA operatives to false passports used to enter the United States in connection with the Letelier case. Providentially, one of those operatives was a U.S. citizen who resided in Chile, allowing the U.S. government to build a strong case for extradition and to place even greater diplomatic pressures on the government.

Pinochet, furious at these developments, called Contreras to tell his side of the story in a cabinet meeting. Contreras, who had always denied that DINA operatives entered the United States on false passports, was forced to reiterate his denial in front of a powerful audience.[67] On March 20, Pinochet asked Contreras to resign from the military for "having lied" to his commander. A reported U.S. threat to break diplomatic relations finally led Chilean officials to turn the DINA operative over to U.S. authorities in early April.[68] A top military official serving in the Interior Ministry declared at the time, "In these moments there is a political crisis that encompasses the whole country."[69]

The chain of events presented here points to human rights pressures and the growth of the rule-oriented faction as the key factors in the demise of the DINA. Accusations of the DINA's involvement in the Letelier murder lent an aura of scandal and crisis to the pre-existing human rights pressures. Civilian advisors and their allies grasped onto increasingly plausible accusations of international terrorism leveled against the DINA and used them as leverage. They argued, ironically, that a security apparatus run amok was only exacerbating the international threat to the military government and thus must be controlled. Furthermore, the lack of a serious domestic threat reduced substantially any domestic costs the government would pay for disbanding the DINA. Finally, the end of the DINA can be viewed as part of the government's new strategy to achieve legitimacy in the late 1970s. The DINA's success at exterminating its opposition paradoxically undermined one of its most important roles within the government. Once the DINA had annihilated short-term security threats, it was no longer an indispensable tool in the war against Marxism.

Although written details of Pinochet's decision-making process are unavailable or nonexistent, substantial interview evidence corroborates this analysis. Of course, the interviewees may have been positioning themselves for a favorable place in history, and thus it is difficult to know for certain what happened. Yet it is significant that most interview testimony given in this respect in the late 1980s and early 1990s was produced under conditions of anonymity and at a time when many Pinochet loyalists still openly admired the DINA and its work. Further, the evidence is consistent among a variety of individuals, and others have not emerged with competing claims. As a result, the evidence is more credible than it might appear at first glance.

Interviews with officials from the time of Pinochet's government almost uniformly stress the combination of human rights pressures and the efforts of rule-oriented officials within the government. U.S. pressures connected to the Letelier case strengthened the arguments of rule-oriented officials and provided tangible evidence of the costs that the DINA generated. An important civilian advisor of the time observed, "Jaime [Guzmán] was very much in favor of ending the DINA. To the extent that he achieved it, I believe it can be attributed in part to his perseverance. I believe the detonator to achieve the victory was the Letelier case. That case was taken advantage of very strongly to put an end to the DINA."[70] A cabinet official with access to Pinochet confirmed that Contreras' involvement in the Letelier case led to his fall. This same official worked to remove Contreras from power by pointing out to Pinochet that if Contreras lied about the Letelier case, then he had lied in other cases and could not be trusted.[71] An army general with regular access to Pinochet summarized it this way: "There was one fact that motivated the end of the DINA and its transformation into the CNI: the Letelier assassination. It motivated the exit of Contreras and the change in the DINA. Contreras had assured Pinochet that he did not know anything about the visas, passports, and travels to the United States. When it was demonstrated that agents of the DINA had gone to the U.S. with false passports, then it was clear that Contreras had not been sufficiently truthful with Pinochet."[72]

Human rights pressures and the political struggle within the government threatened not only the survival of the government broadly but also Pinochet's personal power within it. Pinochet's top civilian legal advisor of the time made this argument, pointing out that by law the DINA answered directly to Pinochet, making him extremely vulnerable to charges leveled against the security agency.[73] A nationalist advisor to Pinochet offered the same observation: Contreras "was becoming a threat to Pinochet's personal power. He was a threat because factions outside the Army, domestic political factions, and international actors were going to think that Pinochet was an accomplice to Contreras."[74] One military general who served in the cabinet at the time said, "I believe the pressure within and outside the country was very great. The whole country was aware that something was rotten. And the country was not willing to accept it. Things [i.e., human rights abuses] that happened in the days following the coup, everyone accepted. But after a few years, No. . . . Within the armed forces themselves there was an enormous rejection of the DINA. Within the military institutions themselves, a very great rejection. There were serious fears about the power of Contreras."[75]

Alternative Explanations

It is difficult to explain the adoption of a human rights discourse or the demise of the DINA without reference to the international social environment within which Chile interacted or the strong normative pressures to which it was subjected. Realist-style explanations focused solely on U.S. military and economic power cannot fully explain the changes occurring in Chile from 1976 to 1977. The United States was the only state to substantially increase sanctions on Chile in this period, yet even these new, and newly enforced, sanctions did not pose a significant threat to Chile. The United States opposed all new multilateral development bank (MDB) loans to Chile, but every one of them was approved anyway.[76] It is possible that U.S. opposition decreased the amount of the loans, as MDB funding rose sharply with the friendly Reagan administration in office in 1981. Still, capital flows from private investors and banks into Chile continued to increase, easily replacing the U.S. cutoff of economic aid and possible reductions in MDB loans, as is evident in table 3. The United States did not implement any trade sanctions, save a small cutoff in direct Eximbank credit amounting to perhaps several million dollars a year.[77] The cutoff of all military sales worried military officials, but did not significantly impact either Chilean arms imports or military budgets, as summarized in table 4.

In any case, if military officials were seriously concerned about U.S. sanctions, we should expect them to take actions that would successfully reverse those sanctions. They never did. Carter's restriction on Eximbank credit was tied to the extradition of suspects in the Letelier case, which never occurred, and then became a moot point when Reagan lifted the restriction. Because of Chile's ongoing human rights abuses, the United States continued opposing MDB loans until the Reagan administration reversed the policy and voted favorably for Chile. Restrictions on economic aid and the ban on military aid and sales remained in place, even into the Reagan years. Chile never demonstrated enough concern about these sanctions to change its human rights policies. Although government officials expressed concern that sanctions could broaden, small-scale sanctions alone simply were not large enough to leverage change.

Democratization theorists often point to domestic opposition groups and softline factions as sources of change in authoritarian governments. While both factors were important in Chile in the mid-1970s, they cannot provide a complete explanation. It seems unlikely that civilian advisors alone – who had little political or economic power in broader Chilean society – would have been able to implement changes to government discourse and to the DINA in the absence of human rights pressures. Military officials were extremely skeptical of the need to create new legislation with constitutional standing, arguing that it would simply tie their hands in the process of remaking Chile. Junta debates make it clear that they viewed the Constitutional Acts as a response to outside pressures and not simply as a good policy initiative. Likewise, Pinochet did not easily sacrifice the DINA or his close relationship with Contreras. Pinochet viewed the DINA as an essential part of his central project to exterminate Marxists, a task he believed had not

Table 3: International Aid for Chile, 1974–78 (by fiscal year, in millions of U.S. dollars)

	1974	1975	1976	1977	1978
U.S. economic aid: Loans and grants	8.5	93.7	82.3	32.1	5.8
U.S. military aid: Loans and grants	15.9	0.7	0.0	0.0	0.0
World Bank and Inter-American Development Bank	110.8	65.5	58.2	128.0	54.0
Private bank funding of Chilean government	304.7	216.6	245.0	871.9	1676.9

Sources: Rows 1 and 2 from Agency for International Development (AID), *U.S. Overseas Loans and Grants and Assistance from International Organizations* (Washington DC: U.S. Government, various years). Row 1 includes all loans and grants from AID and the Food for Peace program, the two major sources of aid. Row 2 includes all forms of loans and grants tracked by AID. Row 3 from Schoultz, *Human Rights and United States Policy*, 283. Row 4 from Brian H. Smith, *Church and Politics in Chile*, 326. Row 4 includes private banks in the United States and Western Europe.

Table 4: Chilean Military Expenses, 1974–78 (in millions of U.S. dollars)

	1974	1975	1976	1977	1978
Military expenditures	627	489	487	566	713
Arms imports	99	25	160	69	65
U.S. commercial arms sales	1.8	0.6	1.4	1.3	0.0

Sources: Row 1 from Stockholm International Peace Research Institute, *World Armaments and Disarmament*, in constant 1979 prices and exchange rates. Row 2 from Arms Control and Disarmament Agency, *World Military Expenditures and Arms Transfers* (Washington DC: U.S. Government, various years). Row 3 from Schoultz, *Human Rights and United States Policy*, 321–22.

yet been completed. Without human rights pressures, it is difficult to imagine him giving up the DINA and its tangible security benefits.

Likewise, domestic opposition began to form in the mid-1970s, but remained weak and incapable of forcing any concessions from the government. Labor leaders first began to publicly criticize the government in 1976 through a series of open letters and press statements, which undoubtedly added to the pressures coming from human rights groups.[78] Inside Chile, labor strikes and unrest were limited in the late 1970s to a few copper mines and to demands for better working conditions and more workers' rights. Transnationally, a regional labor organization backed by the AFL-CIO threatened to boycott Chile in late 1978 for its violation of labor rights. The government responded with repression and by reworking labor laws in such a way that they granted the right to unionize but significantly weakened unions in many ways.[79] Of Chile's previously strong political parties, only the Christian Democrats continued to operate any kind of open opposition. In the 1970s, this consisted mostly of careful public statements and meetings to renew the party's leadership.[80] Many students opposed the government, but were forced to confine their dissent to artistic and cultural productions and refusal to participate in government-sponsored programs.[81] None of this amounted to a serious challenge to government authority or to a fundamental change in the structure of state-society relations. It did, however, reinforce criticisms from the human rights network and raise the specter of widespread domestic illegitimacy in addition to the international problems.

The Changes and Their Implications

From the immediate perspective of government opponents, the changes taking place in Chile from 1976 to 1977 were insignificant. The only concrete short-term benefit was a decline in disappearances and political murders, a salutary improvement but one that hardly signaled the end of other forms of government terror such as torture or prolonged illegal detentions. More widespread repression – the climate of fear, the banning of political parties, constraints on labor unions – remained in place. The end of Contreras and the reorganization of the DINA were hopeful signs, but most opponents dismissed these moves as cosmetic surgery.

With the benefit of hindsight, the changes in Chile can be viewed as more significant because the demise of the DINA changed the face of repression in Chile. Generally speaking, the government opted for less violence and more legalistic repression after 1977. This new strategy ameliorated some of the most heinous human rights abuses in the late 1970s as "the number of fatal human rights violations cases declined dramatically."[82] As Fruhling summarized it, "Compared with the first three years of military rule the intensity of repression was generally low, but it increased whenever the opposition increased in force."[83] Further, the CNI became a more professional organization in the sense that it "concentrated more on political intelligence than on repression."[84] In short, the government after 1977 maintained repression, but reserved some of its most violent manifestations for periods of strong and open opposition.[85]

This change in strategy was especially important because it shaped politics in Chile during the 1980s and into the 1990s in two contradictory ways.[86] First, the changes consolidated the military's grip and helped it hang on to power for the following twelve years. Although the DINA successfully crushed the opposition and strengthened Pinochet's hand, it also ran the risk of generating a new, more radicalized opposition and long-term political instability. By turning their attention to the quest for legitimacy, and by incorporating civilians into the government, military officials shored up their support among civilian allies and planned new political-legal institutions capable of governing the country in the long term. Seen in a long-term historical perspective, this strategy of institutionalization succeeded. In 1980, the military government approved a new constitution that lengthened its rule until 1990.[87] The new constitution helped unify a rather fractured government and allowed the military to govern the country under the pretext of law rather than force. So successful was the military project first born in 1977 that the military-imposed constitution continues to govern democratic Chile today – and to give the military special benefits – with relatively few changes.

Second, events in 1976–77 began to shift the balance of power within the military government in favor of the rule-oriented faction and its plans to build new political institutions that would eventually allow popular participation and a self-described "authoritarian democracy." As I argue in more detail in subsequent chapters, opposition forces in

Chile used these institutions in 1988–90 to remove Pinochet from office, to elect a center-left government, and to ensure a peaceful transition to democracy.[88] The 1980 Constitution – written, designed, and promoted by rule-oriented actors – mandated a plebiscite on Pinochet's continued rule and the creation of a new congress with free and fair elections under universal suffrage no later than 1989. After the opposition failed to topple Pinochet by protests during the dark days of economic depression in 1983–84, they decided to use the military's own constitution as a weapon. In a dramatic change of strategy in 1986, opposition leaders accepted the constitution, pushed the government to adhere to its promised plebiscite and congressional elections, and organized political parties using the government's own rules. Military leaders, for their part, complied with the constitutional mandates, lost a fair electoral contest, and left power peacefully. One of the most remarkable features of the Chilean transition is the extent to which it was guided by the principles and procedures laid down by those who drafted the constitution in the late 1970s.

The end of the DINA marked a significant long-term decline in the power of Contreras and the hardline militaristic position he represented within the government – a process I explore more fully in chapter 4. Contreras was replaced as the head of the newly created CNI within two months, and shortly thereafter he prematurely resigned his rank of army general. In early 1978 a civilian favoring limited political liberalization was named to the powerful post of interior minister and stocked the cabinet with civilian allies.[89] Even the new head of the CNI threw his support behind the efforts to legitimize the government and downplayed the importance of direct force. Military hardliners still earned Pinochet's ear, but with the end of the DINA they lost their previously predominant position with the government.

I have argued that human rights pressures helped lead to limited yet important changes in the discourse and behavior of Chile's authoritarian government from 1976 to 1977. In some ways, these changes probably helped the government solidify its hold on power and thus had the opposite effect intended by human rights activists. With the demise of the DINA, the government got rid of one of its most reviled features without sacrificing much control over society. With the same blow, the government removed a serious source of contention within its own ranks and simultaneously avoided deeper problems with the United States. Other changes, such as the short-term decline in state-sponsored violence, were more in line with the intentions of human rights actors. Even these, however, were not a direct concession to human rights pressure. Rather, such pressures highlighted the government's problems with legitimacy, reinforced and amplified the arguments of rule-oriented actors, and forced government officials to reconsider the costs of repression.

Chile was relatively susceptible to human rights pressures because it was characterized in the mid-1970s by decreasing levels of crisis, by an increasingly powerful rule-oriented faction, and by moderate levels of domestic fit for international human rights norms. After reaching very high levels in the first two years of military rule, security and economic threats declined in 1976–77, thereby decreasing the "need" for repression. By 1976, the authoritarian government had completely decimated leftist groups and faced only minor opposition from moderates. Further, the 1975 economic shock therapy led to economic rebound in 1976, allowing the government some breathing space for changes. It is important not to overstate these conditions. Repression still served important purposes in Chile and was consistent with military-style anti-Communist thought. As time wore on, however, it became marginally less beneficial.

The growing presence of a rule-oriented faction also played a crucial role. Although theories of political liberalization and democratization have long stressed the importance of a softline faction, they say little about where softliners come from and how they increase their influence. The Chilean case suggests that human rights pressures strengthened the rule-oriented faction by creating a threat – an isolated, illegitimate government – which rule-oriented actors could help resolve. Civilian advisors and their allies used human rights pressures to argue persuasively that their policy preferences for new constitutional provisions and a restructuring of the security agency would actually benefit the government.

Chile's moderate levels of normative fit undoubtedly strengthened the hand of rule-oriented actors and forced authoritarian elites to be concerned about the government's legitimacy. Rule-oriented actors recognized that Chile's long history of democracy would eventually generate demands for more participation and greater respect for human rights. They argued that Chile's democratic traditions and vibrant civil society could not realistically be ignored. Even if the military was reconstructing society, Chilean officials could not easily sidestep charges of human rights abuse by claiming, as do many Asian governments, that international norms do not apply in their country. As a result, the government adopted a discourse of human rights and government officials expressed repeated concerns about how to legitimize their rule.

At the same time, Chile's domestic structure cannot help to explain these changes. Human rights groups never gained any meaningful access to government officials. U.S. officials undoubtedly gained access when they demanded changes stemming from the Letelier incident. It is difficult to argue, however, that they formed any kind of "winning coalition" with domestic forces. No Chilean official could have expressed sympathy with the United States and its deeply hostile efforts toward the country. Further, the resulting changes were not completely in line with U.S. pressure, which called for more dramatic changes in Chile's policy. In fact, these moderate changes do not fit with theoretical predictions derived from a domestic structure approach, which suggest that changes instigated by transnational actors should be either nonexistent or far-reaching.

Chilean events in 1976 and 1977 demonstrate an increasing government interest in legitimacy. Within the international relations literature, realists suggest that national interests are self-evident and persist over long periods of time. Constructivists argue that national interests shift gradually over time in response to changing patterns of interaction among states, while liberals look to domestic society as sources of national interests. The Chilean case offers evidence for a combination of liberal and constructivist approaches. Human rights groups and foreign states attempted to systematically isolate Chile from the international community. Not all states would perceive a threat from these activities, especially when they did not involve military or economic isolation. Yet Chilean officials, spurred on by a rule-oriented faction, interpreted the pressures as a serious threat and set about to protect Chile. They rallied around an interest in the government's legitimacy that was constructed by the interplay of human rights pressures and government factions within the existing normative and military-economic contexts.

These arguments complement and flesh out rather than contradict previous studies of the DINA's end. Valenzuela argues that opposition within the government to Contreras and the DINA, aided by U.S. pressure in the Letelier case, finally put an end to the DINA.[90] While partially correct, this explanation places too much emphasis on the sheer struggle for power within the government, fails to see U.S. pressure as part of a broader threat, and does not place the end of the DINA in the historical context of gradual change. Without understanding the government's growing concern for legitimacy, it is difficult to understand how the DINA moved so quickly from preeminent power to disbanded organization. Contreras did not lose favor due to poor performance, nor was he outmaneuvered on internal policy disputes, nor was he simply muscled out by a more politically powerful faction. Rather, his organization stood in the way of an increasingly important government interest – namely, legitimacy. Ignoring the broader pattern of human rights pressure and the way it intersected with domestic conditions in Chile makes it more difficult to understand why U.S. demands for Contreras' extradition would force the government to reorganize its main security apparatus. After all, any number of states, including relatively weak states like Libya, have withstood U.S. extradition demands for years without undertaking domestic reorganizations. The success of U.S. pressure makes more sense when placed in the context of ongoing, widespread human rights pressures placed on a government that had no other pressing problems and that worried about its legitimacy because of the country's democratic history.

This chapter suggests that at least some authoritarian governments concern themselves with the normative bases of their authority and prefer to rely on some form of legitimacy in order to rule. In the modern era, human rights norms have become important standards of legitimacy in many countries. International action that challenges the government's human rights record therefore challenges the government's legitimacy and its long-term political stability. International relations scholars who focus exclusively on the material bases of power – economic and military – are likely to miss this potentially important avenue of international influence in domestic politics. Opposition actors routinely use both norms and power to pressure authoritarian governments to improve their human rights records, and an analysis of both is necessary to understand how governments respond.

FOUR

Building New Political Institutions through the 1980 Constitution

Soon after the dissolution of the Directorate of National Intelligence (DINA) in August 1977, the military government took its first serious steps toward building long-lasting political institutions. The most important of these was the new constitution, approved in mid-1980 and still governing Chile today, though with some important modifications. At first, the new constitution simply institutionalized the existing power arrangements and offered a formal source of legitimacy for the government's sweeping powers. Some provisions of the constitution, however, opened small spaces that the opposition utilized to end military rule.[1]

Both the decision to implement a new constitution in 1980 and the content of that constitution present important puzzles. The military government had long resisted setting limitations on its power and time in office that a constitution implied, and powerful elements within the government opposed creating new political institutions. With respect to content, the new constitution mandated the future creation of political institutions that mixed democratic and authoritarian elements in a formula that the government labeled "authoritarian" or "protected" democracy. Many government officials and supporters opposed the more liberal features of the constitution – even though they would not exist for at least eight more years – including universal suffrage, free and fair elections contested by political parties, specific limitations on the military's remaining time in office, and the adoption of political institutions that were not primarily corporatist.

Why did the military government decide to create a new constitution? Why did it incorporate promises of political institutions with important liberal features rather than opting for a completely authoritarian state? Why did the government commit itself to the establish-

ment of political rights like free elections and political parties that
many officials blamed for facilitating the Marxist rise to power and
the near destruction of Chile? And why commit to a constitutionally
sanctioned timetable for withdrawal from power?

The interplay of human rights pressures and government factions in
the mid-1970s generated substantial concerns about the government's
long-term legitimacy. Human rights pressures in the 1970s forced Chilean officials to think seriously about the long-term stability of authoritarian rule. With the DINA out of the way, rule-oriented officials came
to dominate the military government. They seized on these pressures
to argue that the government needed to gain legitimacy by creating
new political institutions that would enjoy widespread normative approval. Human rights norms limited the range of strategies by which
the government could achieve legitimacy, thereby favoring some concessions to liberal-style political institutions. As a result, civilian rule-
oriented officials promoted "protected democracy," which partially incorporated the language of human rights norms while still meeting
the anti-Marxist interests of military officials.

Chile's ongoing moderate levels of normative fit and crisis levels
from 1978 to 1981 facilitated the effects of human rights pressures and
the dominance of the rule-oriented faction. With respect to domestic
norms, little changed in Chile as civil society slowly continued to rebuild itself, and most government officials understood that a radical,
long-term departure from Chile's traditional liberal norms was un-
workable. Economic recovery and the absence of radical opposition ensured that human rights pressures would gain more attention, even if
a serious conflict with Argentina remained an important background
threat.

At the same time, Chile's unchanging domestic structure contributes
little to the explanation. Network activists never gained access to the
military government, and even though officials from Western governments enjoyed some access and raised human rights issues, there is no
evidence that they had any direct influence. In fact, Chile's responses to
human rights pressures were not what network activists and their state
allies intended. Additionally, functionalist explanations for the constitution that focus on the "natural" need to legitimize the government
cannot explain the content of the constitution and do not fit with substantial evidence that President Augusto Pinochet resisted institution-

alization and would have preferred a more enduringly authoritarian and corporatist formula for the constitution.

Because rule-oriented officials were the most immediate force behind the new constitution and its content, I begin by tracing their effects on Pinochet's decision making. I then examine the growth of the human rights network and analyze the ways in which human rights pressures affected the government's institutional plans in the mid- to late 1970s. Although these effects were more indirect than those analyzed in previous chapters, they were still substantial. Subsequently, I show how Chile's generally favorable domestic characteristics opened it to influence from human rights activists, but not in the way they intended. I conclude by discussing alternative explanations for the institutionalization process and by commenting on the double-edged nature of the constitution for the government and its opposition.

Rule-Oriented Officials and the New Institutionality, 1973–80

Although human rights pressures played a key role, it is important first to understand the constitution as the product of domestic politics. Ideas for constitutional reform predated human rights pressures on the authoritarian government and even predated the government itself. During the years of Salvador Allende's presidency, some Chilean conservatives, upset by the "advance of Marxism" and the decay of the Chilean political system, placed part of the blame on an inadequate constitution. Once the coup occurred, a few conservative legal scholars quickly seized the opportunity to press their ideas on Chile's new military rulers. Although the government obliged by creating a study commission, no real progress occurred until mid-1977.[2] Then, in the midst of growing human rights pressures and increasing concern about the government's legitimacy, Pinochet finally announced a timetable for the end of military rule and set out the essential principles of a new constitution. By 1980, the government was rushing to put the finishing touches on a long-delayed constitution in time for a popular ratification plebiscite on the seventh anniversary of military rule, September 11, 1980.

Rule-oriented officials were the most immediate causal force in the progress of the new constitution and in determining the nature of the political institutions the document would create. As argued in chapter 3, a rule-oriented faction first emerged in 1976 and gained moderate levels of power within the government by sitting on study commissions and serving as junta advisors. The faction actively pushed for a new constitution that would offer the government some legitimacy and would shape politics in Chile for years to come. Beginning in 1978, rule-oriented officials gained nearly complete dominance of the government bureaucracy, a position they never really relinquished for the remaining years of military rule. As I argue below, they skillfully used their bureaucratic positions to persuade Pinochet of the wisdom of their constitutional project.

Genesis

When military officials seized power in September 1973 they were convinced that Chile's traditional democratic political institutions had become corrupted and destroyed beyond repair and needed to be built anew. In an important speech marking the one-month anniversary of the coup, Pinochet claimed that the armed forces would rebuild democracy, "which should be reborn purified of the vices and evil habits that resulted in the destruction of our institutions."[3] In that speech, Pinochet first utilized a phrase, the "new institutionality," that would later become a prominent symbol of the government's project. Pinochet, however, gave little hint of the nature of these institutions, suggesting only that they would rid the government forever of demagoguery and sectarianism, would include a new constitution, and would not be in place in the foreseeable future. Over the next three years, government officials frequently referred to the new institutionality, but did little to back up this discourse or to provide a timetable for its implementation. On the contrary, they often insisted that the government would establish "goals, not deadlines."

Jaime Guzmán, a young, conservative lawyer and one of the most visible intellectual opponents of the Allende government, believed that Chile needed a new constitution that would afford greater protection against Marxism. His celebrity status as an articulate commentator on television talk shows during the Allende years, his lack of strong ties to traditional political parties, and his vehement opposition to the Allende government earned him ready access to junta members. On September 13, 1973, just two days after the coup, the junta met in its first formal, recorded session and noted that "the promulgation of a new Constitution is currently under study, directed by the university professor Jaime Guzmán."[4]

The four original members of the Constitutional Commission first met on September 24 and elected Enrique Ortúzar, a conservative politician and former cabinet minister, as president.[5] The Ministry of Justice formalized the creation of the Constitutional Commission by Supreme Decree No. 1,064 on October 25, 1973, charging it to "study, elaborate, and propose a draft of a new Political Constitution of the state and its complementary laws." The commission eventually expanded to eight members by December 1973 and was composed primarily of constitutional law professors, with the exception of Ortúzar and the only female representative, Alicia Romo.[6] In an effort to build bridges to moderate political sectors and to legitimize its work, the commission included three members from moderate political parties (Radical and Christian Democrat). Whether by design or by happenstance, the commission included no figures who might enjoy political weight or public visibility, except Ortúzar and Guzmán.[7] Both Ortúzar and Guzmán enjoyed access to the junta and Pinochet, and they easily became the most influential members on the commission.

The commission quickly produced two statements of its goals and objectives that demonstrated a remarkably authoritarian bent. Although vague, they reflected the government's preferences for strong military involvement in politics, corporatist-style political institutions, and a depoliticized society. The first statement of goals, approved on September 26, 1973, included large-scale restrictions on political parties, a senate partially elected by a national constituency and partially appointed, a congress made up of experienced legal specialists and technical experts, and the active participation of the armed forces.[8] The commission's second statement on November 26, 1973, included some liberal-democratic principles, but also endorsed a quasi-corporatist role for social organizations, emphasized the minimal role of political parties, and placed key restrictions on human rights guarantees.[9] Significantly, the document identified Chile as a republican democracy whose leaders would be selected by universal suffrage in free, multiparty, secret elections. At the same time, it assigned political parties a relatively minor role and, in a bow to corporatist thinking, emphasized the importance that organized social groups would have in national decisions. Finally, the document recognized the importance of the armed forces in protecting the internal security of the country and envisioned a constitutional role for them that had yet to be determined.

Although he did not object to a study commission, Pinochet opposed the actual creation of a new constitution on the grounds that it was simply too soon to impose limits on military rule. Government officials argued that they needed time to rebuild the economy, to purge society of Marxism, and to evaluate the long-term harmful consequences of the Allende period. As a result, the commission lapsed into a long period of slow progress on the new constitution.[10] The commission maintained a low public profile for the next four years and spent a good deal of its time listening to the testimony of legal specialists and representatives of important social institutions.[11] It did not even draft articles on central political institutions or take up questions about the generation of political power until March 1978. At the same time, Guzmán and Ortúzar remained in close contact with junta members. The junta utilized the commission as a legislative drafting committee for complex or problematic laws, taking time away from the commission's work on the constitution.[12] The commission contributed to legislation dealing with the prohibition of political parties, the expiration of electoral rolls, the constitutional, executive, and legislative powers of the junta, the decentralization of the government, and government administrative procedures, among others.

Trapped between constant international questions about its legitimacy and refusal to enact a new constitution that might help alleviate those pressures, the government adopted some half-measures designed to create new governmental institutions that would serve as a useful facade but have no real meaning. On January 1, 1976, the government created a Council of State composed of distinguished political, military, and social figures designed to serve as a formal advisory body. Because it included former presidents of Chile, former cabinet ministers, and former commanders of the armed forces, legal advisors hoped that the council would give the government some legitimacy. Their hopes were partially dashed when Eduardo Frei, the Christian Democratic president of Chile from 1964 to 1970, refused to participate.[13] Legal advisors then designed three Constitutional Acts as "transitional institutions" (see chapter 3) that would give the government a formal legal-institutional base of support, but would not supercede military authority or endure beyond the period of military rule.[14] In the same speech announcing the acts, Pinochet underscored their limited authority and the military's intention to remain in power indefinitely: "In the face of Marxism, which has become a permanent aggression, there is an urgent need to place power in the hands of the armed forces, as they are the only ones with the organization and the means to combat it."[15] As 1976 closed, further progress on a new constitution seemed unlikely.

Moving Forward

Between July and November 1977, the government unexpectedly altered its stance, first by setting a timetable for the end of military rule (which it did not meet) and then by accelerating the study of a new constitution. On July 9 at Chacarillas, Pinochet used the opportunity presented by Youth Day celebrations to announce his definitive endorsement of a new institutionality that would end military rule in Chile and would endow the country with a new constitution and new political institutions.[16] Most significantly, for the first time Pinochet laid out a specific timetable that would gradually put an end to military rule. In this plan, Pinochet and the junta would appoint a congress by 1980 that would take over legislative functions. In 1985, there would be elections for two-thirds of the members of the legislature. The legislature would also select a president to govern Chile for the next six years. Finally, at the end of this transition period, a new constitution would go into full effect. Other than this general timetable, Pinochet offered few specifics on the new constitution or the role of the armed forces throughout the transition period. Even though the government later ignored this plan, the announcement generated some of the first open political debate on Chile's future and increased Chileans' expectations that military rule would some day give way to democracy.[17]

Once Pinochet had decided to move ahead with a new constitution, the key questions concerned the nature and form of the new political institutions. Pinochet knew what he did not want: liberal democracy as it had been traditionally practiced in Chile. He especially rejected political parties, arguing that they were responsible for the Marxist advance in Chile owing to their narrow self-interests, divisions and quarrels, and spineless leadership. Stressing national unity as one of the highest values, he expressed suspicion of elections because they created divisions as each group attempted to improve its narrow self-interest.

On the system of government that should replace liberal democracy, Pinochet was less clear. "I believe the president did not have a clear path," said one military advisor close to Pinochet in the 1970s.[18] "He had a general idea of where he wanted to go, and he had a very authoritarian vision, but he did not have specific solutions." As a close friend of former president José María Bordaberry in Uruguay, Pinochet was influenced by his ideas about a state built around the armed forces.[19] Pinochet also admired Franco's authoritarian system in Spain and the Catholic Church's hierarchical system of appointing officials. When Guzmán presented the original draft of the 1980 Constitution, which established traditional democratic political institutions with important authoritarian features, Pinochet rejected it. He reportedly told Guzmán to "take your little head and come up with something else. This is not original; it is the same old thing."[20] Pinochet's daughter reflected these sentiments when she declared that the commission's draft constitution did not "reflect the spirit of my father."[21]

Not all government officials and supporters shared Pinochet's view of a state built around the armed forces as the chief political power. Many preferred an authoritarian corporatist solution that would have some trappings of democracy but would channel politics through sectoral groups like business, labor, women, and students.[22] Corporatists argued that a new congress should not represent geographical or ideological groups of Chileans, but rather "organic" or natural social groups, like labor unions and business federations, and that Chileans should indirectly elect the president through these groups. They shared with Pinochet a complete rejection of political parties and liberal democracy, labeling it a "partyocracy." Further, they argued in the mid- to late 1970s that it was still too soon to create more democratic institutions because the military had not yet finished restructuring Chilean society and the economy.

In contrast with Pinochet's military state and corporatists' organic state, rule-oriented officials became increasingly vocal about promoting an "authoritarian" and "protected" democratic state that would establish more authoritarian forms of Chile's traditional democratic institutions.[23] In this governing system, Chileans would select a president and a congress in direct elections with universal suffrage and secret balloting, but severe limitations would be placed on political parties and ideological diversity. Specifically, all totalitarian or Marxist activities would be banned, and political parties would be limited to acting as "opinion channels" that truly reflected Chileans' beliefs rather than the political ambitions of party bosses. Further, social groups like labor unions and business associations would actively shape Chile, but not through political means such as elections or representation in Congress. Rule-oriented officials adopted the discourse of human rights to a much greater extent than either militarists or corporatists, arguing that the future government would fully respect human rights.

In November 1977, Pinochet sent a memo to the Constitutional Commission outlining the structure of future political institutions in which he largely adopted rule-oriented ideas of a protected democracy.[24] The memo proposed that Chile be governed by a president and a congress, just as it always had. The majority of the members of Congress would be elected by direct, universal suffrage and represent geographical regions. A substantial portion of congressional seats (to be decided later) would be designated by the president or would earn the right to serve based on their previous political or social positions. Political parties would play an important, though limited role in contesting political power, and social groups would remain autonomous from the state and completely depoliticized. The memo specifically disavowed corporatist ideas of generating political power through social or economic groups. This document represented an important change from previous government statements that had incorporated corporatist ideas and that had insisted on an end to political parties in the name of national unity. Finally, Pinochet imposed a six-month deadline in which to complete the draft constitution, though it is unclear when he intended it to be put into effect.[25]

It is fairly easy to trace the direct influence of the growing rule-oriented faction on the Youth Day speech at Chacarillas and the constitutional memo. Guzmán played a key role in authoring both documents and persuading Pinochet to adopt them.[26] As Guzmán held no official post on Pinochet's cabinet or personal staff, he relied on allies to promote his arguments and to help him gain access to the general. The most important of these was Sergio Covarrubias, an army general and Pinochet's chief of staff from 1975 to 1979, who regulated the flow of information, memos, and visitors into Pinochet's office. Covarrbuias and Guzmán often met two to three times a week and agreed completely on the need to institutionalize and legitimize the government along the lines Guzmán suggested.[27] Working together, they drafted the Chacarillas speech and urged Pinochet to give it during Youth Day as an appropriate symbol of the future.

Then in early November 1977, Pinochet asked Mónica Madariaga, who was then the justice minister but had previously worked as a trusted advisor in the president's legal office, to produce a memo summarizing government thought on constitutional principles. Madariaga sought the help of Guzmán and together they drafted the memo.[28] Madariaga then presented the memo to Pinochet, who presented it personally to the Constitutional Commission on November 15, 1977. As a result, Pinochet's memo outlining government policy to the Constitutional Commission was actually drafted in part by one of the members of that same commission.

Jorge Alessandri, a conservative politician who served as president of Chile from 1956 to 1962, and a person of considerable influence with impeccable anti-Marxist credentials, played a central role in advancing rule-oriented arguments. In 1977, Alessandri was deeply troubled by the junta's use of the Constitutional Acts, which he viewed as antithetical to Chile's constitutional traditions. In Alessandri's view, the acts were illegitimate because they were being used to build a new constitution in a piecemeal, ad hoc fashion without any attempt to have Chileans ratify the new rules in a formal plebiscite.[29] Chilean traditions held that sovereignty rested with the people, and Alessandri believed the people should voice approval of the constitutional rules of the game that regulated their government. Alessandri in fact believed that Chile's 1925 Constitution was sound and should be amended rather than replaced entirely. Although he was willing to accept a new constitution, if it were enacted properly, he was adamantly opposed to the piecemeal process of the Constitutional Acts. Alessandri used his standing as president of the Council of State and as former president of Chile to ask Pinochet to put a stop to the Constitutional Acts and get on with the business of actually drafting a constitution.[30] In late 1977, the entire council officially asked the government to move forward with a new constitution, suggesting that the sentiment was widespread among a broad segment of government supporters. A few days later, Pinochet produced the constitutional memo.

Outside of the government itself, conservative government supporters picked up and articulated rule-oriented arguments. El Mercurio,
Chile's flagship newspaper and long a bastion of conservative thought,
began to complain in early 1977 that the juridical-political side of the
military government "has advanced in theoretical principle but still
lacks in the planning and construction of the machine itself."[31] For the
next three years, El Mercurio's editors – who were well-connected with
Chile's most important financial sectors – constantly called for continued efforts at institutionalization and faithfully mapped the government's progress on the new constitution. More broadly, businesspeople, rightist politicians, and other conservative sectors responded
enthusiastically to Pinochet's Chacarillas talk, undoubtedly encourag-
ing Pinochet to continue on this path.[32]

The Commission and the Council

From late 1977 to mid-1978, the Constitutional Commission quietly
finalized its draft constitution with minimal direction from the junta
or military officials and without media attention or much public aware-
ness.[33] The final draft represented a blend of principles summarized by
the label "authoritarian democracy."[34] With respect to political rights,
it incorporated liberal principles such as free and fair elections with
universal suffrage (Article 15), the right to associate freely with others
in political parties or other groups (Article 19, clause 14), direct election of the president (Article 31), direct elections of all members of the
Chamber of Deputies and most of the Senate (Articles 47–53), and procedures and institutions to ensure that these elections would be free
and fair (Articles 90–91). The draft constitution contained important
authoritarian elements as well, including an expanded political role
for the armed forces in the National Security Council (Articles 99–100),
restrictions on the president's ability to name commanders in chief
(Articles 97–98), limitations on the political and civil rights of Marxists
(Article 8), and severe restrictions on the ability to reform the constitution (Articles 120–123). Significantly, the draft left to the junta decisions
on when the constitution would go into effect and how Chile would be
governed until then.

Pinochet, who still was not convinced of the need to hurry along a
new constitution, then sent the draft to the Council of State for further

study and revision. Military and nationalist hardliners became alarmed that the constitution was progressing at all. Despite the strongly authoritarian clauses, they believed the constitution looked too much like Chile's previous constitution and leaned too far toward liberal democracy. Arguing that it was still too soon to institutionalize the government, they tried to block further progress by rallying public support and by talking to Pinochet.[35] Among the most important hardliners was Hugo Rosende, a civilian lawyer and intellectual who was close to Pinochet. One high-ranking government official recalled his influence this way: "He used to say, 'You're never leaving, my general, from now until death.' And if there were some sort of public disturbance, Rosende would pound the table, 'My general, tanks in the street! I know that to General Covarrubias this doesn't seem right, but here you need a firm hand.'"[36] Two corporatists sitting on the Council of State, Pedro Ibáñez and Carlos Cáceres, attempted first to delay passage of the constitution and then to substitute corporatist provisions for the existing ones.[37] Pinochet was sympathetic to these arguments and had serious doubts about liberal-style political institutions that rule-oriented officials supported. Government officials from that era recall that when Pinochet would visit cities outside Santiago, hardline government supporters would gather crowds chanting "Mano dura Pinochet, hasta siempre Pinochet" (Hard hand Pinochet, until forever Pinochet). "And Pinochet would come back and say, 'This is what the people want.'"[38]

Rule-oriented officials rallied their forces. Though they controlled the constitutional drafting process in the Council of State, where they defeated corporatist amendments, they could not be assured that Pinochet would accept their draft constitution or would put it to popular vote in the near future. In response, they adopted a two-track strategy. First, they continued to use their government positions to lobby Pinochet and other officials, citing continuing human rights pressures, internal government divisions, and questions among domestic actors about the government's legitimacy as reasons for a new constitution. Second, they formed a political movement called "New Democracy" and maintained a high public profile in the media, hoping to gain some popular support. In January 1980, they scored a key victory when Pinochet promised that he would submit a constitution to a popular plebiscite on September 11 of that year.[39]

Meanwhile, the Council of State made several significant changes to the draft constitution. The most important change concerned when it would take effect. Alessandri strongly believed that the time had arrived for the military to begin sharing power with civilians and saw little need for the junta to retain its full power. The council's draft version therefore specified a transition period of five years beginning as soon as the constitution went into effect. Pinochet would continue to act as president during that time, but his power would be partially circumscribed within the limits of the new constitution. The junta's powers would be limited to choosing a successor president should Pinochet die or resign, approving constitutional reforms, and serving as advisors to the president. A congress designated by Pinochet and the junta would be responsible for all other legislative functions during the transition. At the end of the five-year transition, presidential and congressional elections would be held and the junta would be disbanded.

End Game

Long before the Council of State concluded its version of the constitution, Pinochet and the junta had begun to think about an appropriate transition formula from military to civilian rule.[40] Pinochet thought Alessandri's five-year timetable was too short and preferred a much longer period of sixteen years. Junta members opposed their replacement by a congress, even one in which they designated the members. Military officials also thought it was too soon to put a constitution into effect that would immediately legalize parties and implement human rights guarantees, as would the version presented by the Council of State. In general, Pinochet and the junta believed that they still needed time to complete the transformation of Chilean society to completely rid it of the "vices of the past."

As a result, junta members enlisted the help of a small group of legal advisors and set to work drafting their own transitional articles for the constitution. If the constitution represented civilian attempts to legitimize the government, the transition articles reflected the military's desire to rule with force and its uneasiness about handing over power in the next few years. In contrast to the Council of State's proposal, the junta devised a transition in which Pinochet would retain power for at least eight and probably sixteen more years.[41] The junta would also remain in power for eight more years, carrying out legislative functions.

Its most important role would be to enact "constitutional organic laws" that would flesh out vague constitutional provisions with specific laws regulating sensitive political issues like voting and political parties. Additionally, the transitional articles gave Pinochet and the junta the power to violate many human rights. The fifteenth transitional article, for example, granted Pinochet the right to unilaterally impose (without the junta's approval) a state of emergency, with its accompanying powers, while the twenty-fourth transitional article empowered the executive to order detentions for up to twenty days without court approval, to restrict free association and free speech, and to exile opponents.

The junta completed its revisions of the constitution and the transitional articles in early August 1980 and called for a popular plebiscite to approve them on September 11, 1980 – the seventh anniversary of the military coup. Alessandri strongly objected to the length of the transition period and the special powers granted to Pinochet and the junta, leading to his resignation from the Council of State.[42] Nevertheless, he and others silenced their criticisms in deference to military preferences. After a brief campaign period tightly controlled by the government and without sufficient guarantees of a free and fair electoral process, 67 percent of Chileans (according to official figures) approved the new constitution.

In sum, rule-oriented officials successfully persuaded Pinochet and the junta to adopt a new constitution that had important liberal-democratic features mixed with significant authoritarian elements. At the same time, they quietly acquiesced to military preferences for a long transition period before the constitution would be fully effective. Rule-oriented officials were successful in part because they controlled the commissions that produced the constitution and because they enjoyed access to Pinochet. Although junta members themselves had the final say on the constitution, military officials had remarkably little to do with the drafting process itself.[43] With the exception of the transitional articles, the ideas and the language of the 1980 Constitution were largely a product of bureaucratic institutions and the legal advisors who staffed them, within boundaries placed by Pinochet.

Some rule-oriented individuals, and Guzmán in particular, influenced Pinochet because they presented their ideas in articulate and persuasive ways that made sense to military officials. "The man with the ideas was Guzmán," recalled one top government official.

> The work of convincing others was also Guzmán. He was a preacher of the necessity of advancing the new institutionality and was always talking to people about it. If he saw things weren't going well in one way, then he tried another. For example, he would talk to Pinochet about an idea. If Pinochet wasn't convinced, he asked him [Guzmán] to put it down on paper. Then Guzmán would be back in a few days to see if the president had read the paper. Covarrubias would ask Pinochet, and Pinochet would tell Guzmán to come in and chat. Then Pinochet would agree to the idea under certain conditions. Jaime Guzmán had the greatest power to convince, and the clearest ability to talk. He was an expositor with solid ideas and precise arguments. Pinochet valued him greatly.[44]

Guzmán was also a very patient yet energetic protagonist, proposing and joining numerous study commissions, seeking interviews and lunches with a wide variety of people, and promoting his ideas with everyone he met.

At the same time, dominance of study commissions and a persuasive tongue were not enough to change Chile's course by themselves. Pinochet and other military officials preferred either a long-term military state or corporatist political institutions and would not be easily persuaded otherwise by mere arguments. The commissions were powerless unless Pinochet decided otherwise, and arguments alone are rarely compelling unless they offer persuasive solutions to real-world problems. It is difficult to imagine that rule-oriented officials would have made much progress in the absence of serious normative challenges to the government's legitimacy.

Pressures and the Concern for Legitimacy

The transnational network continued to grow and to expand its activities, especially inside Chile, in the mid- to late 1970s, while state pressures remained relatively constant after the sharp increase in U.S. action in 1976–77.[45] The constant barrage of criticism from human rights groups, foreign states, and, increasingly, other domestic opposition groups, pushed the government to be even more concerned with its own legitimacy, especially as the coup faded into the background and some normality returned to Chile. Government officials viewed a new constitution as the best way to permanently resolve these legitimacy problems. Although human rights advocates hoped that pressures would end repression, the government instead responded by creating a new constitution designed to strengthen the government's long-term legitimacy while preserving its short-term power. Domestic characteristics such as moderate levels of normative fit and crisis ensured that the government would respond to pressures, but not that it would change dramatically in the desired direction.

Even though the outcome – a new constitution – was unintended by human rights activists, human rights pressures still played three key roles in producing this result. First, they posed a serious threat to the government's long-term legitimacy. Second, they strengthened rule-oriented officials by presenting problems that civilian advisors were well-equipped to resolve – by training, temperament, and expertise. Third, they exacerbated divisions within the government and either created or served as the backdrop for internal crises that shook the government's traditional structure, paving the way for the advancement of rule-oriented advisors.

A couple of new human rights groups formed in Chile in the late 1970s, adding vigor and new international contacts to the existing human rights network. The most important of these – and eventually the largest lay human rights organization in Latin America – was the Chilean Commission of Human Rights, founded at the end of 1978 by two prominent Christian Democrats.[46] The commission complemented and reinforced the work of the Vicariate of Solidarity by issuing more aggressive reports that documented more abuse victims drawn from a wider range of sources. Because the commission was staffed with activists from Chile's traditional political parties, it enjoyed a range of contacts among the exile community and like-minded political parties in Europe. It expanded the existing network by setting up formal affiliations with established international human rights groups like the International Commission of Jurists and by hosting a human rights conference in Santiago attended by more than two hundred activists.[47] In 1977, activists founded the Chilean chapter of the Service for Peace and Justice (Servicio de Paz y Justicia – SERPAJ), a transnational nonviolence and human rights group headquartered in Buenos Aires with a large network of contacts throughout Europe and the Americas.[48] Un-

like the Vicariate, SERPAJ focused on popular education and mobilization rather than on legal and medical services and exhaustive documentation. Student activists joined the growing human rights movement in
1978 when they established the National Commission for the Rights of
Youth (Comisión Nacional Pro Derechos Juveniles – CODEJU), adding a
youth dimension to the network.

Not only did the network increase in size, it also became more active
and enjoyed more media coverage after 1977. The Catholic Church and
the Vicariate led the way, punctuated by an extraordinary burst of activity in late 1978 and early 1979.[49] First, the church sharpened its criticism of the government in November 1978 when it essentially accused
the government of lying about the fate of the disappeared and of failing to make any serious investigations. Just two weeks later, the Vicariate hosted a large international conference on human rights with
prominent human rights and religious leaders from forty-four countries. News arrived during the conference that the Vicariate had won
a prestigious UN human rights prize awarded every five years. At the
same time, Vicariate officials, following up on a tip from a desper-
ate old man searching for any clue of his disappeared son, discovered
the decomposed corpses of fifteen people in disused smelting kilns at
an abandoned mining area called Lonquén.[50] The news reverberated
quickly around Chile and shook all parts of the country, resulting in
the appointment of a special investigating judge and the eventual application of a new amnesty law for the presumably guilty policemen.
The Vicariate followed up these stunning events in early 1979 by pub-
lishing an exhaustive study of 613 cases of disappeared individuals in
seven volumes, titled simply ¿Dónde Están? (Where Are They?). These
events made it impossible for the government to seriously claim that
disappearances were a figment of the Marxist imagination. From that
point on, Lonquén served as a symbol and ¿Dónde Están? as irrefutable
documentation of the government's abuses.

Human rights groups formed by victims' families likewise broadened their public activities and also gained important media attention
during this time.[51] The relatives of the disappeared organized a series
of events during the late 1970s, including hunger strikes, demonstrations, petitions to international organizations, efforts to seek an audience with Chilean officials, and, most dramatically, chaining protesters
to the fence surrounding the National Congress.[52] The Lonquén case

and the impossibility of winning justice in the court system led relatives and sympathetic priests and nuns to initiate a hunger strike and to hold a large memorial mass for the victims. Outside of the human rights network, political party officials, union leaders, and others began to criticize the government more openly in the late 1970s, rejecting the notion of an "authoritarian democracy" and criticizing the government's long transition timetable.[53] Among increasingly active, popular-sector organizations, human rights issues formed a central part of their identity and motivated many of their efforts.[54]

The transnational network and associated pressures played three roles in the military government's decision making in the mid- to late 1970s. First, they posed a normative threat that could not be easily ignored, because it raised questions about the government's medium- and long-term viability. Even if this threat was not strong enough to topple the government, or even to inflict tangible damage, it amplified rule-oriented arguments by demonstrating the costs of the government's failure to legitimize itself. As one of Guzmán's closest political collaborators put it:

> One must remember that, in that moment, the government held clear political control domestically. There was no domestic political problem. But yes, there was a very strong international problem. . . . Chile was opening its economy to the world, and one could not expect success unless there was a degree of appreciation in the world about what was happening in Chile. . . . The world had to understand that Chile was not simply another Latin American dictatorship, but rather a country that had suffered an institutional crisis and that the armed forces wanted to resolve this crisis. And this crisis implied a return to a legal framework and the necessity of setting deadlines [to military rule]. I would not say this was the only argument – but it was the most important argument – that Jaime [Guzmán] used to convince Pinochet of the importance of [the constitution].[55]

A conservative journalist who also served as a junta advisor observed that it became conventional wisdom among government officials that international pressures needed to be ameliorated because they could become worse at any moment. Those who downplayed international pressures were received with skepticism, he argued, while civilian officials gained the confidence of junta members by offering solutions to the perceived international problems.[56]

The threat posed to the government's legitimacy helped increase the size of the rule-oriented faction, or at least earned it a serious audience among otherwise hardline officials. Many military officers serving in government posts were clearly concerned about human rights pressures in the mid-1970s and were therefore receptive to rule-oriented arguments for a new constitution. "I was one of the people who believed the sooner the better with establishing constitutional norms, and even then I believe it was too late," said one army general with excellent access to junta members.[57] "I was always of the opinion that things should be normalized because the international criticism was very strong and it affected the country economically." Another general close to Pinochet declared, "There was a lot of worry inside the government about the international front because the threats were constant that the doors would shut. And the United Nations was going to proclaim a condemnation, and that they were going to send commissions and reports of human rights violations and this and that, and the Letelier case. These themes worried *mi general* [Pinochet]."[58] In a secret speech to army generals in late 1977, Pinochet himself invoked human rights pressures from international actors – and the fear of more pressures – as one of the main reasons to adopt a rule-oriented strategy.[59]

As government officials understood, the threat was not only international (that is, state pressure), but in the late 1970s increasingly transnational (within Chilean society as well). A former high-level military and cabinet official argued that the main threat to Chile after 1976 was not Marxism but rather the increasing disunity of Chilean society, fueled principally by criticisms from the Catholic Church and moderate political sectors, as well as by their international allies. "The Church and the Christian Democrats maintained social turmoil and class antagonism. Although they did not engage in terrorism, they gave terrorist attacks resonance through international publications like *Chile América*. They did everything possible to debilitate the military government, and as a result they fortified extremism. Although the government was never in danger of being overthrown, it made the country less governable."[60] Far from being irrelevant owing to its lack of resources and small size, the military government viewed the human rights network as a fundamental threat because it facilitated the spread of Marxism and made it more difficult for the government to govern the country in an orderly way.

Government officials appropriately understood the threat as a long-term problem. While human rights pressures could not topple the government in the short term, they could undermine and discredit the government in the long run. Guzmán and other legal advisors raised the specter that the government would become a simple "administrative period" between two weak democratic governments. They asked key questions about the government's future: How could the government fundamentally reshape Chile's social, economic, and political systems far into the future if the international community – and even Chileans themselves – rejected the government? Wasn't the government in need of long-term, fundamental normative acceptance if it was to succeed in its deep restructuring task? What type of political institutions were the most likely to win normative acceptance? Rule-oriented officials did not yet have all the answers to these questions in 1977, but they knew that the government needed legitimacy.

Second, the transnational network and state pressures posed a problem that civilian advisors were well-equipped to resolve. Normative pressures required not economic or military skill, but rather legal maneuvering, diplomatic skill, and public relations work. The government had already proven itself inept at international public relations and poor at diplomacy.[61] Once these failed, Pinochet was more willing to listen to solutions that involved a reworking of domestic institutions and laws. Rule-oriented officials argued that a new constitution was the perfect way to kill multiple birds with a single stone. It would, they argued, help the government achieve legitimacy both nationally and internationally. By the late 1970s, it was clear that the government could no longer rely on its 1973 coup and brute force to run the country. It needed a stronger juridical basis to govern and to fend off charges of illegitimate authority. At the same time, the constitution would provide an additional legal weapon in the war on Marxism, one that would be increasingly important as the country returned to normality. By writing restrictions into the constitution, the government would ensure that its efforts against Marxism would endure far into the future.

Considerable interview evidence exists to support the contention that Chilean policymakers viewed a new constitution as an important solution to the decline of the government's legitimacy. "There was criticism in all the world," recalled a former military advisor to Pinochet, "and the government believed it was absolutely necessary to give stability and backing to the constitution and clear rules to continue governing. Without a political constitution it appeared like an eternal government, arbitrary in its actions, and so it was necessary to have a constitution. Internationally, it was impossible to carry on with the character of a dictatorship."[62] A civilian advisor to Pinochet expressed similar thoughts: "[Pinochet approved the 1980 Constitution] because he had progressively committed himself to it and found himself bound by his commitments. In international relations, in the fora of the United Nations and in all places, the ambassadors and the representatives always said, 'Next year, we're going to have a constitution, and it will be approved by all the people.' And, quite reasonably, the countries that did business with us began to ask, 'But when will there be a constitution?' And the date was fixed and it got closer and closer. I believe in the end it was a very bitter pill for Pinochet to swallow."[63]

One junta member recalled that he originally opposed a new constitution in the late 1970s because it was too early. Concerns about legitimacy soon persuaded him, however, that a new constitution would "tell the people where we were going. It was better to come out and say where we wanted to go, once and for all, so that everyone knew what the rules would be and where we were going to direct ourselves."[64] Military officials viewed the constitution as a way to earn normative support for the government and to counter opposition discourse. As a former military official put it, "Ideas cannot be fought with sticks. Ideas are fought with ideas."[65] Since the primary threat to Chile in the late 1970s was normative – namely, the discrediting of the government – the proper weapon to combat this threat was also normative – a new constitution.[66]

Additionally, transcripts of the meetings of the Constitutional Commission and the Council of State show that throughout the drafting process, Chilean policymakers continued to feel an urgent need to establish political institutions in order to resolve Chile's international problems and to ease human rights pressures. Alessandri himself often cited international norms and legitimacy concerns as a reason to speed up the drafting process or to create more democratic institutions. During the meeting at which the council first considered the draft constitution, Alessandri argued that even though Pinochet had not set a deadline, there was an urgent need for the country to "return to normality" and "to improve the international image of the country, for which a functioning constitution is indispensable."[67] Later that month, Alessandri once again invoked international concerns, this time in debate with a council member seeking corporatist-style political institutions: "There are those who support a corporatist government, but without anyone being able to define it, for the simple reason that these types of systems have only been able to function under dictatorships such as those of Hitler or Mussolini. We should strive to live in harmony with the Western countries, and for that we need a congress. For while a congress does not exist, they will always label Chile a dictatorship and promote boycotts against us — as some have already announced — or prohibit us from receiving financial aid."[68]

Third, international pressures generally exacerbated divisions within the government and, in particular, provided an opportunity for air force general and junta member Gustavo Leigh to challenge Pinochet's power. The resulting power struggles created a sense of crisis within the government, toppled key officials, and created a power vacuum into which civilian advisors easily stepped.

Since 1974, the air force had been increasingly unhappy with the army's predominance within the government, and Leigh was particularly upset by Pinochet's status as president while other junta members played a less important role.[69] In early 1976, his opposition took on broader dimensions when Leigh proposed an end to the DINA and a speedy return to civilian rule. Although his proposals were swept under the rug, the tension between the air force and other branches continued to simmer just below the surface in 1976-77 and sometimes even burst into public view. In particular, Leigh continued to press for a rapid return to democracy in both public speeches and private meetings.

In December 1977, his relationship with Pinochet neared the breaking point over a dispute involving the fourth consecutive UN condemnation of Chile's human rights abuses. Pinochet scheduled a national referendum to manifest support for the government in the face of the international attacks. Leigh strongly opposed the referendum as a non-democratic procedure designed simply to enhance Pinochet's personal standing. The two military leaders exchanged acrimonious letters filled with charges of personal power-seeking and misconduct. Leigh nearly created a definitive break with the rest of the junta members before finally giving in and signing a law that allowed Pinochet to call for a national referendum in January 1978.

Though Leigh had lost the battle, he continued his war by trying to use human rights pressures as leverage against Pinochet's power. In early 1978 he seized on pressures generated by the Letelier case to issue forthright criticisms of Pinochet's leadership and to call for a swift return to democracy.[70] In a move that especially irritated Pinochet and served as the straw that broke the camel's back, Leigh repeated his critiques in an interview published in an Italian newspaper. By July 1978, Leigh's opposition had become too great to tolerate, and, amid rumors that the air force was planning a coup, the other three junta members forced him from power. The entire corps of air force generals, save one, resigned in solidarity with Leigh, demonstrating the magnitude of the break between the branches of the military.

Human rights pressures either directly shook the military government, as with the end of the DINA and Contreras' retirement, or else provided the context for others to contest Pinochet's power, as with Leigh and the air force. Either way, the turmoil provided a perfect opportunity for rule-oriented individuals to increase their influence. The rule-oriented faction opportunistically used both the problems with the DINA and Leigh's opposition to buttress their own position and to sell Pinochet on the need for a clear institutional plan. Between Leigh's calls for a speedy restoration of democracy and hardliner sentiments for a continued strong hand and unlimited military rule, rule-oriented officials took the middle ground. They drew a bright and important line between Leigh's calls for a *return* to democracy and their own ideas about creating a *new* democracy. They argued that their plan differed from Leigh's because it would not restore traditional Chilean democracy, which was widely denigrated by military officials and conservatives, but rather create a new and better "protected" democracy, complete with a military-controlled transition.

If Pinochet had at first been attracted to a state built around the armed forces, Leigh's actions demonstrated the serious problems in this scheme. In the midst of these problems, Pinochet addressed army generals and declared that the military must work toward removing itself from power. If not, "The armed forces would be compromised for too much time in dealing with trivial matters, with the risk of destroying military prestige among Chileans as well as the ability to serve as reserves for national values, due to their governmental role."[71] Further, Pinochet argued that in many other countries the armed forces spent too much time in power, soon lost their internal discipline and cohesion, lost their prestige, and became the brunt of criticism from a hostile populace.

With the DINA out of the way, Contreras in retirement, and a widening split in the armed forces, civilians promoting new institutions enjoyed an easy path to power. In March 1978, beset by international human rights pressures and internal turmoil, Pinochet cast about for a new political direction. He held two extensive conversations with his recent labor minister, a young civilian lawyer named Sergio Fernández, well-connected with the rule-oriented faction.[72] Fernández spoke of the need for a legal and institutional renovation of the military government and the adoption of a new constitution. Likewise, seven civilian cabinet ministers met with Pinochet at a dinner and argued for a new civilian face to the government and the gradual withdrawal of military leaders from power.[73] Pinochet accepted these ideas, and on April 12, 1978, he reshuffled his cabinet, placing Fernández at the powerful post of interior minister and giving him the authority to pursue plans to institutionalize the government. The new cabinet marked a decisive turning point because it signaled Pinochet's definitive acceptance of the rule-oriented strategy.

The initial success of the rule-oriented faction simply bred further success. Their conquest of Pinochet's cabinet in April 1978 gave them access to important institutional resources, a higher public profile, and more direct control of government functions. They continued to build important alliances with neoliberal economists who also held key cabinet posts. In fact, in 1979–80, some powerful economists like Alvaro Bardón and Pablo Baraona began to address political issues more explicitly and pushed for a new constitution in the media, in business circles, and within the government itself. Further, civilian legal advisors built bridges to influential military lawyers advising junta members, including Fernando Lyon in the army and Mario Duvauchelle in the navy, both of whom fully supported the constitutional-drafting process.[74] Even the new head of the intelligence services, Odlanier Mena, met routinely with civilian legal advisors and shared their ideas about the importance of a new constitution. From mid-1978 until the approval of the constitution – and indeed until the transition to democracy – rule-oriented officials dominated the government. Human rights pressures played a key role in producing this outcome.

Domestic Characteristics

I argued above that a rule-oriented faction came to dominate the government and facilitated the influence of human rights pressures. At the same time, moderate levels of normative fit ensured that human rights pressures would continue to be taken seriously and that government officials would concern themselves with problems of long-term legitimacy. The quick resolution of a security threat from Argentina also helped ensure that the government's attention would be focused on human rights pressures.

Chile's normative fit remained unchanged at moderate levels during this period, reinforcing human rights pressures and government concerns about its legitimacy. Government officials naturally wanted to control the political landscape of the future, but were realistic enough to know that they could not simply shape it according to their own wishes. Expectations of democratic governance and respect for human rights were widespread among Chileans owing to decades of experience and a national identity as a progressive Western state. Rule-oriented individuals in the government astutely observed that democratic norms were ingrained into Chile by long years of practice and that human rights norms formed the basis for the extensive pressures on the government. Thus, they argued that a new constitution could gain long-term legitimacy only if it appealed to norms of human rights and democracy.[75]

Guzmán was especially adept at persuading military officials of this constraint. In 1979, for example, debates on what to do with political parties ran through the military government. Corporatists and military hardliners, including Pinochet, would have preferred to do away with them forever. Nevertheless, Guzmán took on the task of persuading them otherwise. In a memo to Pinochet in early 1979, he argued:

> The suppression of universal free suffrage and of political parties is only possible in real and definitive form through a totalitarian-style political repression, which even the most iron-fisted contemporary governments cannot efficiently impose without vacillating. What is occurring in Iran is eloquent. Even China and the Soviet Union find themselves with dissidence that they still silence with brutal totalitarianism, but even so are not able to eliminate — even with the unlimited repression of the Stalinist epoch. Unity and dissent are es-

sential to all human communities. Dissent is a part of social life. Without it, there is no political freedom. In the other extreme, without a fundamental unity or basic consensus, the community disappears, and paradoxically, the atmosphere of dissent is destroyed. Finding the just equilibrium is the task of all societies that are free and at the same time unified. The grouping together of humans according to their tendencies, call it political party or not, is a natural reality that always has existed and always will exist. Even today in Chile they have not disappeared from real life.[76]

Guzmán neatly played on Pinochet's hatred of Communism, his strategic sense (trying to completely destroy political parties is a waste of resources), and promises of bounded dissent to persuade him of the need for political parties. More fundamentally, Guzmán was arguing that Chile was not China and that Chile was not Iran. If those countries could not possibly rid themselves of political movements despite enormous repression, then how could Chile – with its long tradition of free political expression – ever succeed?

Pinochet eventually bought into these arguments because he was pragmatic and realistic. As a good strategist, he knew the constraints he faced, whether they were tangible or, as in this case, cultural. As one high-level military advisor from the time summarized it, "In the end Pinochet was a realist. He liked to plant ideas with others and see if they would take root. His idea of a political power based in the armed forces did not really take root anywhere, and the people who talked with him convinced him that it wouldn't work."[77]

With respect to crisis levels, I argued in the previous chapter that the economy began to grow again in 1976 and then hit stride in 1977. The ensuing four years were some of the government's best as international investment and petrodollar loans produced an economic boom that led some government officials to predict that Chile would be a developed country by 1990.[78] On the security front, the DINA's effectiveness ensured that no leftist guerrilla movement or widespread social disorder would disturb the government. Even with the end of the DINA, little changed in this respect during 1978-81.

On the international front, however, the government suddenly and unexpectedly met growing hostility from Bolivia and Argentina.[79] Bolivia had a long-standing conflict with Chile over access to the ocean, and relations deteriorated rapidly in early 1978. The situation with

Argentina was even more serious.[80] In January 1978, Argentina rejected a supposedly binding British-mediated solution to a territorial dispute with Chile over three small islands off the southern tip of South America. By late 1978, both countries were mobilizing for war, which was avoided at the last moment through the Pope's intervention. Although the threat of war was relatively short-lived, it undoubtedly distracted the government's attention from legitimacy problems and human rights concerns. The ebbing of the threat created space for human rights pressures to take center stage once again.

Chile's domestic structure remained strongly state-dominated in the late 1970s and was absolutely closed to any human rights activists or their allies. It thus contributes little to an explanation of why the government adopted a new constitution, or to the content of that constitution. Chilean officials generally refused to discuss human rights issues with intergovernmental organizations or diplomats from Western states. Even if some managed to share their ideas with military officials, it seems unlikely that a new constitution with "protected democracy" is what they had in mind. Domestic opposition groups began to show some signs of activity, but absolutely lacked access to government decision makers. In the labor sector, prominent leaders formed the Group of Ten and issued important criticisms of the government.[81] Rank-and-file union members often elected antigovernment officials and, in the copper mines, even engaged in limited strikes and related work protests. Nevertheless, the government maintained heavy repression and unions enjoyed little if any of the mobilization power or unity that they would manifest in the mid-1980s. Popular organizations had progressed to a point where their survival was no longer in doubt, but were nevertheless in a state of "crisis" as they shifted focus to deal with the government's institutionalization and apparent long-term survival.[82] Political parties moved from a state of simple survival and resistance to one of more open opposition, but still lacked mobilizing power, mass media platforms to disseminate their ideas, or any type of strategy or coordinated opposition.[83]

Alternative Explanations

This analysis differs in important ways from previous explanations of the government's institutionalization. Many scholars have adopted a functional argument to explain Chile's new constitution. In Garretón's view, authoritarian governments typically seize power under the pretext of some crisis, but the eventual passing of the crisis and a return to normality undermine their claims on power.[84] As a result, authoritarian governments naturally seek to institutionalize themselves and to create a new basis for their legitimacy. Valenzuela also adopts a functionalist explanation, arguing that Pinochet needed a constitution to consolidate and institutionalize his personal power.[85] In theory, these arguments are essentially sound. Most (but emphatically not all) authoritarian governments seek to institutionalize and legitimize themselves, and Pinochet undoubtedly found institutions and rules useful to consolidate his power.

At the same time, functional explanations are incomplete and are not always supported by the evidence. Functional arguments assume that the government search for institutionalization and legitimization is a naturally occurring process triggered by government age and the leaders' desire to ensure their positions. Yet this approach does not entirely fit with the evidence that Pinochet reluctantly endorsed a new constitution after extended resistance. Nor does it square with government documents and interviews, which show that the process was as much reactive and defensive as it was a natural government initiative. Additionally, functional explanations tell us little about the content of new political institutions or the ways in which a government tries to achieve legitimacy. As a result, they cannot tell us why Pinochet opted for "authoritarian democracy" over a military state or authoritarian corporatism.

Most importantly, functional approaches cannot explain the dramatic variation among different governments in the timing of the institutionalization efforts, in the particular ways in which governments try to achieve legitimacy, or in the content of the institutions. The 1976 military government in Argentina, for example, never wrote a new constitution and wound up reintroducing an old 1853 Constitution in its waning days. It failed to appeal to human rights norms as a source of legitimacy, instead relying on a "vague hope for some kind of restricted democracy."[86] The Uruguayan government delayed institutionalization until the government had lost too much legitimacy and saw its proposed constitution voted down at the polls. Moving beyond the Southern Cone, even more variation is apparent. The authoritarian government in Cuba, born in 1959, did not build new political institutions until the mid-1970s and has sought legitimacy by appealing to socialist principles and nationalist traditions rather than Westernized human rights norms. Any number of other authoritarian governments – from South Africa (until the 1990s) to Yugoslavia (under Milosevic) – have legitimized themselves by appealing primarily to norms of racial or ethnic superiority.

A focus on human rights pressures and domestic factors, in contrast, helps explain both the timing and content of the new constitution. In this respect, I assign a larger impact to the international dimension of these pressures than previous studies. Other scholars agree that international pressures played a role, but insist that they had relatively minor consequences, especially in the 1970s. Muñoz argues that human rights pressures "probably saved many lives and shortened many jail sentences."[87] Portales is even more skeptical, pronouncing the government "unmoved" by external pressure up until 1982–83.[88] If we consider only the intended and desirable consequences of the human rights campaign, these analyses are essentially correct. The human rights situation as a whole did not significantly improve during the 1970s, although some victims undoubtedly benefited from international pressure.

By looking only at the intended consequences, however, these analyses miss all of the unintended consequences, mixed results, and complex government reactions. Although human rights activists intended to improve Chile's human rights situation, their efforts helped push the government to implement a new constitution that, in the short run, strengthened its repressive power and in the long run opened some important spaces for the domestic opposition (see chapter 6). Cause and effect are present, just not always in the normatively desired or intended directions, unfortunately leading some scholars to downplay the impact of human rights pressures. Human rights pressures mattered, just not in the way intended by network activists.

Although Chile's new constitution was not primarily addressed to human rights activists and Western states, it is difficult if not impossible to explain the timing or the content of the constitution without reference to human rights pressures. Transnational human rights groups and Western states made it clear in the mid- to late 1970s that they would never accept the military government's legitimacy and that they would continue to criticize the government's abuses despite minor reforms. The strength of hardliners in 1976–77, the military's extreme nationalism, and Pinochet's personal preferences for ongoing authoritarianism made it seem unlikely that Chile would respond in any significant way.

At the same time, Chile developed a very strong rule-oriented faction in the context of moderate levels of normative fit and moderate security threats to produce a growing interest in the government's legitimacy. Legalistic civilian officials dominated government legal posts and study commissions and developed allies among military officials and economists. They used excellent informal access to Pinochet to argue that human rights pressures could undermine the government's long-term influence and that a new constitution was essential to establish the government's legitimacy. The government's absolute dominance of the opposition and a robust economic recovery decreased other threats, allowing human rights pressures and long-run concerns to take center stage. Chile's democratic history and the depth of human rights norms in domestic culture helped convince Pinochet that political schemes to institutionalize endless authoritarian rule would never work in Chile. As a result, he pushed ahead the constitutional drafting process and opted for political institutions that would eventually integrate some liberal features into authoritarian rule.

Critics might argue that even if human rights pressures influenced the timing and content of Chile's new constitution, these changes were essentially meaningless at best, and harmful at worst. Most North American academics and Chilean opposition groups during the 1970s and 1980s dismissed the institutionalization process in Chile as a sham. During the mid-1970s, military government officials promised to create new political institutions, but refused to commit to a timetable for setting them up and discussed them in vague terms. This behavior, argued critics, demonstrated that the military government was not serious about establishing new political institutions and leaving power.

Once the new constitution was approved, critics argued that it simply served as a facade for Pinochet's personal power. Valenzuela and Valenzuela went so far as to argue that Chile in the 1980s was a personalistic "dictatorship of the commander in chief of the armed forces" rather than a military government and that it was an "authoritarian situation" rather than an authoritarian government because it lacked institutions.[89] Likewise they argued that the 1980 Constitution simply reflected "some codification in legal norms of Pinochet's unipersonal power" rather than an institution binding Pinochet to certain rules and procedures.

While Pinochet certainly held enormous political power, the endurance of the 1980 Constitution well beyond the end of military rule demonstrates that it was much more than the window dressing for Pinochet's personal power. Further, as I argue in chapter 5, the constitution ensured that the government would stick to its transition schedule — in stark contrast with the schedule laid out at Chacarillas, which the government simply ignored. As the plebiscite date approached, government officials often wished they could alter either the timing or the method, or both, or call the whole thing off altogether. Yet such an action was impossible without jeopardizing the legitimacy of the constitution and the entire period of military rule. As Valenzuela conceded in 1991, "Ironically, the constitution would eventually come to constrain the regime, and the transitional formula of 1989 would prove to be a much greater challenge to Pinochet than his advisers imagined in the euphoric days of 1980."[90] One might add that it posed a much greater challenge than academics imagined as well.

The constitution had two-edged implications for human rights issues in the 1980s. In most ways, it cut in favor of more government repression. Article 8 prevented individuals from propagating Marxist doctrine, declared all Marxist political parties unconstitutional, and authorized severe penalties for violations. Article 41 granted the president wide latitude to violate a number of rights in legal states of exception. The transitional articles in force from 1981 to 1988 were particularly repressive, granting Pinochet the exclusive authority to detain people indiscriminately, to restrict free assembly and free speech, to exile those who undertake acts "contrary to the interests of Chile," to restrict freedom of movement inside the country, and to impose states of emergency that would give him even more powers. More generally, the constitution maintained centralized power in the hands of Pinochet and the junta with few checks and balances.

In some ways, however, the new constitution established procedures and institutions that unintentionally hindered the government's ability to violate human rights at will. Although I discuss many of these in chapter 5, it is worth noting here that some provisions opened the door ever so slightly to opposition groups, who took full advantage of them. Article 19, clause 15, for example, placed a few general restrictions on political parties, and authorized the creation of an organic law to further regulate parties and to devise penalties for failure to abide by the restrictions. With the junta due to be replaced by an elected legislature in early 1990, the government had a strong incentive to write this organic law in the mid-1980s and put it in operation so that it would carry over to the post-junta period. Yet regulating political parties required legalizing them, and thus the junta both legalized and regulated political parties in March 1987. Parties quickly took advantage of this small opening in time to organize opposition to Pinochet in the 1988 plebiscite.

More broadly, the constitution raised Chileans' expectations of a return to democracy and respect for human rights. Opposition parties eventually used constitutional provisions to press for this result. Garretón has aptly summarized these paradoxical features of authoritarian political institutions: "Thus, they are instruments of consolidation which provide the space for the imposition of a new social order. At the same time, they delineate the space in which new contradictions and social conflicts arise; the place and the instrument through which social movements, with difficulty, reconstitute themselves; the gap through which the immobility of the first phase is broken."[91] At the same time that opposition groups reject and denounce new institutions, they simultaneously take advantage of small breathing spaces to regroup and press their demands. Such was the case with Chile's constitution.

FIVE

Legitimacy and Elections
in the 1980s

I will die and the person who succeeds me will also die. But there won't be any elections. — Augusto Pinochet, June 23, 1975

In the first fifteen years of military rule, Chileans went to the polls only twice, in 1978 and again in 1980. Both votes consisted of simple yes/no questions. The first asked citizens whether they supported Pinochet and Chile against international condemnations in the United Nations and the second asked voters to approve a new constitution. Neither vote met minimal standards of freedom and fairness.[1] In 1978, the government announced the plebiscite only two weeks before it occurred, utilized pro-government election officials, and maintained repressive state-of-siege conditions. As a result, the climate of terror ensured that opposition forces could not meet, protest, or even communicate their concerns in the media. Further, voting procedures were far from fair. To cite one egregious example, the line on the ballot supporting Pinochet was marked by a Chilean flag and the opposing line by a black flag. In 1980 conditions improved, but not by much. There were no independent election officials or observers, the state of emergency imposed severe restrictions on free speech and free assembly, and a variety of voting irregularities were reported.

On October 5, 1988, Chileans went to the polls for a third time to answer another yes/no question in a vote that was mandated by the 1980 Constitution: Should General Augusto Pinochet continue as Chile's president for the next eight years? In stark contrast to the previous plebiscites, government officials took a number of steps to ensure that the voting procedures were comparatively fair and that no one could question the outcome.[2] Although the government did not create a completely level playing field, it offered enough guarantees of a fair election that it found itself voted out of office. Its efforts to hold a fair election included legalizing political parties, allowing public demonstrations, facilitating voter registration, lifting the state of emergency, and allowing the opposition limited but free advertising time on television stations.

Opposition forces used these small political openings to great advantage, breaking the climate of terror and scoring a surprising and conclusive victory at the polls. After a tense late-night meeting of junta members and other top officials, a government spokesman conceded defeat at 2 A.M.[3] When the dust had settled, the opposition had garnered nearly 55 percent of the vote to Pinochet's 43 percent. A stunned Pinochet was thereby forced from office, paving the way for Chile's democratic transition and the election of a new president in 1989. These events give rise to the central question driving this chapter. Why did the military government risk its political life by facilitating the right to vote in a relatively fair election?

As with previous political changes examined in this book, I argue that human rights pressures played a crucial role. After the 1982–83 economic recession, political parties and a variety of social groups dominated the government opposition. The transnational human rights network suddenly became a smaller fish in a bigger pond, making it more difficult to sort out its influence from that of other opposition groups. Over time, a large number of opposition groups, human rights groups, and foreign states came to focus intently on the question of voting rights in the 1988 plebiscite. They laid out clear standards that would have to be met for the plebiscite to be considered a valid expression of popular will and pressured the government to meet these standards.

These pressures forced the government to recognize that large segments of domestic society and the international community rejected the legitimacy of the government generally and its 1980 Constitution specifically. Realizing that the military could not hold onto political power forever, government officials began to think strategically about the ways in which they could influence Chilean politics in the future. As a result, they constructed an interest in achieving widespread legitimacy for the 1980 Constitution. If the opposition and international actors accepted the 1980 Constitution, then many of the government's attempts to restructure Chilean society and politics would remain intact. Government officials adopted the strategy of enticing the opposition to participate in the upcoming presidential plebiscite, thereby ensuring de facto recognition of the constitution's legitimacy. To entice the opposition to participate, they adopted rules that would ensure a minimally fair vote.

In 1982–83, large-scale economic and political crisis blocked any serious positive changes from occurring in Chile and in fact prompted the government to increase repression. By the mid- to late 1980s, however, Chile's domestic characteristics made it particularly susceptible to human rights pressures even though those pressures were largely intangible. Perhaps most importantly, the 1982 economic collapse reactivated domestic social groups, which in turn began to champion domestic human rights norms and to make them more salient. As a result, the normative fit of international human rights standards increased to high levels. Beginning in 1984, economic recovery and the decline of mass protests signaled the end of the crisis, and by 1987 the government faced minimal economic and security threats. These improvements ensured that human rights pressures would get the attention of government officials.

Finally, rule-oriented individuals dominated central institutional positions in the 1980s, including the cabinet, legislative bodies (the junta and other study commissions), and a constitutional court. They believed that a transition to democracy was inevitable and sought to legitimize the constitution and its associated laws as a way to structure the rules of the game in Chile's emerging democratic government. As a result, the government's interest in legitimacy was stronger than ever. In fact, the government essentially traded an election loss for legitimacy of its constitution – although this trade was not its intention.

Other factors either fail to explain Chile's relatively fair plebiscite, or must be supplemented by the explanation offered here. Chile's state-dominated domestic structure clearly cannot explain why the government undertook such important changes. Transnational human rights groups never gained meaningful access to Chile's decision makers, while U.S. officials gained access but never formed any kind of "winning coalition" with Chilean officials. Nor was the plebiscite simply a colossal miscalculation caused by false confidence in Pinochet's victory. Rules establishing a relatively fair contest began to be set up long before victory could be assured, and government officials often debated whether Pinochet could in fact win the plebiscite. Finally, the domestic opposition certainly played a more influential role in the 1980s than during the 1970s, yet it would be a mistake to disconnect this opposition from broader international and historical processes.

I argue these points as follows. I first demonstrate how economic crisis and social unrest threatened to topple the government and produced escalating levels of repression and violence as the government fought to survive. The next section examines the human rights pressures on the government by looking at the human rights network and foreign states and illustrating the relationship between these actors and the newly invigorated domestic opposition. I then analyze the ongoing development of a strong government interest in legitimacy by looking at the establishment of an independent Electoral Qualifying Tribunal, the ending of legal states of exception and the easing of restrictions on free expression, the decision about when to hold the plebiscite, and the military's role in these political processes. Three of Chile's domestic characteristics – in particular, low crisis levels, high levels of normative fit, and a strong rule-oriented faction – help explain why government officials became so concerned about holding a minimally fair plebiscite. Yet a fourth characteristic, Chile's domestic structure, cannot explain these changes because network activists and their allies never gained any meaningful access to the government, which refused to negotiate seriously with anyone. I conclude by examining alternative explanations and the ways in which my arguments illuminate the origins and development of state interests.

Increase in Repression, 1982–84

After implementing the 1980 Constitution, a sense of complacency and triumph pervaded government officials. The government had destroyed Marxist groups, launched the country on seemingly steady economic growth, planned for the political future, and – it hoped – resolved its legitimacy problems. Then in 1982, government officials received a rude shock. The revered neoliberal economic policies that had brought strong economic growth and capital flows to Chile presided that year over the country's economic collapse. Financial difficulties precipitated a crisis when international capital flows dried up, leading to a steep drop in Chile's international reserves and a massive balance of payments deficit in 1982.[4] The government's initial refusal to devalue the Chilean peso – pegged at thirty-nine to a dollar by the Chicago Boys – and a sharp climb in interest rates as capital became scarce only exacerbated the problem. As a result, Chile's economy shrank 14.1 percent in 1982 and an additional .7 percent in 1983.

The 1982 economic crash produced the first open and widespread opposition to the military government. Massive popular protests rocked Chile during 1983, and smaller-scale protests continued in the following years. After quietly gathering steam for several years, the opposition finally exploded into action on May 11, 1983, when labor union leaders called for a national day of protest because of Chile's deteriorating economy and the government's continuing repression. A large segment of the population, including many of Santiago's middle- and upper-class neighborhoods, participated in public demonstrations, work slowdowns, keeping children from school, and banging pots and pans at night. So successful was the protest that opposition leaders called for similar protests in ensuing months. As the popular protests continued, they opened space within which opposition political parties, media outlets, and social groups could organize.[5] Although the protests focused on any number of grievances, protesters and organizers alike routinely denounced the government's repression. The widespread nature of the protests took the government by surprise and demonstrated a significant erosion of government support, even within some of its traditional power bases.

The government responded with a strategy of splitting the opposition by negotiating with moderate elites while simultaneously unleashing a new wave of violent repression on the massive street demonstrations. In early August 1983, Pinochet named a new interior minister – Sergio Jarpa, a well-known conservative politician – and declared the need to increase "the margins of human liberty."[6] Jarpa began negotiations with moderate opposition leaders and promised to implement "an open and full democracy, just like the traditional democracy that existed in Chile before the Marxists intervened."[7] At the same time, Pinochet met protesters in the street with increasing levels of deadly force and repression, killing dozens and jailing tens of thousands. In November 1984, the government reimposed a state of siege on Chile, not lifted until June 1985. The state of siege drove the final nail in the coffin of the promised reforms and gave legal status to the increased levels of repression.

This increasing repression can be ascribed to the high levels of crisis facing the military government because of the widespread domestic protests. Concerns about government legitimacy, so prominent during the mid- to late 1970s, simply vanished as the government faced threats to its survival. As a result, the government fought back with intense force and careful political strategies designed to ensure its short-term stability rather than its long-term legitimacy. Rule-oriented individuals continued to dominate key government positions, but they supported short-term repression as necessary for salvaging long-term institutions. Chile's domestic structure changed little in 1982–84 and thus cannot explain the increasing levels of repression.

Renewing Human Rights Pressures

During and after the economic crisis, the human rights network actively continued documenting and denouncing an array of abuses and created ties with grassroots organizations instrumental in organizing some local protests. At the same time, a large variety of other social and political groups, often funded by international donors, prioritized human rights themes in their opposition to authoritarian rule and became so visible that they overshadowed the work of the human rights groups themselves. Sensing change in the air, the United States distanced itself from Chile and joined other Western states in a renewed effort to delegitimize the government. Over time, human rights groups, political parties, a variety of social groups, and foreign states all came to focus on one particular event and one specific right: the 1988 plebiscite on Pinochet's rule and the right to vote in a free and fair election.

The Human Rights Network

Important developments within the human rights network in the 1980s included the rise of groups focused on nonviolent protest and the efforts of national human rights organizations to create and mobilize grassroots groups. Inspired by the death of a construction worker who lit himself on fire to protest the torture of his children, activists formed the Sebastián Acevedo Movement against Torture and held a series of nonviolent surprise demonstrations beginning in 1983 that directed considerable media attention toward the government's ongoing use of torture.[8] The Chilean Commission of Human Rights developed a series of base committees in the 1980s — eventually numbering around 90 and encompassing some 1,100 members — that documented and protested human rights abuses in their local areas.[9] The Committee for the Defense of the Rights of the People (Comité de Defensa de los Derechos del Pueblo – CODEPU), founded in late 1980, also formed a variety of base committees that actively protested human rights abuses in their communities. Unfortunately, the organization's Marxist orientation made these grassroots committees prominent targets of repression, which eventually forced their dissolution. Rather than give up mobilization efforts, CODEPU focused instead on holding human rights training sessions for other social groups, such as labor unions and women's organizations.

Internationally, human rights groups continued to document widespread abuses in Chile, to circulate the information among Western states, and to provide points of transnational linkage for domestic groups in Chile. Although these activities became more routine and thereby lost some of their earlier vigor and novelty, they constantly reinforced the fundamental international illegitimacy of the military government. Human rights pressures reminded the government that domestic repression would continue to adversely affect its foreign relations, despite the adoption of a constitution that promised a return to democracy and future respect for human rights. Throughout the 1980s, the Inter-American Commission on Human Rights continued to document abuses, punctuated in 1985 by the release of a fourth comprehensive report on human rights in Chile that strongly denounced the government's practices.[10] Yet this report was undermined by the failure of the General Assembly of the Organization of American States to condemn Chile by name. The United Nations General Assembly, in contrast, continued its overwhelming condemnation of Chile during each year, except in 1985.[11] For its part, the UN Human Rights Commission designated a special rapporteur to deal with Chile on a more consistent basis and repeatedly condemned Chile's behavior. In the United States, human rights groups faced a far more conservative administration and Congress, but continued to circulate information and press for changes in U.S. policy and in Chile.

State Pressures

Ronald Reagan's 1980 election to the U.S. presidency had weakened international human rights pressures by removing a major source of state pressure on Chile. Over time, however, the Reagan administration began to view Pinochet as more of a liability than an asset, owing to the waning Cold War and the rebirth of the Chilean opposition.[12] In late 1984 the United States signaled the end of its "quiet diplomacy" with the military government when prominent State Department officials, and even Reagan himself, began to criticize Chile publicly. More substantively, the United States abstained on a $430 million loan to Chile from the Inter-American Development Bank in January 1985 because of human rights concerns. In April 1985, the United States appointed a new ambassador, Harry Barnes, who repeatedly criticized the Pinochet government and made it clear that he expected a democratic government to take its place soon.

Over the next few years, the United States consistently called for a return to democracy in Chile, though it only intermittently penalized Chile for human rights abuses.[13] In actions that apparently reflected the competing views of different U.S. bureaucracies as well as perceived progress or obstructionism in Chile, the United States sometimes favored and sometimes abstained on multilateral development bank loans and voted inconsistently on multilateral condemnations of Chile's human rights situation. As the plebiscite approached, however, the United States adopted tougher, more consistent stances. In December 1987, Reagan issued a signed statement that laid out the U.S. view on the conditions necessary for free and fair elections in Chile. As 1988 dawned, the United States announced the first new bilateral sanctions against Chile since the Carter administration. After a study of labor repression in Chile, the Reagan administration decided to exclude Chile from the Generalized System of Preferences (which offered Chile lower tariffs on goods exported to the United States) and to terminate Chile's eligibility for the Overseas Protection Investment Corporation (OPIC), a U.S. government program that insured U.S. investments in Chile.[14]

The Domestic Opposition

Unlike the 1970s, when small human rights groups constituted the most visible opposition, antigovernment forces in the 1980s varied widely in membership, goals, tactics, and values. Relying on tactics ranging from direct dialogue to armed confrontation, opposition forces included lower, middle and even some segments of the upper classes, labor unions, student groups, women's groups, political parties, labor unions, and popular organizations. Although the search for human rights was not their main goal or principal value, a variety of social and political groups routinely used human rights issues to discredit the government and challenge its legitimacy. As a result, domestic opposition groups complemented and strengthened the efforts of the human rights network and its state allies.

After the mass protests diminished in 1984, in part because of economic recovery and in part because of effective repression, many opposition groups rallied behind a new strategy in 1985. Rather than toppling the government through a show of force in the streets, moderate opposition leaders planned to achieve a rapid transition to democracy through dialogue and negotiation. They carefully built a coalition of leaders that ranged from moderate left to moderate right in the hope that through unity and moderation they would represent a movement that the government could not ignore.[15] Twenty-one political leaders representing eleven political "movements" fired their first salvo in late August 1985 with the publication of the *National Accord for a Full Transition to Democracy.*[16] To give the document unquestionable legitimacy and visibility, it had been negotiated and signed under the guidance of Santiago archbishop Francisco Fresno.

Human rights issues were given a prominent place in the accord and in the opposition's broader strategy of undermining the government's normative approval. The accord called on the government to terminate the states of exception, to re-establish "public liberties" and constitutional guarantees, to end the practice of exile, to legalize political parties, and to pass electoral laws that would ensure free and fair election of the president and members of Congress. Specifically, the accord called for "universal, personal, free, secret, informed and impartially controlled suffrage, assuring free expression and equal access to the means of communication of the state and the universities," a reference to television and radio stations. Although the accord soon fell apart in the face of squabbling among its supporters and the government's refusal to respond, opposition forces continued to criticize the government's human rights record at every possible opportunity. A series of high-profile human rights abuses offered ample opportunities to challenge the government's legitimacy, and the rebirth of an independent media ensured more vigorous attention to these problems.

Long after it became clear that the government would not engage in serious dialogue, opposition forces finally decided on a strategy change in early 1988. After months of internal wrangling and indecision, a coalition of thirteen parties announced they would participate in the government-sponsored plebiscite and organize a No vote. At this point, the opposition became extremely focused on one right in particular – the right to "participate in government" through "secret ballot that guarantees the free expression of the will of the voters."[17] Coalition leaders continually challenged the government's legitimacy in the ensuing months by arguing that a vote for Pinochet would be a vote for eight more years of fear and terror. They pushed hard for electoral guarantees that would make the plebiscite a true expression of popular will and taunted the government by claiming that Pinochet "only can win via fraud, and if he does it, this can touch off a national and international repudiation which can destroy him."[18]

Linkages between States and Opposition Groups: The "Pro-Democracy" Network

At all stages, transnational support played a key role in strengthening the domestic opposition. A new transnational pro-democracy network sprang up in the mid-1980s that overshadowed – and to some extent incorporated – the pre-existing human rights network. The common thread running through this network was the desire to remove Pinochet from power. For some network groups, this goal represented a principled commitment to improving the human rights situation, but for others it was a strategic attempt to lay the groundwork for a return to political power. Despite the fact that network groups were not motivated solely by principled commitments, the connections among them resembled a network in the sense that they passed money, information, and other resources among themselves in a rapid fashion.[19] As much as $55 million a year poured into Chile from international donors between 1985 and 1988 and was disbursed among a variety of social and political groups, including media organizations, labor unions, student groups, political parties, neighborhood organizations, human rights groups, women's groups, and intellectual centers.[20]

Significantly, the United States and other Western states played a key role in this process. German political foundations funded by the German government and closely affiliated with German political parties and trade unions provided a large part of this aid.[21] From 1983 to 1988, German political foundations transferred $26 million to Chilean trade unions, political parties, neighborhood self-help organizations, media sources, and other social groups. Nearly two-thirds of this money was provided by the Konrad Adenauer Foundation, which used it to fund Christian Democrat groups in Chile. Overall, close to 90 percent of Germany's aid went to the coalition of moderate-left groups, who provided the most prominent opposition to the military government, while the remainder went to moderate-right groups, who supported Pinochet but called for a quick and complete transition to democracy.[22] The United States also provided $6.8 million in political aid between 1984 and 1988, much of it to ensure that Chile held a free and fair plebiscite in 1988. Additionally, political parties, trade unions, political foundations, and NGOs in Italy, Holland, and elsewhere provided an unknown amount of money for the Chilean opposition during this same period.[23]

As 1988 approached, international actors targeted their money toward efforts to win the plebiscite and to ensure that the government held a fair vote. This aid enabled domestic groups to hold face-to-face gatherings in Chile and abroad, facilitated communication among opposition factions, and encouraged them to share political ideas and strategies. The availability of funds helped create a network of organizational ties among various opposition groups and between domestic groups and international actors who shared similar antigovernment goals. Foreign funding enabled researchers at academic centers to carry out extensive public opinion polls.[24] Drawing on foreign funding, Chilean academics and opposition politicians brought the U.S. political consulting group Sawyer, Miller to Chile to teach them modern political campaign techniques. Foreign-funded polls and campaign expertise were essential in formulating the opposition's successful strategy to unseat Pinochet.

International aid helped ensure that free and fair voting procedures would be respected in the 1988 plebiscite. Widespread doubts that the government would hold a fair plebiscite led international actors to provide money for voter registration drives, the training of poll watchers, and election-night monitoring activities.[25] Most significantly, foreign funding allowed the opposition parties to install a nationwide system to tabulate votes that would provide an independent check on the government's vote tally.[26] The night of the plebiscite, opposition parties announced accurate election results, taking away any government opportunity to announce fraudulent numbers.[27] The presence of hundreds of international election monitors – many from foreign countries – also helped ensure that the plebiscite would be clean.

The Government's Quest for Legitimacy

As the 1980s dawned, government officials believed they had resolved the government's legitimacy problem. The eruption of popular protests in 1983 quickly disabused them of this notion. Almost overnight, the government's ten years of work to restructure Chilean society appeared to be in jeopardy. Using a mixture of repression, pretended concession, and renewed economic growth, the government survived the most serious threats and regained the political advantage by late 1984. At that point, the constitutionally sanctioned timeline for the phasing out of authoritarian rule became an overwhelming political reality. The constitution mandated that a referendum on the junta's candidate for Chile's next president be held by February 9, 1989. It also required that an elected congress replace the junta by 1990 and that many of the temporary repressive powers handed to the president would come to an end.

Faced with the end of authoritarian rule within about five years, government officials began to worry about how they could ensure that the changes they had imposed on Chile would not be undone. One option – pushed by powerful government supporters and considered by Pinochet up until the very end – was to ignore or amend the constitution and to simply extend authoritarian rule indefinitely. A second option was to gain legitimacy for the new constitution so that it would continue to shape Chile's political future and to win the elections so that the new government would be dominated by constitutional sympathizers. In 1985, the government explicitly chose the second option – though it never entirely disavowed the first – calculating that legitimacy would achieve similar results with fewer costs and that the government could prevail in the elections.

As the 1980s progressed, the government discovered that the twin strategies of gaining legitimacy for the constitution and winning the presidential plebiscite sometimes conflicted with each other. One of the best ways to gain legitimacy was to ensure that Chileans would participate in the plebiscite and that international observers would accept the vote as a valid expression of popular will. By participating, the opposition would explicitly accept the legitimacy of the government's rules and therefore implicitly accept the broader constitutional framework. Yet facilitating opposition participation was risky because it raised the possibility that Pinochet might lose the plebiscite – an outcome the government downplayed but never dismissed entirely. Constant opposition pressure in the latter part of the 1980s repeatedly reminded the government that large segments of the population and the international community had not yet accepted the constitution's legitimacy.

As I argue in detail below, the government responded by developing an even stronger interest in legitimacy and by implementing measures that would ensure a minimal level of electoral fairness. These measures included establishing an independent Electoral Qualifying Tribunal, lifting states of emergency, and allowing sufficient time for voter registration rather than calling a surprise plebiscite. Together, they marked an important change in the government's repressive strategy and paved the way for a fair vote on Pinochet's rule. As it turned out, these efforts to legitimize the constitution paradoxically cost Pinochet the presidency. Trying to put a good face on the loss, Interior Minister Sergio Fernández later summarized this paradox when he wrote, "A new presidential period had not been won, but the new institutionality was consolidated. That which had not been consolidated by winning, had been consolidated by losing. This was the great merit of the transition that had been designed nearly a decade previously."[28] In short, human rights pressures caused the military government to pursue legitimacy to such an extent that the government unintentionally sacrificed Pinochet's presidency to attain it.

An Independent Electoral Tribunal

Concerns for the government's legitimacy were strongest in the junta, which served as the legislative branch in the 1980s and included an army general as Pinochet's representative. These concerns led to important conflicts between the junta and the executive branch, headed by Pinochet as president. In early 1984, the executive drafted its first constitutional organic law relevant to the 1988 plebiscite. The law mandated the future establishment of an Electoral Qualifying Tribunal to tabulate final vote counts and to review and adjudicate any claims of electoral irregularities after the results were tallied. In June 1984, the executive dispatched the law to the junta, where it was delayed for several months. Junta members, led by navy admiral José Merino, held the bill hostage in an attempt to force the executive to speed up the drafting of other organic laws that would regulate Chile's political life.

Chief among the junta's concerns was the government's legitimacy. Junta members generally felt that the disparity between the government's words and deeds was too large and privately chided the executive for this gap.[29] The government had repeatedly promised that it would carry out a transition to democracy, as outlined in the constitution, yet it did almost nothing of substance to achieve this goal. Junta members felt that the government's legitimacy would be strengthened by good faith efforts to pass legislation that would pave the way for the transition. Their reasoning was summarized by a memo drafted by a legal advisor and circulated among junta officials in late 1984:

> In effect, the constitutional state of exception that the country is living through at these moments – imposed by the necessity of repressing anarchistic excesses and terrorist threats – should not be interpreted, under any circumstances, as a lack of willpower in the government to carry out the transition foreseen in the constitutional text. One of the pillars of the democratic government consecrated in the 1980 Constitution is the public electoral system. . . . At the same time, the independent Electoral Tribunal forms a substantial part of this public electoral system, as its task should fundamentally consist of overseeing the electoral processes of the Republic. Therefore, it is beyond doubt that this is a politically convenient moment to legislate on this matter.
>
> On the other hand, it frequently occurs that, as much in the domestic plane as in the international, the desire of the government to democratize the country is put in doubt. Therefore, a permanent and sustained legislative advance toward the full implementation of mechanisms that will make it possible to exercise the right to elect public authorities – a fundamental characteristic of democracy – will call into question any assumptions about the supposed antidemocratic nature of the current government.[30]

With the domestic protests fading in late 1984, however, the executive did not feel the same urgency to move the institutionalization process forward in the immediate future. The executive dug in its heels, refusing to draft further electoral laws until it could more clearly discern the shape of the political landscape at the end of the decade. Exasperated junta members finally decided that one electoral law on the books was better than none and approved the Electoral Tribunal law in July 1985.

The most important and hotly debated provision of the law during the approval process was the question of when the Electoral Qualifying Tribunal would begin its work. The eleventh transitional article of the 1980 Constitution stipulated that the tribunal would start work in conjunction with the first congressional elections that would not be held until late 1989 at the earliest. The constitution thus apparently prevented the tribunal from functioning during the presidential plebiscite that would be held in late 1988 – an obvious advantage to the government candidate. Some junta members and legal advisors thought it might be better to have the tribunal function during the 1988 plebiscite, just to give the process a legitimate stamp of approval.[31] An air force legal advisor summed up this argument in the following way: "... we are interested that the process be free, sincere, secret, informed, and that there be no possibility of constitutional reproach."[32] Others argued that the constitution must be interpreted literally, and thus the Electoral Qualifying Tribunal could not function before 1989. In the end, the junta chose the literal interpretation.

After approving the legislation, the junta sent it to the Constitutional Tribunal, whose duty was to review laws to ensure their compatibility with the constitution before being promulgated. This seven-member court was set up in March 1981 and was composed of three Supreme Court justices and other distinguished legal scholars appointed by Pinochet, the junta, and a new government institution known as the National Security Council. Given its makeup and origins, most observers expected that the Constitutional Tribunal would simply rubber-stamp the junta's legislation. However, in September 1985 the court surprised observers when it ruled precisely the opposite of what junta members had decided. That is, the Constitutional Tribunal argued in a four-to-three decision that the spirit of the constitution required completely fair and legitimate elections. Thus, the court struck down the clause that would have created the Electoral Qualifying Tribunal in time for the congressional elections, requiring instead that the tribunal be established for the 1988 plebiscite, or any other plebiscite the government might hold. The Constitutional Tribunal's decision was not subject to appeal, and the junta soon complied with the court's wishes.

Concerns about legitimacy played a key role in the decision of the Constitutional Tribunal.[33] Although the constitution itself expressly noted that the Electoral Qualifying Tribunal should begin functioning in conjunction with congressional elections in 1989, only three of the court's seven members adopted the literal interpretation of the constitution. The remaining four members perceived an overriding interest in the legitimacy of the new institutions and protecting the democratic "spirit" of the constitution. A key phrase in the majority argument noted, "A contrary opinion would not only wound the spirit of the constitution but also common sense, which is the basis of all logical interpretation, because such an opinion could expose the very plebiscite to fundamental questions about its legitimacy, with grave damage to the normal development of future institutions."[34]

This decision was the first clear indication that the 1988 plebiscite would be held under completely different circumstances than the two previous plebiscites. The 1985 ruling of the Constitutional Tribunal reflected a commitment to democratic governance by its insistence that the plebiscite would be a valid expression of popular will. In addition, the Constitutional Tribunal made it clear that an organic law regulating elections themselves would also have to be in place prior to the plebiscite, in order to ensure the legitimacy of the vote. The opposition rejoiced, declaring it a sign that some government institutions had begun to lose their fear of Pinochet. Even conservative elites welcomed the ruling because it helped ensure that the plebiscite would be respected by other domestic groups.[35]

States of Exception and Free Expression

In the 1978 and 1980 plebiscites, an existing state of siege (1978) and state of emergency (1980) combined with government harassment of journalists and opposition leaders to muzzle almost all public debates or protests related to the vote. By the mid-1980s, the terrain had changed somewhat. In the wake of the mass protests and renewed political activity, a significant opposition media had emerged, especially in newsmagazines and radio stations. However, the government retained control of the most influential medium, television, and maintained broad authority under the existing states of emergency to restrict press freedoms and to detain individuals for causes related to the exercise of free expression. Most opposition leaders and international observers expected the government to retain these advantages throughout the plebiscite process. Government officials hinted that they would do so, arguing that a variety of elections had occurred under state-of-siege conditions in Colombia and elsewhere and been accepted by most observers as legitimate expressions of the popular will.

As early as 1983, however, the junta began to worry that the legal states of exception were widely viewed as fundamentally illegitimate and that their imposition resulted in greater costs than benefits. In response to the second mass protest in June 1983, Pinochet formally asked the junta to impose a state of siege. Junta members resisted and ultimately killed the request due to concerns about the government's legitimacy and its tangible repercussions in the renegotiation of foreign debt.[36] In the junta, Merino led the opposition to Pinochet's request: "In my opinion, a state of siege in this moment is very poorly aimed politically because we are negotiating the foreign debt and we are practically saying that the political situation is similar to that ten years ago. . . . In the domestic arena we are cutting off all of our leverage with the forces in the country that can or want to support the government. And in the international arena we are virtually filling out a type of death certificate for the current regime."[37]

Even army general Raúl Benavides, who represented Pinochet in the junta and was under his direct authority in the military chain of command, expressed his doubts about the state of siege. Suggesting that the international press – especially in the United States – was becoming more critical of Chile, Benavides argued that Chile's international opponents wanted the government to impose a state of siege so they would have even greater incentive to hurt Chile. Merino raised an additional concern: A state of siege implied that military courts would begin to function again and so the military would once again have to be in charge of the "dirty part" of the problem – clearly a prospect the military men did not relish.[38] Air force general Fernando Matthei agreed, arguing that a state of siege was not the best way to govern the country: "No matter what we do to sit ourselves atop the lid of the pot, in the end it is only going to blow off, because it is a problem that exists. We get nowhere by trying to cover the problem. First, let's recognize the problem, confront it, and resolve it. By sitting each time on top, just as the general says, 'And then what?' And if the pressure is so great that it explodes, we are going to be blown far away."[39]

Continued pressure from the executive and ongoing social unrest convinced the junta in late 1984 that a state of siege would be necessary to help the government regain complete control of the political situation.[40] Still, junta members worried about the normative repercussions and how the decision would affect Chile's international legitimacy. They discussed precedents set by other Latin American countries that had recently imposed states of siege and noted that they were limited to certain regions of the country. Junta members expressed their hope that the executive would use state-of-siege provisions in fine-toothed ways that would target certain segments of the population rather than as a blunt instrument to bludgeon the whole country.

None of this suggests that junta members opposed the use of force on moral grounds. Rather, it demonstrates that they recognized conflicting interests between intangible government legitimacy and short-term domination, and they attempted to balance those interests even when they deemed it necessary to unleash higher levels of repression. The state of siege lasted from November 1984 to June 1985 and then was briefly reimposed from September to December 1986, after the attempt on Pinochet's life. At this point, the junta insisted on an end to the states of siege, in part because there was little evidence of ongoing social disturbances and in part because its effect on Chile's foreign relations was, as Merino put it, "tremendously negative, as we all have witnessed through the international and national press."[41]

In some ways, the lifting of a state of siege made little difference because a state of emergency remained in place and the government enjoyed other extraordinary powers to abuse human rights under the constitution's transitional articles. As the plebiscite date approached, domestic and international actors increasingly pressured the government to end these states of exception and to foster a political climate in which free expression would be guaranteed. In August 1987 the Bishops' Conference of the Catholic Church set forth four basic conditions that must be met for the plebiscite to have moral authority. One of these four stated that "all sectors of opinion must have equal access to the television and other means of social communication and to the various forms of political publicity, in order that the voters express their vote with the proper information."[42] Similarly, in December 1987, the U.S. government declared that freedom of expression was one of the basic conditions for Chile's plebiscite to be recognized as valid and one that could not be achieved with the existing states of exception. Domestic opposition groups continually questioned the legitimacy of any plebiscite that would be held with official states of exception in place and that did not allow opposition access to television.

In mid-1988 with the plebiscite date fast approaching and Pinochet's advisors publicly taking a hard line on lifting the states of emergency, Carabinero commander and junta member Rodolfo Stange joined the fray by declaring that the states of emergency should be lifted: "I am of the opinion that a plebiscite cannot be undertaken in a state of exception. The pre-plebiscite period should occur without states of exception because we all want the plebiscite to be as perfect and as clean as possible."[43] At one level, the declaration was significant because the Carabineros were those who enforced state-of-emergency provisions and could generally be expected to take the hardest line on these "law-and-order" issues. At another level, the declaration was not so important because the decision to lift Chile's two legally distinct states of emergency could only be taken by Pinochet, who did not need the concurrence of the junta.[44] Within Pinochet's circle of advisors, however, many adopted Stange's position, arguing that Pinochet must win a plebiscite that was as clean and as fair as possible.[45] Pinochet himself hinted as early as June 1, 1988, that the states of emergency could be lifted, and he in fact lifted them on August 24, 1988.[46] It marked the first time since the coup that Chileans lived without any states of exception imposed upon them.

Lifting state-of-emergency provisions aided free expression by easing the climate of terror, but represented only half the battle. Government critics insisted that free expression did not exist if the opposition did not enjoy access to television, the most important mass media. Television stations in the 1980s were managed either by the state or by universities under close government supervision, and so coverage consistently favored the government. Most observers considered access to television time a crucial test of the fairness of the plebiscite process.[47] In January 1988, the junta approved the final and most important electoral law on voting procedures and vote counting, but failed to lay down any rules for television access.

In its April 1988 review of this law, the Constitutional Tribunal noted this omission and argued that the government had thereby left open the possibility of a one-sided media campaign. Although it had little real power to force compliance, it called on the government to draft new legislation that would govern television access.[48] The government could have ignored the tribunal's ruling or drafted rules that appeared to be fair but in fact favored the government. For example, the government could have required political groups to pay for their television ads and allowed access based on the ability to pay – as in the U.S. political system. Such regulations would have favored the government, which had greater resources and the loyalty of those who managed the television stations. Likewise, government regulations could have banned all campaign spots on television, which would have again favored the government owing to the pro-government news coverage.

Rather than pursue these options, however, government legal advisors drafted legislation in mid-1988 that guaranteed free television time to both the pro-government and anti-government positions. Further, it ensured that both sides were given an equal amount of time, fifteen minutes per day during the official campaign period that would be initiated thirty days before the plebiscite. Legal advisors modeled the legislation on historical precedent, which allowed free but limited television access to competing political groups during an electoral cycle.[49] When challenged by Merino on why the law did not require payment for campaign spots, legal advisors replied that they were following Chilean tradition. When the regulations were later challenged by a prominent television station (which wished to be paid for the campaign spots), the Constitutional Tribunal again came into play when it held unanimously that free television time is "in perfect harmony with the duty of the State to assure a fair and equal participation of the people in plebiscites and elections, through which the people exercise sovereignty."[50]

Granting the Yes and No forces fifteen minutes each on nightly television did not create a level playing field because Pinochet enjoyed all the advantages of an incumbent president and received consistently positive coverage from admiring reporters during regular news programming. At the same time, the legislation at least allowed the opposition onto the playing field. Opposition forces took full advantage of the small opening by creating memorable television spots that focused on Chile's bright future and undoubtedly helped sway voters against Pinochet.

It is difficult to explain why the government would have allowed even this limited television time without invoking the government's interest in legitimacy. No mass protests or economic sanctions centered around television time for the opposition. Opposition leaders did not appeal to the moral sensibilities or to the pocketbooks of television executives, who wanted to be paid for their air time but were not. Rather, government officials wanted to hold a fair plebiscite that could not in any way be discounted as fraudulent, thereby enticing the opposition to accept the legitimacy of the 1980 Constitution.

The Plebiscite Date

Although few expected the government to use outright fraud, conventional wisdom dictated that the government would hold the plebiscite on short notice to ensure its victory. The constitution left the timing of the plebiscite up to the commanders in chief of the four branches of Chile's armed forces, stipulating only that it occur within thirty to sixty days of their nomination of the candidate, and that the nomination occur no later than December 11, 1988.[51] Thus, it left open the possibility that the plebiscite could be held months earlier, if conditions seemed favorable. A constitutional loophole would even have permitted the government to keep the nomination a secret until very close to the plebiscite date, thus allowing precious little time for opposition campaigning. The expectation that the government would hold the plebiscite early and on short notice was quite reasonable, especially in light of the historical precedent. In 1978, government officials offered only two weeks' notice of the upcoming "consultation," and in 1980, the government unveiled the new constitution and announced that Chileans would vote on it just one month later. This strategy gave antigovernment forces little time to organize and debate such an important document.

In 1987–88, at least three specific strategies were available to government officials with respect to the plebiscite date. First, they could announce the plebiscite for late 1987 or early 1988, before many Chileans had registered to vote. Because pro-government forces had been initially more effective at conducting voter registration drives, the government had a greater advantage with a smaller voting pool. In late 1987, government strategists calculated that the best month for the plebiscite would be March or April 1988. At that point, around 50 percent of Chileans would have registered to vote, thus legitimizing a vote without jeopardizing the pro-government nature of the pool of registered voters.[52] Pinochet fueled speculation that the government would attempt this strategy by suggesting in November 1987 that the plebiscite could occur "any one of these days."

Opposition to this strategy stemmed primarily from the junta. Beginning in mid-1987, individual junta members publicly opposed an early plebiscite. Air force commander Matthei announced that "there cannot be a plebiscite" unless 70 to 80 percent of Chileans participate, a condition that other junta members would reiterate in the following weeks.[53] After Pinochet's November 1987 declaration, Matthei and Merino publicly contradicted him by saying that the plebiscite would not be held before September 1988. Matthei argued that any plebiscite prior to this date, "would not be accepted by the Chilean people, and much less, by the rest of the world." And Merino suggested that the constitution would have to be amended in order to hold the plebiscite earlier than September.[54] If the executive had any serious plans to hold an early plebiscite, this opposition buried them because Matthei and Merino held two of the four votes necessary to nominate a candidate and set the date.

Second, the government could wait until late 1988, thereby ensuring that most Chileans had registered to vote, but then call the plebiscite on very short notice, perhaps as little as fifteen days in advance. Because the Chilean media were mostly pro-government, the government's candidate would have a clear advantage in a shortened campaign season. Both junta opposition and a ruling by the Constitutional Tribunal prevented Pinochet's advisors from seriously pursuing this strategy.[55] Again, Matthei and Merino publicly declared throughout late 1987 and 1988 that Chileans needed sufficient time to think about how they would vote in the plebiscite, and thus announcing the date only two weeks in advance would be illegitimate. As Matthei put it, the plebiscite "deals with something serious that cannot be a surprise. Therefore, all Chileans have to have the opportunity to think and to listen to the arguments for one side and another."[56] Junta members also made it a practice to publicly announce that the plebiscite would occur between September and December 1988. By early July 1988 the pressure to specify the date had grown so intense that Pinochet himself announced that it would be about ninety days away, providing the opposition plenty of time to prepare their forces for the final assault.[57]

Even within this time frame, however, the government had some room for maneuver. Although the commanders in chief of the armed forces were required to nominate a candidate thirty days prior to the plebiscite, the constitution did not explicitly require them to announce their choice or to notify the public of the plebiscite date immediately. In other words, the commanders could have nominated the candidate secretly and then waited until shortly before the plebiscite to announce the name of the nominated candidate (almost surely Pinochet) and the specific date, thus allowing a very short time for the opposition to mount an official campaign. Legislation proposed by the executive in late 1987 left this option open. The junta, however, amended the law to require public notification of the nominee within forty-eight hours of the official nomination. After reviewing the law, the Constitutional Tribunal further limited Pinochet's options by requiring that the government hold the plebiscite no earlier than thirty days from the time in which the nomination of the candidate was made public.[58] This ruling would thus allow nearly thirty full days for the official campaign, a boon to the opposition.

The third possible strategy was not discussed publicly nor did it enter the strategic planning of opposition figures to the same degree. However, it was discussed intensively by military government officials and helped trigger a reshuffling of Pinochet's cabinet in July 1987.[59] Under this scenario, the government would pass legislation that would alter the plebiscite formula to allow direct and open elections of Chile's next president. Many of Pinochet's strategists believed that the general would fare better in an electoral race against other real-life contenders than he would in a straight thumbs up-thumbs down vote. Additionally, strategists believed that the announcement would catch the opposition by surprise and give them little time to reach agreement on which candidate to put up against Pinochet. As a result, they expected the opposition to split behind at least two candidates, each of whom would poll less than Pinochet in an election.

In contrast to the previous two strategies, the struggle over the plebiscite formula took place entirely within the executive branch. Two of Pinochet's most influential ministers, Francisco Javier Cuadra and Ricardo García, argued that the government should take a flexible approach to the plebiscite formula. If polls showed that the government's candidate would win with open elections rather than a one-man plebiscite, then the government should change the election procedure on short notice.[60] Others within the government, including former Interior Minister Sergio Fernández, opposed this strategy. They reasoned that the move would be seen as illegitimate because it would be undertaken on such short notice and thus might backfire on the government candidate and cause him to lose. Further, they argued that Pinochet should be the only candidate in the plebiscite due to his preeminent position in recent Chilean history. Pinochet eventually supported Fernández, reinstalling him as interior minister and sending Cuadra as ambassador to the Vatican in July 1987.

It is difficult to explain why the government passed up the opportunities to hold a surprise plebiscite without invoking the government's interest in legitimizing the 1980 Constitution. The three strategies outlined above would have helped ensure Pinochet's victory, but would have triggered widespread condemnation of the government's machinations. Merino and Matthei consistently cited the need for a fair, honest, and legitimate plebiscite throughout 1987–88, and Pinochet either bought the logic or found it impossible to gain their acquiescence to more devious plans. Either way, an interest in legitimacy guided the government's actions.

The Military and Legitimacy

Although military officers strongly supported Pinochet, they also jealously guarded their tradition of professionalism, which included compliance with the constitution and the rule of law. As Valenzuela has noted, "Pinochet was the most powerful person in the country, but Chile's institutions were not 'personalized.' Even in the army, institutional loyalties and respect for 'legality' were more important factors than allegiance to the ambitions of the commander in chief."[61] Any effort to subvert the transition laid out in the constitution would have faced a steep uphill struggle in the Chilean military. Military commanders went to great lengths in 1988 to demonstrate their professional commitment to the constitution. For example, two of the three editorials published in the army's journal, Memorial del Ejército, in 1988 centered on the army's commitment to the rule of law and, more specifically, to the constitutionally ordained transition process.[62] In the January-April issue, the editorial declared:

The armed forces of the nation have, among other missions, that of guaranteeing the existing juridical order. . . . The violation of law by authority in a particular case, even if in the name of an ideal of justice and with good intention, will always constitute an arbitrary act. An arbitrary act is in opposition to law; it is the very denial of law. . . . Law implies the existence of a clear and precise regulation to which everyone is subject, even the very head of state. On the other hand, an arbitrary act is something unstable, subject to capriciousness, that destroys all security and guarantee, and therefore, is not stable nor does it guarantee inviolability by public authority.[63]

Soon after the October plebiscite, the *Memorial* published the following editorial:

After having completed the plebiscite on October 5, as established in the constitution, the citizens of Chile and the world have been able to appreciate the exemplary behavior of the armed forces in their mission of guaranteeing with absolute impartiality this transcendent occasion. It has been made manifest in the international arena that Chile is a country with a profound democratic feeling and that the institutions that Chile has enjoyed over a long historical process are maintained without alteration. These facts have confirmed the professionalism and the morally correct way of proceeding of the institutions that make up the national defense.[64]

Even military officials serving in government posts emphasized their loyalty to the constitution rather than the person of Pinochet. When asked why the military government placed so much emphasis on establishing fair voting procedures, one high-ranking military officer and government official responded:

It's that the constitution already existed. And we had sworn to uphold that formal, solemn document. It was not just one more piece of paper. And it had to be legitimate. We could not try to win this plebiscite in whatever way we wanted. We had to win it legitimately. And if we didn't win it legitimately, then so be it, and it was lost. When I said that Chileans were going to have the last word, I said it willing to die for that. I say this in all seriousness. It's not idle talk. Willing to die for that. It was more than important, it was absolutely fundamental that the world leaders could see that the plebiscite was completely legitimate. Because the honor of the armed forces and all of the government was at stake. Look, in the military government many things were done badly, arbitrarily, and with human rights crimes as well, but with respect to this plebiscite, it had to be perfect.[65]

In short, the military as an institution and individual military officials accepted the constitution as a legitimate document to which they owed obedience, and they expected other Chileans to feel the same way. This sense of duty and the strong interest in fostering constitutional obedience in other Chileans led them to support a fair plebiscite.

Domestic Characteristics

Chile's relatively favorable domestic characteristics in the mid- to late 1980s ensured that government officials would respond to human rights pressures to delegitimize the government. Three of the four domestic factors changed in ways that facilitated human rights pressures while domestic structure remained unchanged and of little importance.

Normative Fit

The economic crash and subsequent widespread demonstrations revitalized Chilean society. Labor unions, which had been "poor and politically impotent," increased in size, visibility, and level of association after 1983. Some 62 federations and confederations with 630 affiliated unions in 1982 blossomed into 180 federations and confederations with 2,308 affiliated unions in 1987.[66] Although firm numbers are not available, women's groups also dramatically expanded their membership base and mobilization efforts after 1983, contributing significantly to the broader pro-democracy movement in Chile.[67] Popular organizations, which had long been the victims of some of the government's fiercest repression, became more numerous and active after 1983, paced by a threefold increase in the number of subsistence organizations.[68] Although social groups still lacked any formal representation within the government, they increasingly had a public voice and used it to define their identities, articulate grievances, and make demands.

Very often, these demands centered around human rights issues, and expectations spread quickly that military rule would some day give way to a democratic government. A 1985 public opinion poll showed that 97 percent of Chileans thought that democracy was necessary or very necessary to resolve the country's problems.[69] More importantly, 65 percent thought that the transition to democracy should occur that year or the following year, and only 5 percent expressed a preference for endless authoritarian rule. With respect to human rights, 71.5 percent of the population in early 1988 thought that human rights problems remained unsolved, while 70 percent wanted the guilty to be punished and 59 percent believed that the military government committed more human rights abuses than every other government in Chile's history combined.[70] Even more telling, 57 percent of those who voted against Pinochet in the plebiscite cited human rights concerns as a reason for their vote, second only to the economic situation.

The change in the normative climate can be seen by examining prominent cases of human rights abuses in the mid-1980s when compared with the 1970s. Three Communist Party members found with their throats slashed would have created barely a ripple in the 1970s. Yet in 1985, when it occurred, an investigating judge connected the crime to Chile's militarized police, the Carabineros. The revelations forced General César Mendoza – head of Carabineros and one of the original four members of the junta – to resign abruptly.[71] The idea that a junta member would resign for his association with a gruesome human rights abuse had been unthinkable a few years earlier. The episode demonstrates crucial changes in domestic normative expectations. Human rights norms certainly existed in Chile in the 1970s, but they became much more salient in the 1980s. They became part of the political arena and media reports and actively shaped government actions by restricting the government's ability to simply ignore human rights problems.

Crisis

The government faced a serious crisis when the economy crashed in 1982 and focused for a time on simple survival. By late 1984, however, Pinochet was once again firmly in control of the country as mass protests lost steam and splits among opposition forces became more apparent. Although Chilean society had been reborn and would never return to the state of shock it experienced in the 1970s, the protests were clearly too weak to threaten the government. Antigovernment terrorist forces became active again and even mounted an unsuccessful attempt on Pinochet's life in 1986, but did not inflict any significant economic or military damage. A modified neoliberal economic plan produced moderate to strong economic growth ranging from 2.4 percent to 7.4 percent from 1984 to 1988.[72] As the economy recovered and the opposition began to grudgingly accept the constitution, it became clear that the government faced its lowest threat level since it seized power.

The ebbing of security and economic threats created political space for government officials to worry about the long-term stability of the political and economic restructuring they had imposed on Chile. The 1980 Constitution mandated an end to the junta in 1989 and the end of Pinochet's presidential tenure by 1997, at the latest. Government officials began to ask what would happen once the military no longer controlled the government. How could they ensure that the government's political-economic projects would endure beyond the elections scheduled for the end of the decade? Francisco Javier Cuadra, Pinochet's principal political strategist in 1985–86, summarized this concern: "We should project ourselves in time beyond 1989. Time may pass by one or another individual, but the ideas should remain. The ideas, principles, values, and social, political, and economic styles that have governed the country for the past twelve years should be projected, therefore, farther into the future. The year 1989 is certainly an important stage. It marks a change of juridical government, but it is not the end of the government. The government will project itself beyond the year 1989, and it is absolutely necessary that many people begin to understand that."[73]

In short, the lack of a serious threat and the ever-closer electoral calendar allowed, or forced, the government to concern itself with the long-term political situation. In this context, concerns about the constitution's endurance and legitimacy naturally found fertile soil.

The Rule-Oriented Faction

Rule-oriented officials retained a firm grip on power throughout the 1980s, despite the fact that Pinochet kept some hardline advisors close to him and was often drawn to hardline solutions.[74] Militarists believed that continuing domestic opposition demonstrated that Marxism was still not extinct in Chile, and thus the government's task was not finished. This view received a dramatic boost when Pinochet barely escaped with his life after guerrilla forces ambushed his motorcade in late 1986. Officials holding this view – located most often in the intel-

ligence agencies and among extremely conservative civilian sectors—
believed that Chile would once again fall into chaos if the military
government were to lose the upcoming plebiscite. Chileans had been
profoundly affected by Marxist doctrines and practices, they argued,
and the military government had not yet finished its work of restructuring and purifying the country. As nationalists, hardliners deemed
the international arena as hostile but relatively unimportant. In their
view, international efforts to influence the upcoming plebiscite unquestionably represented an intolerable interference in internal affairs,
one that should be rigorously denounced.

Strategically, military-style nationalists proposed an indefinite post-
ponement of the 1988 plebiscite and the use of force to rule the country.
They were deeply committed to Pinochet's personal rule, but felt little
commitment to the 1980 Constitution and its plans for a transition
to democracy. Hugo Rosende, a hardline civilian lawyer who served as
justice minister for much of the 1980s, used a striking image to try to
persuade Pinochet not to hold the plebiscite: "They are going to stick
you in a cage like a little bird and they are going to make you go up and
down the Alameda [Santiago's main thoroughfare] so that people can
spit in your face."[75] As it became clearer that the plebiscite would indeed
be held, hardliners formed a short-lived political movement, Avanzada
Nacional, to support Pinochet's candidacy. Despite their prominence in
the media and Pinochet's apparent sympathy with many of their positions, however, hardliners held few key executive branch posts in the
1980s and were almost entirely absent from the junta.

Rule-oriented officials, in contrast, dominated key decision-making
institutions, including Pinochet's cabinet, the junta, and legislative
study commissions. At first glance, this claim appears to fly in the face
of common sense. The military government in the 1980s remained extremely repressive, although intermittently less violent than in the
1970s. How can one claim the dominance of rule-oriented actors in a
government practicing systematic repression?

Rule-orientation, however, does not imply opposition to repression.
As I have defined them, rule-oriented officials are, after all, pro-authoritarian. They are not believers in the universal application of human
rights, nor do they wish to see the demise of authoritarian rule. Rather,
they wish to strengthen it by opening up some limited political space
and gaining some popular support for the government. They advocate

the eventual legitimation of the government, often through limited political liberalization, in order to ensure the government's survival. It is not at all inconsistent for rule-oriented officials to favor sharp repression for a period of time if it enables a government to survive an economic crisis or to face down strong political opposition. Rule-oriented officials can also favor ongoing repression against some segments of the population at the same time that their plans for broader political liberalization proceed. Rule-orientation and repression are not mutually exclusive terms.

One of the most important and visible government posts, interior minister, was filled through most of the 1980s with men who espoused rule-oriented positions: Sergio Fernández, Sergio Jarpa, and Ricardo García.[76] Although these officials presided over various abuses of government power, they also urged Pinochet to stick to the constitutional calendar and they sometimes implemented limited reforms. Soon after taking over in the Interior Ministry, for example, Jarpa announced specific plans to lift the state of emergency, legalize political parties, implement electoral laws, hold congressional elections in 1985, and engage in a dialogue with non-Marxist opposition forces.[77] Although the government later reversed course and opted for a much more gradual transition, under civilian guidance it never stopped preparing for electoral legitimation.

Key military officers also adopted rule-oriented positions. Julio Canessa, Pinochet's number two man in the army in the early 1980s and, for a time, the army's representative on the junta, made it clear as early as 1984 that the military was deeply committed to the government transition scheduled for the late 1980s. Throughout the 1980s, a variety of generals consistently echoed this position and insisted that the constitution would be respected fully, implying that the government would not use force or subterfuge to maintain power beyond the mandated deadlines.[78]

Rule-oriented officials interpreted human rights pressures as a threat to the legitimacy of the 1980 Constitution and its accompanying political institutions. Some government officials emphasized the threat from the international arena: "I feared for an international pressure that would make things very difficult for us. . . . The theme of the foreign front was always very important. I feared an eventual united front of Europe, the United States, and the Church."[79] Others focused more on domestic threats, arguing that Chile's new rulers would attempt to amend or discard the constitution unless they were somehow forced to accept it. In the rule-oriented view, the two different levels of threats reinforced each other, and the best solution was to achieve electoral legitimation for the constitution through opposition participation in the presidential plebiscite.

Beginning in 1984, key junta members adopted rule-oriented positions, an important development because they enjoyed considerable media access, some political power, and some independent standing vis-à-vis Pinochet. Matthei, the air force general, was the most outspoken and consistently rule-oriented member of the junta. As early as September 1984, he called for a quicker transition to democracy, pronounced himself ready to negotiate with Marxists, sanctioned opposition protests as a legitimate activity, and declared that future investigations of human rights abuses were inevitable.[80] He was the first junta member to respond favorably to opposition calls for a dialogue and repeatedly tried to speed up electoral and political legislation that would demonstrate the government's good-faith commitment to a democratic transition. Other junta members, including navy admiral Merino and, after 1985, Carabineros general Stange, adopted similar positions and even repeatedly refused to endorse Pinochet as the government's official candidate up until the final days before an official decision was required.[81]

Rule-oriented individuals successfully dominated the government in part because they offered reasonable solutions to the international and domestic normative challenges. After the protests died down in 1984, most domestic opposition forces took a more moderate stance that focused on dialogue and negotiation. The economic crash had let the genie out of the bottle, so to speak, and it became clear that no amount of force could push it back in. Rule-oriented individuals successfully argued that this style of opposition could never be completely repressed and must therefore be channeled in the right direction. In this view, the government's best shot at shaping Chile's political future lay in legitimizing the 1980 Constitution. Pinochet was eventually persuaded that enticing the opposition to play by the government's rules would ensure that the government's political restructuring of Chile would not simply be undone by future politicians.

Domestic Structure

As with other periods in Chile's history, domestic structure seems to add little, if anything, to the explanation. Ambassador Barnes certainly met with officials to let them know of the U.S. views, but few other transnational actors ever gained any access. Never did any military official seriously consider any kind of "winning coalition" with human rights advocates or the representatives of Western states. Nor did the government ever adopt the ideas promoted by transnational networks and their state allies. Rather, the government responded to normative and tangible pressures that threatened its legitimacy. Its authoritarian structure was important only to the extent that it drew the attention of a wide variety of critics. The structure may have blocked access, but it did not prevent changes.

I have argued that strong human rights pressures, supported through transnational channels, backed by foreign states, and reinforced by a vibrant domestic opposition posed a serious threat to the legitimacy of the government's constitution and thus the government's long-term political influence. Faced with the choice of legitimizing the constitution or extending its rule through electoral subterfuge or force, the government chose legitimacy as a core interest because of favorable domestic factors. This interest in legitimacy led the government to adopt guarantees of a minimally fair presidential plebiscite in an attempt to entice the opposition to participate and to recognize the government's rules of the game.

This analysis does not deny that Pinochet was motivated by the desire to retain power. It helps resolve the puzzle, however, of why a dictator seeking power would hold a fair plebiscite on his rule. Most observers agree that outright fraud was out of the question because it would have triggered mass protests that would have made the country ungovernable. Nevertheless, the government still could have held an unfair plebiscite by enacting a pattern of rules that would have favored the government and guaranteed Pinochet's re-election without simply miscounting votes. Surprisingly, government officials adopted a third strategy in which they made it possible for the opposition to win the election on an uneven playing field. It is difficult to imagine this result in the absence of strong domestic human rights norms that set expectations about the nature of a fair election and strong pressures to adhere to those norms.

The government's confidence that it would win the plebiscite undoubtedly contributed to its decision to hold a fair election, but the importance of false confidence should not be overstated. The government certainly had plenty of reasons to think it would win, including complete control of patronage resources, a "mammoth financial and media advantage" over the opposition, solid support from economic elites, and a growing economy.[82] At the same time, numerous and credible public opinion polls showed that the anti-Pinochet forces had a very good chance of winning. Although government officials undoubtedly thought they could win, it is difficult to say how confident they were in that result. Both interview evidence and memoirs suggest that government officials clearly had their doubts about Pinochet's ability to win.[83] Conservative elites constantly debated among themselves whether Pinochet would even be the best candidate, with many arguing that a civilian would fare far better in the plebiscite. As noted earlier, others argued that Pinochet would lose a simple yes-no vote against an idealized imaginary opponent and that he should run against flesh-and-blood candidates offered by opposition parties.

The government's repeated predictions of victory and Pinochet's reluctance to concede defeat do not constitute sufficient evidence that the government engaged in unbridled self-delusion. All electoral contestants engage in optimistic predictions of victory – if only for strategic purposes of rallying their supporters – and find it difficult to accept the reality of defeat, yet not all are deluded. In the final analysis, some key decisions affecting the fairness of the plebiscite – the creation of an independent Electoral Tribunal and the junta's efforts to ease the legal states of exception – were taken long before economic recovery had set in and before any prediction of victory could reasonably be made. The desire for legitimacy seems to be at least as important as self-delusion in explaining the government's decisions.

The explanation presented here is not entirely novel, but it complements previous analyses by identifying the source and historical evolution of the government's interest in legitimacy. Other scholars have argued that opposition pressures combined with the government's interest in legitimizing the 1980 Constitution led Pinochet to hold a fair plebiscite.[84] Yet these explanations are incomplete because they do not tell us why government officials cared so much about legitimacy. Not all authoritarian governments develop such a strong interest in legitimacy that they are willing to risk the leader's future in an honest vote. In fact, one might expect just the opposite, that Pinochet's cronies would sacrifice a certain degree of legitimacy in the name of his re-election.

The construction of a government interest in legitimacy was a historical process marked by extensive uncertainty about the nature of the government's interests generally. Officials had a clear interest in shaping Chile's political future, but this statement is rather banal. Moving beyond the self-evident, government officials debated whether they had a greater interest in maintaining their influence by legitimizing the constitution, or by using force to keep Pinochet in power. These debates over appropriate policies and interests were resolved only across time in a series of historical steps that shut off some options and made others appear more feasible or desirable. Government officials began planning for the plebiscite at least as early as 1984. Each new voting guarantee was adopted only slowly and reluctantly after bruising political battles. Drafting the electoral legislation was a time-consuming political process that pitted different government factions against one another. Different institutions within the military government, including the executive bureaucracy, the junta, and the Constitutional Tribunal each played a role in shaping election policies over the course of five years. Each time a decision was made regarding electoral processes, it closed off possible strategies in the plebiscite and provided a precedent for future decisions.

As the plebiscite drew closer, this interest in legitimacy began to conflict with the government's interest in a Pinochet victory. If government officials worked to make the rules of the plebiscite acceptable to domestic and international actors, they undermined their chances of winning. If they tilted electoral laws in their favor, they risked the legitimacy of the constitution. Government officials eventually chose legitimacy. Government elites had long claimed that they were committed to a return to democracy; human rights networks and domestic opposition groups called their bluff in the 1980s. By holding a free and fair plebiscite, the authoritarian government gained legitimacy for its constitution, but paradoxically sacrificed its domination of the government.

SIX

Chile in International and Comparative Perspective

Consistent with realism's traditional emphasis on power politics and unitary states, analysts often argue that international norms have little effect unless powerful states enforce them through substantial economic pressure or military force.[1] While not denying that power enforcement can be useful, this book makes two alternative arguments. First, states care not only about their material well-being, but also about their legitimacy (that is, their normative standing) among both domestic society and foreign states. As a result, vigorous efforts to shame noncompliant states can produce important changes in the targeted state even in the absence of overwhelming economic sanctions or military force. In human rights issues, these changes are not always anticipated or intended, and they do not always improve the situation, but they are nevertheless the results of norm-based pressures. Second, human rights pressures can influence a state's repressive policies when they are calibrated to domestic conditions.[2] In fact, the impact of human rights pressures depends more on domestic conditions in the targeted state than on the overall power differential between the actors employing the pressure and the targeted state. Even weak states can resist strong human rights pressures, given the right set of domestic conditions, and relatively powerful states can be responsive to pressures that fall well short of coercion.

A detailed examination of authoritarian Chile provides important support for these arguments. In the face of extensive and unprecedented human rights pressures, authoritarian elites in Chile demonstrated a growing concern for the government's legitimacy, and altered government discourse, policy, and institutions as a result. The evidence suggests that three domestic characteristics account for all of the variation in repressive strategies in the face of strong human rights pressures: crisis levels, normative fit, and the strength of a rule-oriented faction. One variable commonly discussed in the literature, domestic structure, contributes little if anything to the explanation. I summarize these results in more detail below.

To strengthen this evidence and to demonstrate that Chile was not uniquely vulnerable to human rights pressures, I then briefly examine two other cases of network and state efforts to promote human rights: Cuba, 1960-present; and South Africa, 1960-94. To illustrate the ways in which human rights networks might operate in a democratic context, I next summarize post-1990 efforts to pursue justice for former President Augusto Pinochet in Chile, Spain, and Britain. Although I cannot focus on these cases in such detail, they offer supportive evidence for my arguments in other countries and contexts.

Cuba and South Africa offer appropriate case study comparisons because, similar to Chile, they have faced high levels of pressure to ease repression. At the same time, their domestic political situations differ substantially, thereby producing variation in the key variables hypothesized to produce the observed outcomes. Such variation is essential in making valid inferences about hypotheses.[3] Comparing highly similar cases like Argentina and Chile, for example, would not yield the same kind of analytical payoff as comparing countries with different domestic characteristics. Further, Cuba and South Africa have responded in remarkably different ways to human rights pressures, thereby satisfying the requirement for variation in the dependent variable.[4] Obviously, these cases are not randomly generated and so do not constitute a hypothesis test, in a strict sense. Nevertheless, they help increase the validity of the inferences by adding additional cases (and observations) that vary across time and space.[5] They help improve the generalizability of the argument by examining countries from different regions of the world and with different political traditions. Following these case study summaries, I offer some concluding remarks about the policy and theoretical implications of this study.

Comparative Perspectives

Chile

Although norms and their effects cannot be observed directly, a careful analysis of the decision making within the Chilean authoritarian government suggests that at least some states develop a strong interest in their legitimacy at both domestic and international levels. Indeed, contrary to conventional wisdom, Chile's ruling elite often seemed more concerned about the government's international normative approval than its domestic legitimacy. This observation was especially true in the 1970s, as shown in chapters 3 and 4, when officials repeatedly expressed explicit concerns about the government's international standing and image. Government documents and interviews demonstrate that officials consciously and strategically incorporated human rights language into their discourse principally as an attempt to improve Chile's international legitimacy. More significantly, they reformed the chief security apparatus and adopted a new constitution in an effort to gain legitimacy in the face of persistent human rights pressures.

Government officials worried more about international legitimacy in the 1970s because they could more easily control domestic society. Chilean social groups, many exhausted by the Allende period and others devastated by repression, could not seriously challenge the government's power in the 1970s. Transnational human rights groups, including some operating in Chile, and many Western states formed the only active opposition to authoritarian rule. Although these pressures were often intangible, they seriously concerned government officials and prompted a series of increasingly significant changes within the government. In the 1980s, the revival of civil society forced the government to become far more worried about its domestic legitimacy – though without leaving behind international concerns.

The government's interest in legitimacy developed and became stronger over time in response to increasing human rights pressures and fading memories of the initial justifications for authoritarian rule. Garretón argues that all authoritarian governments naturally become concerned about their legitimacy as a function of time.[6] This is because the crisis that initially produced a justification for a new government eventually fades and the government must seek other ways to convince society of the necessity of its rule. Although the passage of time undoubtedly plays a role, not all governments seek legitimacy with the same intensity or determination, and not all seek legitimacy in the same ways. The Chilean government was particularly concerned with human rights issues in the mid- to late 1970s and the mid- to late 1980s. Given the military government's disdain for human rights principles generally, it is difficult to imagine such attention to the issue in the absence of strong human rights pressures.

The government's growing interest in legitimacy prompted important changes, but these changes did not always result in an improved human rights situation, especially in the short run. In fact, some changes undoubtedly strengthened the government by resolving internal conflicts about the appropriate nature of government institutions in ways that pleased many government supporters without activating government opponents. The end of the DINA in 1977, for example, signaled a significant decline in disappearances and the use of violent repression, yet it strengthened the government's grasp on power by eliminating an institution that generated significant opposition. The 1980 Constitution provided the government a political path that helped it survive economic collapse and intense domestic opposition in the mid-1980s at the same time that it offered opposition forces a way to defeat Pinochet. That these results were paradoxical and unanticipated should not detract from the argument that human rights pressures have important causal effects.

Changing conditions in Chile help explain why the government responded to human rights pressures, although not all factors matter equally. Table 5 summarizes the correlation between the theorized conditions and changes in the government's human rights strategies over time. Except for domestic structure, which is a nominal variable, it ranks each conditioning factor on a three-point ordinal scale of low, medium, and high. It assesses changes in the government's repressive strategy on a five-point ordinal scale as follows: no change toward greater conformity with norms (includes periods of increasing repression), minor change (agenda/discourse changes), moderate change (some changes in practices), institutional change (some changes in institutions, but without improving respect for human rights in the short term), and significant change (changes in both institutions and practices that substantially alter the existing patterns of repression).

Four implications may be drawn from these results and serve as tentative guideposts for future research. First, no single factor acting alone is sufficient to produce the observed variation. Domestic structure and normative fit did not change in the 1970s (and generally change

Table 5: Case Summary – Chile

Years	Conditions				Outcome
	Domestic structure	Normative fit	Crisis level	Rule–oriented faction	
1973–75	State–dominated	Medium	High	Low	Minor change: human rights on agenda
1976–77	State–dominated	Medium	Medium	Medium	Moderate change: end of DINA
1978–81	State–dominated	Medium	Medium	High	Institutional change: new constitution
1982–84	State–dominated	High	High	High	Increased repression, within existing institutions
1985–88	State–dominated	High	Low	High	Significant change: fair plebiscite and democratization

slowly), yet the government altered its discourse, policies, and institutions in important ways. The rise of a rule-oriented faction correlates perfectly with the changing outcomes in the 1970s, but the ongoing strength of the faction in the 1980s cannot explain the widely varying outcomes. Economic and security crises prevented positive change in 1973-75 and 1982-84, and the absence of crisis was associated with significant change in the mid- to late 1980s. Yet moderate levels of crisis cannot distinguish between moderate change and institutional change in the mid- to late 1970s.

Second, crisis level is most strongly correlated with the outcomes and could be viewed as a necessary but not sufficient condition for explaining variation in repressive strategies. In particular, high levels of crisis are associated with high levels of repression and minimal beneficial changes. In the Chilean case, crises prevented human rights pressures from influencing government decisions. Low levels of crisis (the absence or near-absence of economic and security threats), on the other hand, were necessary for the highest level of change to occur. Moderate levels of crises were consistent with medium levels of change reflected in behavior and institutions.

Third, crisis level, elite factions, and normative fit are each necessary and jointly sufficient to explain variation in the government's strategy in the context of strong human rights pressures. Crisis and normative fit acting together can explain all of the changes except the institutional change in the late 1970s, when these two conditions remained at moderate levels, and yet the government moved ahead with a new constitution. Crisis and a rule-oriented faction acting together can explain all of the changes except the early changes in agenda and discourse, when high levels of crisis and the dominance of force-oriented actors produce the expectation that Chile would completely ignore human rights pressures. Thus, all three variables are necessary to explain the changes over time.

In more specific and narrative terms, high crisis levels from 1973 to 1975 prevented human rights pressures from making much of an impact, yet medium levels of normative fit also ensured that human rights would be placed on the government's agenda. Strong human rights pressures mattered more in 1976-77 when declining crisis levels facilitated moderate change in the context of moderate levels of normative fit and the presence of a growing rule-oriented faction. Then from 1978 to

1981 a powerful rule-oriented faction implemented important institutional changes in the context of medium normative fit and crisis levels. High crisis levels from 1982 to 1984 prevented human rights pressures from having any impact and in fact produced an increase in repression, despite high levels of normative fit and a powerful rule-oriented faction. Then in the mid- to late 1980s, strong human rights pressures produced far-reaching changes under the combined domestic conditions of the absence of crisis, high levels of normative fit, and the dominant presence of a rule-oriented faction.

On the surface, this result raises the possibility that human rights pressures are not important and that the domestic variables acting together are sufficient to explain changes in repressive strategies. Such a claim could only be made by examining this case summary in isolation from the careful process tracing pursued in previous chapters. Senior Chilean decision makers, and especially Pinochet, clearly preferred outcomes that differed from the choices they actually made. As they made their decisions, they did not simply seize the initiative and act on their own; indeed, many senior military officials argued against changes in repressive strategies. Rather, Chilean officials consistently reacted to human rights pressures, although not in ways that human rights activists intended. In the 1970s, for example, there was little domestic opposition and therefore little need to alter a successful strategy of repression. Process tracing in previous chapters suggests that human rights pressures triggered the changes in government strategies; they did not simply occur naturally in a given set of domestic conditions.

Finally, domestic structure contributes the least to the explanation. Domestic structure never changed during this period, and yet important changes occurred in the government's repressive strategy. This problem might be surmounted if it could be shown that the observed variation was the result of varying levels of access by human rights activists within the same domestic structure. Yet the evidence shows that no network actors ever gained meaningful access to high-level decision makers, and no government decision ever embraced network preferences in any case. Further, the original hypothesis on domestic structure suggested that the resulting changes would either be negligible or significant, and yet the pattern that emerges in Chile is one of incremental steps.

Cuba

Like Chile, Cuba has faced substantial human rights pressures. These were generally moderate during the Cold War, but have been quite strong since 1991. The United States first imposed sanctions on Cuba in 1960, and they cost Cuba an estimated 4.4 percent of its GDP per year from 1960 to 1990, even taking into account increased aid from the Soviet Union during the Cold War.[7] Although no comparable estimates are available for the post–Cold-War era, analysts generally agree that the sanctions contributed to Cuba's sharp economic contraction in the mid-1990s and slowed the pace of recovery at the end of the decade. U.S. sanctions have broadened since 1990, but the real problem is that their effects have been magnified by the collapse of Communism. From 1990 to 1992, the Soviet Union and its Eastern European allies halted arms shipments, ended favorable trade agreements, reduced oil shipments, ended subsidies for oil exports to Cuba and sugar imports from Cuba, halted the practice of extending hard-currency credits, and insisted on converting Cuba's accumulated debt from rubles into dollars.[8] With respect to intangible pressures, the United States and Latin America (with some notable exceptions) condemned and isolated Cuba during the Cold War, yet Cuba simultaneously enjoyed strong support from Soviet-bloc countries and the admiration of many developing countries. Since the end of the Cold War, intangible pressures have been quite high, as symbolized by resolutions against Cuba in the UN Human Rights Commission every year from 1991 to 2000, with the exception of 1998.

Unlike Chile, Cuba has maintained essentially the same set of repressive policies without significant change since the emergence of a stable regime in the early 1960s in the aftermath of the revolution. Cuba created new, formalized institutions in the mid-1970s, but these institutions did not create any new political dynamics affecting human rights, as they did in Chile, and did not promise a future democratic regime, no matter how far off.[9] Also in sharp contrast to Chile, Cuba has two distinct networks pushing for liberalization: one that strongly favors the U.S. embargo and one that favors dialogue and economic engagement. While groups in the Chilean network had their differences, no issue split the opposition to the Pinochet government like the U.S. embargo, which has polarized the transnational opposition to authoritarian rule in Cuba. The pro-embargo network has long held the upper hand in the

United States, although the strength of the pro-engagement network grew dramatically in the 1990s. In Cuba, Europe, and Latin America, the pro-engagement network is stronger, although both networks have a lower profile than in the United States.

Until the late 1970s, militant groups enjoying close ties to the U.S. government and seeking the violent overthrow of the Cuban government dominated the transnational opposition.[10] Beginning in 1981 with the formation of the Cuban American National Foundation (CANF), a new generation of conservative, anti-Communist NGOs with purportedly peaceful intentions rose to prominence.[11] Although CANF is the best known, many other domestic and transnational groups are committed to forcing the collapse of the Castro government through extreme economic and diplomatic pressure.[12] These groups form a network because they share a normative commitment to ending Communist rule in Cuba, and they exchange information and ideas regularly. In contrast with some other networks, the pro-embargo network receives most of its funding from its individual members, the majority of whom are Cuban exiles.[13]

Although its center of gravity is in southern Florida, the hardline network is transnational in nature and should not be dismissed as exclusively a Miami phenomenon. Important network NGOs have members in a variety of Latin American and European countries who attempt to influence policies toward Cuba. For example, CANF developed ties to Russian President Boris Yeltsin, even before he came to power, in the hope of ending Russian subsidies to Cuba.[14] More recently, the human rights arm of CANF relied on the organization's office in Madrid to file legal briefs for the arrest of Fidel Castro on human rights violations, using the same methods and legal venues that other human rights groups employed to successfully snare Pinochet in late 1998. Finally, pro-embargo NGOs have developed stable contacts with individuals and groups in Cuba by telephone and personal visits, even though the Castro government fiercely condemns and ridicules the "traitors" in Miami.

The United States government is of course the most powerful ally of the hardline network – though it is also the only important state adopting pro-embargo policies in the post–Cold-War era. Network actors enjoy such large influence in the United States that they successfully pushed to strengthen the embargo in the 1990s, despite the declining threat from Cuba and the lifting of U.S. embargoes against similar countries, such as Vietnam.[15] In 1992, conservative NGOs helped push through the Cuban Democracy Act (also known as the Torricelli Bill), which tightened the embargo by prohibiting subsidiaries of U.S. corporations from trading with Cuba (among other measures) and which simultaneously encouraged the transnational flow of ideas, information, and resources to Cuban NGOs.[16] In 1996, network groups successfully urged the adoption of the hardline Helms-Burton Bill after the Cuban government shot down two civilian aircraft operated by the Cuban-American group Brothers to the Rescue.[17] The bill sought to widen economic pressure by penalizing foreign companies doing business in Cuba with the expropriated property of U.S. owners. More recently, the network demonstrated its continuing grip on U.S. policy by torpedoing initiatives designed to force a fundamental rethinking of the embargo.[18]

The pro-engagement network is less well-known and has fewer resources, but it grew dramatically in the 1990s and enjoys stronger transnational linkages, especially in Cuba. Prominent dissidents released from Castro's prisons since the late 1970s have founded many of the core groups in this network.[19] Many, such as the Cuban Committee for Human Rights, were established in Havana but have become transnational through exile and through the creation of support groups in a variety of countries. With the end of the Cold War, the pro-engagement network experienced rapid growth, both in terms of adding new groups and in expanding ties to broader human rights groups like Amnesty International.[20] Most dissident groups inside Cuba adopt a pro-engagement stance and have developed working relationships with their foreign counterparts despite strong pressure from the Castro government.[21] The pro-engagement network widely distributes information on human rights abuses in Cuba and urges states to exert diplomatic and political pressure on the government while simultaneously engaging Cuba economically. Most states – especially in Europe, Latin America, and Canada – have adopted this strategy and use information provided by the network to try to pressure Cuba to free political prisoners and improve the human rights situation.[22]

Despite their expanding size and intense efforts, neither of the networks has achieved much success in Cuba so far, either on its own or by first changing U.S. policy. Since they were first established in the mid-

1970s, Cuban political institutions have lost "prestige, authority, and effectiveness," but their basic structure and repressive patterns of behavior have remained essentially unchanged.[23] Glasnost in the Soviet Union prompted some discussion of liberalization during preparations that led up to the Fourth Congress of the Cuban Communist Party in October 1991.[24] In the end, however, the congress implemented relatively minor changes (such as allowing nonatheists into the party), while either ignoring or eviscerating proposals to liberalize the political system. Repression in Cuba is often harsh but relatively nonviolent.[25] The government uses pervasive fear, personal harassment, the loss of economic benefits like jobs, and selective imprisonment to keep opposition from forming. As in many authoritarian governments, repressive policies tend to be cyclical and responsive to the level of open opposition. A thaw sometimes occurs, as when the government released dozens of political prisoners following the Pope's January 1998 visit, but is often followed by wide-ranging crackdowns.

In sharp contrast to Chile, Cuba lacks the conditions that facilitate government response to human rights pressures. Cuba's state-controlled domestic structure is even less tolerant of domestic human rights groups and transnational ties than was Chile's state-dominated structure. Low levels of normative fit ensure that domestic groups and individuals rarely articulate the importance of international human rights norms, or are even much aware of them. Popular revolution gave birth to the Cuban government, and the intensity of public support for government policies in the 1960s is well documented. Although that support has eroded badly, nationalist revolutionary social norms remain at odds with liberal ideals and policies pushed by transnational networks and Western states.[26] Many Cubans, for example, equate Castro's leadership with nationalism and sovereignty. As Domínguez argues, "To oppose Fidel meant to oppose national sovereignty, which is the revolution's central legacy; to oppose national sovereignty was to deny the very meaning of their lives."[27]

Human rights groups attempting to influence Cuba from the outside are thus viewed as fundamental threats to Cubans' identities. Further, liberal political institutions are deeply tainted in Cuba because of their association with corruption, underdevelopment, and poor governance during their brief existence from 1940 to 1952.[28] Cuba's democratic experiment ended in the misery of a brutal authoritarian dictatorship when Fulgencio Batista seized power in March 1952. These prerevolutionary years were marked by uneven economic development, especially widespread disparities between rural and urban areas.[29] Socialist authoritarianism, on the other hand, is associated with social equality and a higher standard of living – although both achievements have been undermined since 1990. To the extent that Cubans buy into the argument that the revolution has improved their lives – and there is evidence that a large number of Cubans believe this – they are less interested in demanding human rights and democracy.[30]

Further, rule-oriented individuals are essentially absent from the upper reaches of the Cuban government.[31] A close reading of public pronouncements of top Cuban leaders reveals an absence of reform ideas and a profound silence on questions of Cuba's political future.[32] The last high-ranking official to speak publicly in ways that suggested rule-oriented thinking was Carlos Aldana, who spoke favorably of Mikhail Gorbachev's brand of reform Communism in 1990–91 and who even suggested that dissidents might participate in parliamentary elections.[33] In December 1991, however, Aldana issued a *mea culpa* and harshly attacked the dissidents. His about-face did not save him: he was removed from office nine months later and disappeared from view.

Another key indicator of the lack of a rule-oriented faction is the 1996 crackdown on Cuban social scientists. In the early 1990s, Cuban social scientists – many of them affiliated with the Centro de Estudios sobre America (CEA) and with contacts among U.S. academics – began to develop and publish ideas about how to make Cuba's political institutions more participatory and more democratic. Their arguments caught the attention of the Cuban government, which harshly clamped down on them.[34] In March 1996, the Political Bureau of the Cuban Communist Party issued a report implying that CEA scholars were fifth columnists, counterrevolutionaries, and imperialist pawns.[35] The government then harassed the CEA scholars into silence, dispersed them to a variety of academic institutions, and installed a hardliner at the helm of the CEA. Given this punishing crackdown on scholars who do not hold high-level political positions, it is difficult to imagine any government official expressing rule-oriented views, even if some may secretly hold them.

Crisis is the only factor to change in significant ways in the past twenty-five years, increasing from medium levels during the Cold War to high levels after the collapse of the Soviet Union. In the late 1970s and early 1980s, Cuba enjoyed relatively strong economic growth and social development. At the same time, the continual security threat from the United States ensured that Cuban officials could never let down their guard, concern themselves with the rhetoric of human rights groups, or alter their relationship with the Soviet Union. The end of Soviet subsidies and trade with the Soviet Union and Eastern Europe, a process that began in 1989, drastically altered Cuba's situation by inducing economic collapse.[36] From 1989 to 1993, the gross domestic product fell between 35 percent and 48 percent, real salaries dropped by 50 percent, and as much as a third of the labor force was unemployed.[37] These macroeconomic figures cannot describe the suffering of the Cuban people in the mid-1990s, who often lacked everyday necessities such as adequate food, electricity, oil-powered transportation, and prescription drugs. Cuba's attention since then has focused on surviving economic crisis and rebuilding the economy; concerns about the protests of transnational networks and conforming with international norms have a low priority.

The Cuban case demonstrates that even high levels of human rights pressures do not trigger changes in government responses if domestic conditions are unfavorable. In Cuba, these conditions tend to reinforce each other, making it unlikely that the government will alter its repressive policies any time soon. Cuba's civil society is currently too weak to produce new cultural understandings centered on liberal ideas, and the socialist and collectivist norms of the Cuban revolution make it difficult for an independent civil society to develop. The economic crisis has helped unify the government in the face of a serious threat to its survival, thereby preventing the development of a rule-oriented faction and allowing the government to justify ongoing state-dominated rule. Taken together, these factors impose formidable obstacles to the influence of human rights pressures and make it unlikely that Cuba will change, even in moderate ways, in the short run.

South Africa

South Africa stands as the most prominent target of transnational human rights campaigns and human rights pressure in history. Few if any countries have suffered the same level of scornful attention from the international community. Transnational human rights networks enjoyed extraordinary success convincing Western states to join the campaign against South Africa in the 1970s and 1980s.[38] Important segments of the domestic opposition in South Africa became closely tied to the transnational network and undoubtedly benefited from international patrons.[39] South Africa differs from Chile and Cuba because the government not only violated widely recognized civil and political liberties, but also employed systematic racial discrimination that generated a new set of international norms against policies of racial separation. Those antiracism norms were then routinely invoked by an array of international actors to condemn the white government.

Scattered international efforts to confront South Africa's human rights abuses date at least from the creation of the modern apartheid state in the late 1940s, but did not receive much attention until the March 1960 Sharpeville Massacre.[40] The murder of sixty-nine peaceful protesters served as a catalyst for international actors, who successfully engineered a series of resolutions in the United Nations General Assembly and Security Council against Pretoria's racist practices. International activists also created an international treaty condemning the practice of apartheid, labeling it a crime against humanity. Despite U.S. support for South Africa until the mid-1980s, UN-mandated sanctions first imposed in 1962 cost the country 2.8 percent a year throughout the 1960s, 1970s, and 1980s.[41] When the United States finally imposed sanctions in 1985, they cost South Africa an additional .8 percent per year – though the symbolic blow suffered by South Africa in losing its staunchest ally was probably even more damaging.

From the first strong human rights pressures in the early 1960s until the Soweto riots in the mid-1970s, conditions in South Africa made the government resistant to change. Although Western ideals of human rights and democracy circulated in South Africa, religious and political leaders justified and defended the political system by appealing to nationalism and racial superiority in ways that won the normative approval of white South Africans. The National Party, which built and championed apartheid, enjoyed widespread normative approval in the 1960s. In the March 1966 elections, for example, the National Party won 126 of 166 seats, while anti-apartheid parties took a single seat.[42] South Africa did not face a strong economic or security threat in the late 1960s, especially as it became clear that Angola, Mozambique, and Rhodesia would remain under white control for a time.[43]

Nevertheless, human rights pressures still ensured that issues of racism received a place on the government's agenda, and the government responded with an emphasis on the discourse of self-determination and the illusion of reform.[44] In the 1960s, South African officials constructed an elaborate scheme to grant "independence" to ten "states" covering some 13 percent of South Africa's territory. Although these plans were implemented in the late 1970s, they never received any international support and fell well short of constituting meaningful change. These changes in discourse in the 1960s may be traced to the moderate presence of a rule-oriented faction concerned about the government's long-term viability and its international legitimacy. As Black summarized it, "As the government of a self-consciously 'Western' or 'European' polity, the National Party regime never denied the validity of key international and liberal norms such as self-determination, the rule of law, or representative democracy. Rather it sought, both through its rhetoric and reforms, to reinterpret these norms and principles (often virtually beyond recognition) in an effort to persuade external observers that its policies in fact conformed with them."[45]

Events in the mid-1970s shattered South Africa's apparent calm. In 1976, labor unrest in Natal and the Soweto uprising shook South Africa and focused world attention on the horrific racial repression. In response, states and corporations took stronger actions. Banks and governments increased restrictions on loans, and the United States increased efforts to restrict nuclear technology transfer. A variety of multinational corporations began endorsing the Sullivan principles of ethical business practices, and a new wave of student protests led to a strengthening of the divestment movement.[46] In November 1977, the UN Security Council made the previously voluntary arms embargo mandatory. When South Africa responded in superficial ways, international actors increased the pressure again in the mid-1980s.[47] Intangible normative pressures included awarding the Nobel Peace Prize to anti-apartheid activist Bishop Desmond Tutu and launching the Free South Africa Movement at the South African embassy in Washington DC. More concrete measures included new sanctions from the United States and Europe that banned direct investment in South Africa, loans to the South African government, imports of key South African materials like coal and steel, and exports of oil and some computers. Most surprising were the decisions of commercial banks to tighten lending policies in the mid-1980s, ensuring that South Africa was "effectively cut off from international capital markets."[48]

During this period, South Africa faced a moderate security threat from newly independent and deeply hostile countries such as Angola and Mozambique, which were freed from colonial control in 1975. At the same time, the normative fit for human rights norms grew to moderate levels as a significant minority of white South Africans began to register their disapproval of apartheid at the ballot box in the mid-1970s.[49] The Progressive Party, which favored black majority rule with guarantees for minority whites, held a single seat in Parliament in the 1960s. From 1977 to 1989, in contrast, the progressives consistently captured from 17 to 20 percent of the popular vote. Clearly, most white South Africans continued to support apartheid, yet the normative consensus in favor of systematic discrimination was broken.

In response to the human rights pressures and the shifting attitudes among white South Africans, the National Party became increasingly concerned with the legitimacy and long-term stability of the apartheid regime. P. W. Botha became prime minister in 1978, proclaiming a "new dispensation" and "apartheid is dead." Gaining international legitimacy was one of the most fundamental goals of Botha's administration.[50] In an effort to regain that legitimacy, Pretoria attempted to control blacks through decentralized and indirect means, rather than relying so heavily on the coercive arm of the central state, and by redesigning the constitution in order to allow black political participation in a form that would not threaten ultimate control by whites.[51] This "neo-apartheid" was "a pragmatic attempt to reconstitute domination in a less coercive form in new historical conditions in which the mass of the people can less easily be kept in line by the old hard-line methods."[52] The government did not cease its coercive practices; rather, it attempted legal-institutional changes that would divert attention from coercion and that would buy some legitimacy. These changes, which took place from 1978 to 1983, may be classified as a combination of moderate and institutional change, similar to that undertaken by Chile from 1977 to 1981.

Unfortunately, direct force and extreme repression once again took center stage soon after the constitutional reforms were approved in

1983. Indeed, it was the effort to implement these reforms that triggered widespread and often violent domestic protests that swept South Africa from 1984 to 1986.[53] These protests threatened to topple the regime and made several areas of the country ungovernable. At the same time, South Africa faced growing security threats from neighboring states. Most of South Africa's military raids into Angola, Mozambique, Zimbabwe, and other states occurred between 1982 and 1986.[54] Domestically, South Africa responded to these high-level security threats with open violence and fierce repression, but without disavowing the legal-institutional reforms previously implemented. The government imposed a state of emergency in July 1985 and again in June 1986 and generally gave security forces a free hand to do what they needed to restore order.[55] At the same time, the government did not completely abandon its effort to achieve some legitimacy. Indeed, "[m]ore reform policies were introduced in the eighteen months between January 1985 and July 1986 than during the previous six-year period."[56]

In 1988, the security situation began to improve, especially with the sharp decline in violent mass protest in black townships. In August, South Africa's international security took a turn for the better with the signing of the Angola/Namibia Accord, a regional peace agreement that linked military withdrawal from Angola with Namibian independence.[57] The accord was cemented in December 1988 when South Africa, Cuba, and Angola agreed to a specific set of implementation plans, and troop withdrawals then proceeded despite cease-fire violations. For the first time since 1975, South Africa faced declining security threats from its neighbors. The successful international agreement strengthened the arguments of reformers that South Africa should seize the moment to break out of international isolation by making "some dramatic new gesture to the black majority."[58]

In the face of strong human rights pressures and in the midst of these declining security threats, the "internationalist-reformer" wing of the National Party ascended to power in early 1989 as F. W. de Klerk replaced Botha first as party leader and then as state president.[59] After confirming his leadership in a September 1989 general election, de Klerk stunned the world on February 2, 1990, by announcing the unbanning of the African National Congress (ANC) and other prominent opposition groups, the end of the state of emergency, the release of Nelson Mandela and other black leaders, and an invitation to negotiate a new power structure.[60] By mid-1990, government-ANC talks were in full swing.

From 1989 to 1994, human rights norms enjoyed high levels of normative fit at the same time that security threats to the state diminished dramatically. In March 1992, 68.7 percent of voters favored the reform process in a white-only referendum, demonstrating a remarkable shift in domestic norms about the need to dismantle apartheid.[61] The collapse of the Soviet Union and the end of Cuban interest in the region ensured a further easing of tensions with respect to security issues. By 1991, South Africa felt confident enough about the new security environment to sign the nuclear nonproliferation treaty and to come to terms with its former enemy in Namibia. With the security situation resolved and with public opinion solidly behind the reform process, de Klerk signed a democratization pact in late 1993 that ensured majority rule and extended human rights guarantees to all South Africans.

The varying conditions and outcomes for South Africa and Cuba are summarized in table 6. This table generally confirms the analysis of the Chilean case that crisis level, normative fit, and elite coalitions are each necessary and jointly sufficient to explain changes in repressive strategies in the face of human rights pressures. Cuba faced moderate human rights pressures during the Cold War and strong pressures afterward. Yet its lack of change can be attributed to low levels of normative fit combined with the absence of a rule-oriented faction and medium to high levels of crisis. Cuba's best opportunity to change was during the Cold War, when crisis levels were not so high. Yet the absolute unity of the government under Castro's control and the lack of domestic norms that would facilitate social resistance both prevented ideas about the need for long-term legitimacy from even surfacing.

The South African case is remarkably similar to Chile, though with an extended time horizon. Strong human rights pressures in the 1960s placed the issue on South Africa's agenda thanks to the moderate presence of a rule-oriented faction. The relatively low levels of crisis facilitated South African leaders taking notice of human rights concerns. In the late 1970s and early 1980s, medium levels of normative fit in the context of medium levels of crisis produced moderate changes in South Africa's repressive policies. Increasing repression in the mid-1980s also parallels the Chilean case, but was a response to security threats more than to economic difficulties. With the collapse of those security threats

Table 6: Case Summaries – Cuba and South Africa

Country/Years	Conditions					Outcome
	Domestic stucture	Normative fit	Crisis level	Rule-oriented faction		
CUBA						
1960–89	State-controlled	Low	Medium	Low		No change
1990–present	State-controlled	Low	High	Low		No change
SOUTH AFRICA						
1960–76	State-dominated	Low	Low	Medium		Minor change: human rights on agenda; discourse of "self-determination"
1977–83	State-dominated	Medium	Medium	Medium		Moderate/institutional change: constitutional changes
1984–88	State-dominated	Medium	High	Medium		Increased repression, within existing institutions
1989–94	State-dominated	High	Low	High		Significant change: new constitution; end of apartheid

in 1989-90, South African elites became more willing to make large-scale changes, especially in the context of the increasing acceptance of norms of racial equality among white South Africans. As a result, a rule-oriented faction came to power and implemented significant changes.

As with the Chilean case, domestic structure explains very little with respect to changes in repressive strategies. The absence of change in Cuba could certainly be attributed to its state-controlled domestic structure, but only if Cuba is viewed in isolation from the other cases. The incremental changes in South Africa are not associated in any way with the domestic structure of the state. As in the Chilean case, human rights advocates did not gain any meaningful access to South African decision makers until the early 1990s, and most changes adopted by South Africa did not reflect the policy preferences of human rights advocates in any case. Unlike Chile, the government ultimately negotiated directly with domestic opposition leaders who advocated human rights, yet this outcome can itself be viewed as a result of human rights pressures.

Further, a larger number of observations across cases confirms that domestic conditions are superior to international power differentials in predicting government responses. Although the power differential between the United States and Cuba is vast, Cuba has failed to alter its repressive strategies. During the Cold War, it seemed unlikely that the U.S. embargo would work, because the Soviet Union sustained Cuba's economy. With the Soviet collapse, the Cuban economy contracted sharply while the United States increased its economic pressure. Although the power differential between the United States and Cuba widened dramatically, the result has been the same: no change. In Chile, the United States and a few other countries exerted much less pressure in the late 1970s – cutting off economic and military aid but not trade, investments, or loans – and yet the military government implemented some changes. In the late 1980s, when Chile made its most profound changes, Western states employed even fewer economic sanctions and threats. The only place where power differentials are correlated with change is South Africa, where increases in international sanctions – and especially U.S. involvement – correspond to changes in the government's repressive strategies. Yet these are also correlated to changes in domestic conditions, making the case for power less conclusive. Looking at all the cases together, power differentials cannot explain the variation in government strategies.

Pursuing Pinochet, 1990–

Increasingly, many human rights groups are pressuring not only authoritarian regimes, but also democratic governments to improve human rights conditions – in part because democracies are now more common than they used to be. Human rights groups also pressure democracies to penalize repressive governments abroad and to seek justice for the most heinous abuses, as with the Yugoslav and Rwandan war crimes tribunals. The transition to democracy in Chile marked a sharp decline in human rights pressures, but did not spell the end of the effort. A variety of human rights groups and individual activists launched a new strategy to pursue justice for Pinochet and other government officials, pressuring Chile and other Western states to bring human rights criminals to justice.

With the transition to democracy in Chile, the human rights network shrank in size and visibility, in part because the need was no longer so urgent and in part because international donors and the Catholic Church turned their attention elsewhere.[62] The new democratic government formed by a coalition of center-left parties attempted to achieve some sort of resolution to the abusive legacy of the authoritarian government, but was continually hampered by the military's intransigence. The new democratic government named a truth and reconciliation commission whose mandate was limited to investigating cases of death and disappearance, thereby excluding all other types of human rights abuses. The Rettig Commission, as it became known, produced a report in early 1991 that detailed the death and disappearance of 3,178 human rights victims but did not assign blame to particular individuals.[63]

A variety of circumstances made it impossible to successfully prosecute those responsible. A 1978 law guaranteed amnesty for perpetrators of abuse from 1973 to 1978, and a Supreme Court ruling initially prevented even the judicial investigation of abuses dating from this period. Further, the military made it clear through public displays of military might and private discussions that it would not tolerate vigorous efforts to prosecute human rights criminals. Indeed, on the few occasions when high-profile human rights cases made significant progress in the court system, the military closed ranks to protect the accused.

Some Chilean human rights groups, especially the Association of Relatives of the Detained-Disappeared and leftist political parties, upset by the lack of justice, advocated derogating the amnesty law and punishing the accused.[64] They continued to pursue human rights cases in the courts and received some symbolic justice when the former head of the DINA, Manuel Contreras, and another top DINA official received Chilean prison sentences of seven and six years, respectively, for their role in the car bomb that killed Orlando Letelier in the United States in 1976. The convictions had been made possible nearly twenty years earlier when, under strong U.S. pressure, the military government had specifically excepted that crime from the 1978 amnesty law. Hoping to put an end to the politically sensitive issue, Christian Democratic president Eduardo Frei then proposed a bill in 1996 closing the books on most human rights investigations, but the legislation fell apart in a divided Congress.

Although the imprisonment of Contreras (after he was sheltered for months by the military) salved some wounds, others continued to demand justice. Rebuffed by conservative Chilean courts and frustrated by the government's fence-sitting, human rights groups attempted a new approach. Building on the anger in Spain over the Chilean Supreme Court's refusal to punish the DINA officials who had tortured and killed a Spanish diplomat in 1976, human rights groups successfully promoted a criminal complaint against Pinochet and other top officials in the Spanish courts. Originally filed for the death of Spanish citizens in Chile and Argentina under military rule, human rights groups broadened the complaint to include all victims of Pinochet's abuses. Spanish investigators vigorously pursued the complaint and issued a warrant for Pinochet's arrest, which British officials executed on October 16, 1998.

The detention of Pinochet is the tale of a transnational human rights network in action. A Spanish lawyers group, the Progressive Association of Prosecutors, filed the first complaints against Chilean and Argentine military officials, and a Spanish political party, United Left, officially presented them to the National Audience, a branch of the Spanish judiciary. A transnational group, the Salvador Allende Foundation, worked to broaden the charges to include not only Spanish citizens but all abuse victims. A variety of Chilean human rights groups offered testimony and documents to help build the case against Pinochet. Amnesty International in Britain discovered that Pinochet was visiting the country and notified Spanish lawyers at the Salvador Allende Foundation. After Spain issued its request to detain Pinochet, Amnesty then launched a public campaign to pressure Britain to comply. In other European countries, rights groups filed similar criminal complaints seeking Pinochet's extradition. In the United States, victims' families and human rights groups pressured the U.S. government to provide any available documentation on Pinochet's crimes. And in Chile, human rights lawyers opened new cases against Pinochet for genocide, kidnapping resulting in death, and illegal exhumation. Even though Pinochet ultimately escaped a trial, few would have imagined even this level of success just a few years ago. In addition to demonstrating the continuing relevance of human rights networks, these results suggest that access to an independent judiciary is an important variable in determining network success in their efforts to alter state policies in democracies.

Policy Implications

What policy implications can be drawn from these cases? What should states do to promote human rights in abusive states? Although these conclusions are necessarily tentative, because I have not systematically evaluated different types of policies, the theoretical approach and case histories suggest some important steps.

Debates on U.S. foreign policy and human rights are often dominated by discussions on the effectiveness and desirability of economic sanctions. Scholars who study sanctions are themselves sharply divided among those who think that sanctions do not matter and those who think they do, at least in some cases. For those who think sanctions do not matter, imposing sanctions can only make sense for moral reasons (cutting ties with a repressive government) or domestic political reasons (appealing to constituents who favor such moral positions).[65] In this view, if sanctions do not matter, then words surely do not matter. As a result, efforts to promote human rights abroad are empty, if well-intentioned, gestures.

For those who think they matter, sanctions should – among other factors – target weak states, be costly to the target but not the sender, be applied decisively, and be maintained for a long time.[66] These scholars also tend to downplay the importance of rhetoric, arguing that low-cost sanctions induce little change in the targeted country. As Hufbauer, Schott, and Elliott summarized it, "Sanctions that bite are sanctions that work."[67] While agreeing that sanction success is correlated with its cost for the targeted country, Drezner argues that sanctions are especially successful if the targeted country anticipated a relatively conflict-free relationship with the sanctioning state.[68] In other words, sanctions are more effective on friends than on enemies. These authors – and others that study sanctions – essentially assume that sanctions matter more than rhetoric, and they suggest that sanctions should be employed only if tangible economic costs to the targeted country are quite high.

The analysis in this book challenges these policy conclusions by emphasizing two additional factors: (1) the importance of rhetoric and intangible costs, and (2) the domestic characteristics of targeted countries. Chile and other case studies suggest that normative pressures can be important and should not automatically be dismissed as mere lip service.[69] In the lexicon of foreign policy critics, rhetoric (verbal condemnation) is often contrasted with reality (sanctions). While this distinction is useful, the Chilean case suggests it should not be overdrawn. States do not clearly fear the loss of foreign aid – the most common sanction – more than the loss of legitimacy. Words matter because they encourage others to become more critical, because they give hope and credibility to the domestic opposition, and because many governments, perhaps surprisingly, think they matter.

As a result, Western states seeking to promote human rights abroad should unceasingly document the nature of abuses, articulate agreed-upon appropriate standards, and criticize states verbally for unacceptable behavior. The purpose of these efforts is to challenge the legitimacy of the abusive government; therefore, rhetorical actions should be publicly stated and endorsed by a wide variety of states and nonstate actors. Words can be of little use if they are consistently shrouded in secrecy. Certainly, quiet diplomacy has a place in some circumstances. States unwilling to cave in to public pressure may be persuaded to change their behavior through unseen diplomatic channels. At the same time, quiet diplomacy does not jeopardize a government's legitimacy or give hope to the opposition. Further, quiet diplomacy may simply make the targeted government believe that the pressuring governments are not serious or that problems can be avoided with illusionary closed-door deals. As a result, quiet diplomacy may be combined in some cases with public pressures, but should not serve as a substitute. Public rhetorical pressures are always essential.

Additionally, intangible pressures are probably the most effective when they are adopted by a wide variety of states over a sustained period of time. States fear the long-term loss of legitimacy within domestic society or the international community, not the short-term souring of relations with particular states. Articulating clear and widely accepted human rights norms is an essential first step. States must first gain general agreement on the basic principles of human rights, a process that has been ongoing since the end of World War II. Abstract human rights norms are not empty rhetoric, but rather a necessary first step in the effort to condemn abusive governments. By getting a large variety of states to buy into the abstract principles of human rights, activists have ensured that the subsequent condemnations based on those standards are more forceful. Of course, convincing states to actually condemn each other for violations of those standards is a difficult process fraught with politics. Yet widespread, sustained pressure is a useful policy goal that is sometimes achieved, as in South Africa and Chile. Shrill denunciations from only a few states or for a short period of time, as with international efforts to condemn China's policies, are much less likely to be effective.

I am not claiming that rhetorical pressures are more effective than sanctions or that they can replace sanctions. On the contrary, Chile and other cases suggest that human rights pressures work best when they combine intangible attacks with tangible activities. The international rhetoric of the first few years of military rule triggered some changes inside Chile, but more important changes did not occur until the United States started enforcing some sanctions and threatened to impose others. In the 1980s, in turn, international rhetoric combined with substantial domestic opposition produced change in Chile. My position might be summarized as "rhetoric plus." Rhetoric is essential, but to become more effective it should be combined with action. These actions need not be extremely costly economically or politically, yet they should be substantial enough to demonstrate that the targeted state cannot become a fully accepted member of the international community as long as human rights violations persist.

In this respect, sanctioning states make a mistake if they focus only on the tangible economic costs of their actions. They should also consider the effects of their actions on the targeted government's legitimacy. Admittedly, such calculations are difficult to make and require judgment calls. They require assessing whether or not a targeted government hopes to base its rule on the consent of the people domestically or seeks to become an influential member of the international community. Yet such assessments do not need to be made on imagination alone. Policymakers can evaluate the statements and patterns of behavior of repressive governments to discern the extent to which that government is concerned about its legitimacy. Governments that take out public relations advertisements in the *New York Times*, as the Chilean military rulers did in the 1970s, are clearly more interested in their legitimacy than governments that consistently denounce the unjust global economic and political structure, such as Cuba. By accumulating such evidence systematically, policymakers can make reasonable judgments about a government's relative concern with its own legitimacy and can act accordingly.

Of equal importance, the policy implications of this study favor methods that are finely tuned to the domestic characteristics of each country. International political and economic pressures, such as shame and sanctions, are more likely to work in countries where international norms enjoy domestic resonance and the state faces no serious crisis. In a world of scarce resources where it is impossible to pressure all abusive governments, norm-supportive states would do well to focus on the most vulnerable targets. An assessment of the country's normative fit should be high on the list. States with some history of human rights and democracy are more likely to care about their legitimacy and to possess civil societies capable of building on human rights pressures. The Chilean case illustrates these points. Chilean elites viewed themselves as important leaders in the Western community of states and were shocked that their fellow states would criticize them for violence against Marxists. They routinely expressed their desire to return Chile to its rightful international standing, though they were not willing to jettison repression. Chile's traditionally vibrant civil society and long respect for human rights made it easier for human rights pressures to find an important echo in domestic society.

Where states face economic or security crisis, lack rule-oriented factions, or have low levels of normative fit, even very strong human rights pressures are unlikely to induce change. Any number of repressive states (for example, Cuba, North Korea, Burma, even tiny Haiti prior to the U.S. invasion) have stood up to stiff international sanctions that fall short of military force. In these cases, policies should aim at first changing the state's domestic characteristics. International actors can alter a country's normative fit by diffusing new ideas through social and cultural contacts and can alter crisis levels by helping resolve security threats and promoting economic growth. States can probe for the existence of a rule-oriented faction and identify ways to raise the costs of noncompliance and the benefits of compliance in ways that will strengthen the faction.

The difficulty with this approach, of course, is the length of time it takes to alter a state's domestic characteristics. Altering widespread domestic cultural understandings and ending serious security threats are among the longest of long-term projects. Skeptics appropriately question whether these factors are even amenable to international action. What can foreign states do to alter domestic patterns in cultures and lands they do not understand and that they should stay out of anyway?

Admittedly, altering a government's domestic characteristics is a time-consuming task, and states are not always the best vehicle to accomplish this. At the same time, working for long-term change is better than doing nothing, and states have resources that can be used in partnership with nongovernmental organizations who might be better suited for the task. In the Chilean case, foreign states played a key role in funding and providing moral support for domestic opposition groups. These activities included meeting with opposition leaders either in exile or in Chile and using diplomacy to seek the freedom of prominent dissidents. Foreign states' condemnations of Chile's practices placed human rights abuses in the national media and lent credibility to domestic groups who were otherwise dismissed as Communist dupes. Other nonstate international actors can be crucial in efforts to change the political landscape inside countries. Charitable donors funneled money into Chile in the 1970s and 1980s, thus helping preserve political space and bolster the opposition. Intergovernmental organizations such as the United Nations and the Inter-American Commission on Human Rights gave hope to domestic groups in Chile and validated reports of widespread abuses.

Of the conditions that influence the success of human rights pressures, the role of rule-oriented individuals is the most susceptible to short-term policy manipulation. States would do well to focus their pressures on those governments where rule-oriented factions can amplify international pressures and use them to promote domestic changes. Viewed strictly from a practical perspective, this principle suggests that strong pressures on states with extremely unified governments are a waste of time and effort and have little chance of succeeding. States such as Iraq, Cuba, and North Korea have no visible rule-oriented officials and few identifiable government supporters who could be coerced or enticed into dissent and thus apparently have extremely high thresholds of resistance to human rights pressure. In these cases, widespread sanctions would have to be justified on moral rather than on practical grounds.

Although these policy recommendations may seem commonsensical, they are often ignored in practice – in part because they require a long-term commitment to gradual change rather than a quick strike intended to procure an immediate reversal of behavior. Such long-term strategies may be practically difficult or morally objectionable, but they are more likely to be ultimately effective in states with unfavorable domestic characteristics.

Domestic Politics and International Relations

Scholars have made important strides in the last several years at conceptualizing the ways in which international and domestic politics interact. One theoretical strand retains the state at the center of analysis and posits that state elites must calculate the costs and benefits of their actions at both an international and a domestic level.[70] This insight, however, has been applied almost exclusively in the two-level game literature to cases of international negotiations and bargaining. Human rights pressures generally fall outside this domain.

Human rights interactions between states, nongovernmental organizations, and repressive governments are characterized not by negotiations, but rather by strategic pressures and threats. Strategic interaction differs from bargaining because there is no agreement to negotiate and no interest in achieving any sort of formal or informal common position. Chilean elites, for example, never placed their repressive strategies or their new political institutions on the negotiating table. As a result, many of the theoretical propositions developed in the two-level game literature do not fit the Chilean case or related cases. These include arguments about the importance of "win sets" (international agreements acceptable to a domestic constituency), the two-step process of negotiation and ratification, and the important role of negotiating strategies.

Yet the central insight of the two-level games literature still applies to nonbargaining strategic interactions exemplified by the Chilean case. That is, state elites calculated costs and benefits at both domestic and international levels, and strategies pursued at one level had important repercussions at the other level. A Level I decision maker (Pinochet) set domestic policies and pursued international strategies. A set of Level II actors (top military officials, legal advisors, economists, and other government officials) held their own preferences with respect to domestic policies and international strategies. In responding to international pressures, Pinochet had to calculate not only foreign costs and benefits, but also the domestic viability of his strategies. Even in a centralized polity such as authoritarian Chile, Level II actors played a key role in pressing their policy preferences and eventually in convincing Pinochet to pursue a different course. More theoretical work is needed to distinguish different types of international interactions (bargaining, strategic interaction, and war) and the ways in which the logic of two-level games may differ between these domains.

One promising path of research, for example, would examine the importance of reverberation. Reverberation refers to international pressures that trigger realignments in domestic alliances or preferences and may occur in situations of both bargaining and strategic interaction.[71] Putnam has written of "suasive reverberation" in which one country attempts to persuade the domestic audience in another country of the benefits it will receive from international agreement. Rather than suasive reverberation, international actors routinely employ what might be termed "punitive reverberation" in cases of human rights abuse. Punitive reverberation relies on international threats or penalties to trigger changes in domestic coalitions. In the 1970s, for example, international pressures helped forge an alliance among government factions opposed to the DINA by providing them with a tangible example of the costs of severe repression. Of course, both suasive and punitive reverberation may backfire and create a nationalistic response against foreign interference. More research is needed to investigate which types of reverberation are used and why and to lay out the conditions in which reverberation will be successful.

Viewing states as Janus-faced strategic actors fits well with my argument that they care about both domestic and international normative approval. Although many scholars have discussed government legitimacy at the level of domestic politics, fewer have explored the international dimension of a state's legitimacy. International legitimacy is fundamentally important because state sovereignty also has two dimensions: the domestic control of territory and international recognition. Governments that lack international normative approval jeopardize their sovereignty because they make it far easier for other states to justify intervention. One avenue of research along these lines would be an exploration of patterns of foreign intervention in domestic politics. The line of reasoning developed here suggests that norm-violating states are more likely to be targeted for intervention because they lack international legitimacy. Alternatively, a realist approach might suggest that weak states are more likely targets of intervention.

A second theoretical strand tying domestic politics to international relations conceptualizes the state as an object of influence rather than as the central actor. In this perspective, transnational and domestic groups use international norms in domestic political debates to influence state behavior. Risse-Kappen argues that transnational actors carry international norms into the domestic arena and influence states by building "winning coalitions" with domestic actors. "To influence policies, transnational actors need, first, channels into the political system of the target state, and second, domestic partners with the ability to form winning coalitions. Ideas promoted by transnational alliances or epistemic communities do not matter unless these two conditions are met."[72] In this logic, whether transnational networks succeed at these tasks depends in large part on the state's domestic structure. Where states are too closed, transnational actors have difficulty gaining access; where they are too pluralistic, transnational actors have difficulty being heard.

Other scholars view autonomous domestic actors as the mechanism by which international norms become translated into domestic politics. Moravcsik argues that an independent civil society and robust domestic legal institutions can take advantage of international actions to pressure governments from within.[73] In a similar vein, Cortell and Davis argue that international norms matter when influential state or societal actors appeal to those norms in policy debates or when they are incorporated into national legislation.[74]

Yet none of these arguments helps explain outcomes in Chile or related cases. Because of Chile's personalized, hierarchical state structure and the atmosphere of fear, transnational actors made little headway in the late 1970s and certainly fell far short of building a "winning coalition." In the 1980s, transnational actors gained access to Chilean society, but developed no allies in the government and thus should have lacked influence, according to Risse-Kappen's reasoning. Likewise, Chile lacked an independent civil society, robust domestic legal institutions, and politically relevant actors who could appeal to human rights norms as the correct path. Domestic actors such as human rights groups and the Catholic Church certainly raised issues such as human rights norms, but did not influence government behavior in the ways conceptualized above.

The difficulty is that these analyses assume that at least some powerful decision makers accept the validity of the relevant international norms and are open to persuasive arguments or legal rulings that rely on those norms. These features are more characteristic of liberal democratic polities than of authoritarian governments targeted by human rights pressures. Yet even when government officials reject the validity of international norms, they realize that other powerful actors accept the norms and sometimes back them up with normative pressures and sanctions. As a result, the officials strategically modify their discourse and behavior to correspond more closely to the norm. Complying (or claiming to comply) more closely with norms allows the government to shore up its authority and legitimacy and to deflect international pressures. This avenue of international influence does not require a strong autonomous civil society, nor does it require that government elites accept the international norm, and thus applies more clearly to human rights pressures on authoritarian states.

More generally, the ever-increasing number of rules and norms in the international arena suggests the growing importance of understanding whether and why states comply with these rules. Some rules are enforced by powerful states and others clearly benefit a large number of states; hence, compliance is less problematic. Yet a large number of rules, including all human rights norms, are rarely enforced and provide no clear benefits to states. Why then comply? In some cases, domestic or transnational actors may gain direct access to state decision makers or institutions and persuade them to comply. Yet this path of influence is quite unlikely in the case of human rights norms and authoritarian states, and it did not happen in Chile, South Africa, or Cuba.

Nevertheless, it would be a mistake to see human rights norms as completely devoid of influence. As I have argued throughout, transnational actors and their state allies are capable of seriously threatening a state's legitimacy through intangible pressures backed up by tangible sanctions. Further, even authoritarian states often care about their legitimacy, both domestically and internationally, and so respond to these pressures. In short, even unwanted international norms that have no politically powerful supporters inside a targeted government can still influence state behavior under the right conditions.

Notes

INTRODUCTION

1. Within a large literature, see Donnelly, *Universal Human Rights* and *International Human Rights*; Forsythe, *Human Rights in International Relations*; and Montealegre, *La Seguridad del Estado*.
2. Donnelly, "Progress in Human Rights," 312-58.
3. Krasner, "Sovereignty, Regimes, and Human Rights," 139-67.
4. Wendt, "Anarchy Is What States Make of It," 391-425; Wendt, *Social Theory of International Politics*.
5. Moravcsik, "Taking Preferences Seriously," 513-53.
6. Kamminga, *Violations of Human Rights*, 88.
7. Sánchez, "Las Resoluciones Internacionales sobre Chile," 61-97.
8. Geldenhuys, *Isolated States*.
9. For a prominent example, see Linz, *Breakdown of Democratic Regimes*.
10. Keck and Sikkink, *Activists beyond Borders*.
11. Risse-Kappen, "Transnational Relations," 3-33.
12. Checkel, "Norms, Institutions, and National Identity," 83-114; Cortell and Davis, "Domestic Impact of International Norms," 65-87.
13. Checkel, *International Political Change*, 8-11.
14. O'Donnell and Schmitter, *Uncertain Democracies*.
15. George and McKeown, "Organizational Decision Making," 21-58.
16. Harry Eckstein, "Case Study and Theory in Political Science," 79-138.
17. King, Keohane, and Verba, *Designing Social Inquiry*, 217-28.
18. Garretón, "Institutionalization and Opposition in Chile," 144-83; Varas, "Crisis of Legitimacy," 73-97.
19. Arturo Valenzuela, "Military in Power," 21-72.
20. Muñoz, "Chile: The Limits of Success," 39-52; Portales, "External Factors and the Authoritarian Regime."

1. HUMAN RIGHTS PRESSURES

1. Diamond, "Promoting Democracy in the 1990s," 311-70; Farer, ed., *Beyond Sovereignty*; Shin, "On the Third Wave of Democratization," 135-70.
2. Wendt, *Social Theory of International Politics*; Risse, "Communicative Action in World Politics," 1-39.

3. Risse-Kappen, "Transnational Relations"; Evangelista, "Transnational Relations and Security Policy," 1–38; Cortell and Davis, "How Do International Institutions Matter?" 451–78.

4. Moravcsik, "Explaining International Human Rights Regimes," 157–89.

5. Finnemore, National Interests; Checkel, "Norms, Institutions, and National Identity," 83–114.

6. Risse and Sikkink, "The Socialization of International Human Rights Norms," 1–38.

7. Krasner, "Sovereignty, Regimes, and Human Rights," 139–67; Tony Evans, U.S. Hegemony.

8. Keohane, After Hegemony.

9. Checkel, "The Constructivist Turn," 324–48.

10. Moravcsik, "Taking Preferences Seriously," 513.

11. Moravcsik, "Explaining International Human Rights Regimes"; Risse-Kappen, "Transnational Relations."

12. Checkel, "International Norms and Domestic Politics," 473–95; Finnemore and Sikkink, "International Norm Dynamics," 887–917.

13. Donnelly, "Progress in Human Rights"; Forsythe, Human Rights in International Relations; Lauren, Visions Seen.

14. Forsythe, Human Rights in International Relations; Farer, "Inter-American Human Rights Regime," 510–46.

15. Keck and Sikkink, Activists beyond Borders, 10–12, 89–92.

16. Sikkink, "Latin American Human Rights Network," 59–84.

17. Keck and Sikkink, Activists beyond Borders, 2.

18. Sikkink, "Power of Principled Ideas," 139–70.

19. Schoultz, Human Rights and United States Policy.

20. Keck and Sikkink, Activists beyond Borders, 16–25.

21. Hufbauer, Schott, and Elliott, Economic Sanctions Reconsidered.

22. On the constitutive role of international norms, see Wendt, "Agent-Structure Problem," 335–70; Dessler, "Agent-Structure Debate," 441–74.

23. Medina, Battle of Human Rights, passim.

24. Even observers sympathetic to the use of sanctions find that they are not strong enough to make a difference in most cases. See Hufbauer, Schott, and Elliott, Economic Sanctions Reconsidered, vol. 1, 92–93.

25. Poe, "Human Rights and U.S. Foreign Aid," 499–512; Forsythe, "Congress and Human Rights," 382–404.

26. Falk, "Theoretical Foundations," 33.

27. Martin and Sikkink, "Argentina and Guatemala," 330–62; Sikkink,

"Principled Issue Networks," 411–41; Risse and Sikkink, "Socialization of International Human Rights Norms."

28. Schoultz, *Human Rights and United States Policy*, 344–64.

29. Martin and Sikkink, "Argentina and Guatemala."

30. Crawford and Klotz, eds., *How Sanctions Work*; Thomas, *Helsinki Effect*.

31. Brysk, *Human Rights in Argentina*.

32. This discussion draws on Keck and Sikkink, *Activists beyond Borders*, 25–26.

33. Huntington, *Third Wave*.

34. McCormick and Mitchell, "Human Rights Violations," 510–25; Poe and Tate, "Repression of Human Rights," 853–72.

35. Ron, "State Violence," 275–300.

36. Garretón, "Institutionalization and Opposition in Chile," 144–83.

37. Linz, *Breakdown of Democratic Regimes*, 16.

38. Suchman, "Managing Legitimacy," 574.

39. Weber, *Economy and Society*, 213.

40. Mainwaring, "Transitions to Democracy," 294–341.

41. O'Donnell and Schmitter, *Uncertain Democracies*; Diamond, Linz, and Lipset, "What Makes for Democracy?" 1–66; Linz and Stepan, *Democratic Transition and Consolidation*.

42. Forsythe, *Human Rights and Peace*, 61–76.

43. For a treatment of this process with respect to women's rights, see Fraser, "Becoming Human," 853–906.

44. Forsythe, *Human Rights and Peace*, 61–76.

45. Hedley Bull, *Anarchical Society*; Keohane, "Neoliberal Institutionalism."

46. David Forsythe, "Human Rights and U.S. Foreign Policy," 111–30.

47. Nye, *Bound to Lead*.

48. Barkin and Cronin, "The State and the Nation," 113.

49. Mercer, *Reputation and International Politics*, 6–10.

50. Morgenthau, *Politics among Nations*, 67–79.

51. Morgenthau, *Politics among Nations*, 68.

52. Franck, *Legitimacy among Nations*, 24; Hurd, "Legitimacy and Authority," 381.

53. Franck, *Legitimacy among Nations*, 195–207.

54. Finnemore, *National Interests*, 3–7; Ron, "State Violence," 277–79.

55. Risse and Sikkink, "Socialization of International Human Rights Norms," 17–35.

56. Risse and Sikkink, "Socialization of International Human Rights Norms," 25–28.

57. Risse-Kappen, "Transnational Relations"; Evangelista, "Transnational Relations and Security Policy"; Checkel, "International Norms and Domestic Politics."

58. Risse-Kappen, "Transnational Relations," 3–33.

59. Risse-Kappen, "Transnational Relations," 23–25.

60. Risse-Kappen, "Transnational Relations," 14–28.

61. Checkel, "International Norms and Domestic Politics."

62. Evangelista, "Transnational Relations and Security Policy."

63. Cortell and Davis, "Domestic Impact of International Norms," 65–87; Keck and Sikkink, Activists beyond Borders, 26–28.

64. Keck and Sikkink, Activists beyond Borders, 66–72.

65. Legro, "Which Norms Matter?" 31–63.

66. Keck and Sikkink, Activists beyond Borders, 26–28.

67. Keck and Sikkink, Activists beyond Borders.

68. Gourevitch, Politics in Hard Times; Keeler, "Opening the Window"; Checkel, International Political Change.

69. Checkel, International Political Change, 10.

70. O'Donnell and Schmitter, Uncertain Democracies, 26–32.

71. O'Donnell and Schmitter, Uncertain Democracies, 27.

72. Moravcsik, "Taking Preferences Seriously."

73. Carr, Twenty Years Crisis, 92–98, 132–45.

74. Morgenthau, Politics among Nations, 50–60.

75. For an interesting exception, see Mastanduno, Lake, and Ikenberry, "Realist Theory of State Action," 457–74.

76. Martin and Simmons, "International Institutions," 729–57.

77. Meyer et al., "World Environmental Regime," 623–51; Price, "Chemical Weapons Taboo," 73–103; Legro, "Which Norms Matter?"; Keck and Sikkink, Activists beyond Borders; Finnemore, National Interests.

78. Finnemore and Sikkink, "International Norm Dynamics," 910.

79. Moravcsik, "Explaining International Human Rights Regimes."

80. Cortell and Davis, "How Do International Institutions Matter?"

81. Checkel, "International Norms and Domestic Politics," 488.

2. PLACING HUMAN RIGHTS ON THE AGENDA

1. Vergara, Auge y Caída del Neoliberalismo en Chile, 17–20.

2. Cavallo, Salazar, and Sepúlveda, Chile, 12–13.

3. By agenda setting, I do not refer to a nationwide debate in the media and within various political and social institutions. For even the most innocuous issues, such a debate would have been nearly impossible, given Chile's authoritarian context of the 1970s. Rather, I refer to the extent to which top government officials discussed the issue of human rights and the problems it created for Chile.

4. The events leading to the demise of the Allende government and the causes of authoritarian rule in Chile have been widely debated in a voluminous literature. Some of the most prominent sources include Davis, *Last Two Years of Allende*; de Vylder, *Allende's Chile*; Garretón and Moulián, *Análisis Coyuntural*; Sigmund, *Overthrow of Allende*; and Arturo Valenzuela, *Breakdown of Democratic Regimes: Chile*.

5. Chilean National Commission on Truth and Reconciliation, *Report of the Chilean National Commission*, 129–46.

6. Although the published work on human rights violations in Chile is voluminous, no summary or comprehensive assessment of the period exists. Perhaps a comprehensive record is impossible, given the scope of terror. The two most complete and balanced sources are the 1993 Rettig Report (authored by the Chilean National Commission on Truth and Reconciliation) and the 1985 report by the Inter-American Commission on Human Rights (IACHR). The Rettig Report was commissioned by the democratic government installed in 1990. It provides a comprehensive report of deaths and disappearances from 1973 to 1990, complete with analysis of the political and institutional contexts. Unfortunately, other types of human rights abuses, including torture, fell outside the commission's mandate. The 1985 IACHR report summarized a wide variety of human rights violations during the previous twelve years of military rule. However, it was published in 1985, five years before the military government left office and under conditions in which it was difficult to gather complete and accurate information. Other sources providing a general overview of human rights abuses of the military government include Ahumada et al., *Chile: La Memoria Prohibida*; and Fruhling, "Stages of Repression."

7. Remmer, "Political Demobilization." Useful overviews of the church's opposition to the authoritarian regime may be found in Lowden, *Moral Opposition*; Correa and Viera-Gallo, *Iglesia y Dictadura*; and Brian H. Smith, *Church and Politics in Chile*.

8. Arriagada, "Armed Forces in Chile," 117–43; Arriagada, *Pinochet*; Arturo Valenzuela, "Military in Power," 21–72.

9. Vergara, *Auge y Caída del Neoliberalismo en Chile*, 17–27.

10. See especially Pinochet's speech marking the one-month anniversary of the coup, October 11, 1973, reprinted in the government's pamphlet *Realidad y Destino de Chile* (Santiago: Editora Nacional Gabriela Mistral, n.d.) and the March 11, 1974, *Declaración de Principios del Gobierno de Chile* (Santiago, 1974).

11. Arriagada, *Pensamiento Político*, 92–107.

12. Carmen Hasbún, "Salvar a Chile Era un Compromiso," *La Segunda* (Santiago), late September 1973.

13. Arriagada, *Pensamiento Político*, 219.

14. Arriagada, *Pensamiento Político*, 183–93.

15. Cavallo, Salazar, and Sepúlveda, *Chile*, 42–50; Salazar, *Contreras*.

16. Chilean National Commission on Truth and Reconciliation, *Report of the Chilean National Commission*, 471–78.

17. For summaries of the Chilean military's political thought, see Vergara, *Auge y Caída del Neoliberalismo en Chile*; Arriagada, *Pensamiento Político*; and Varas and Agüero, *El Proyecto Político Militar*.

18. Arturo Valenzuela, "Military in Power," 51.

19. Vergara, *Auge y Caída del Neoliberalismo en Chile*, 63.

20. The best analyses are: Lowden, *Moral Opposition*; Fruhling, "Stages of Repression"; Fruhling and Orellana, "Organismos No Gubernamentales de Derechos Humanos"; Fruhling, "Nonprofit Organizations," 358–76; Orellana and Hutchison, *Movimiento de Derechos Humanos*; Medina, *Battle of Human Rights*.

21. Keck and Sikkink, *Activists beyond Borders*, 90.

22. Medina, *Battle of Human Rights*, 263–64.

23. Lowden, *Moral Opposition*, 31–32.

24. Lowden, *Moral Opposition*, 32; Smith, *Church and Politics in Chile*, 312–13.

25. Lowden, *Moral Opposition*, 32.

26. Bornand, interview, July 9, 1992.

27. Fruhling, "Stages of Repression."

28. Bornand, interview, July 9, 1992.

29. Detzner, "Mecanismos Internacionales," 92–96. After 1979, the Vicariate switched strategies and began preparing human rights reports that focused on the general situation rather than on individual cases.

30. Fruhling and Orellana, "Organismos No Gubernamentales de Derechos Humanos," 28.

31. Lowden, *Moral Opposition*, 40.

32. Orellana, "Derechos Humanos en Chile," 40.

33. Schoultz, *Human Rights and United States Policy*, 74–88.

34. Keck and Sikkink, *Activists beyond Borders*, 91–92.

35. John Barnes, "Slaughterhouse in Santiago," *Newsweek*, 8 October 1973, 53–54.

36. Jonathan Kandell, "Death Toll in Chile May Now Be 2,000," *New York Times*, 12 October 1973.

37. Muñoz, *Gobierno Militar Chileno*, 21–25.

38. "Actas de Sesiones de la Honorable Junta de Gobierno" (hereafter "Actas de la Junta"), no. 2, September 13, 1973.

39. "Actas de la Junta", no. 4, September 17, 1973.

40. An account of the ineffective Chilean public relations efforts in the United States may be found in Schoultz, *Human Rights and United States Policy*, 52–58.

41. "Actas de la Junta," no. 5, September 19, 1973.

42. "Actas de la Junta," no. 7, September 21, 1973.

43. "Actas de la Junta," no. 28, November 5, 1973.

44. "Actas de la Junta," no. 10, September 27, 1973.

45. "Actas de la Junta," no. 14, October 3, 1973.

46. "Actas de la Junta," no. 17, October 8, 1973.

47. "Actas de la Junta," no. 83, January 28, 1974.

48. "Actas de la Junta," no. 29, November 6, 1973.

49. "Actas de la Junta," no. 5, September 19, 1973.

50. "Actas de la Junta," no. 20, October 15, 1973.

51. "Actas de la Junta," nos. 50–51, December 17, 1973.

52. A number of early government documents make the case for the government's legitimacy. See Bando no. 5, reproduced in Loveman and Davies, *The Politics of Antipolitics*, 181–83; Decree Law no. 1, also known as the Act of Constitution of the Governing Junta; Pinochet's speech marking the one-month anniversary of the coup and Huerta's first speech before the United Nations, both reprinted in the government pamphlet *Realidad y Destino de Chile* (Santiago: Editora Nacional Gabriela Mistral, n.d.); and the government's official account of the coup, found in the *Libro Blanco del Cambio de Gobierno en Chile*, first distributed in October 1973.

53. Medina, *Battle of Human Rights*, 263–65.

54. Vargas, "El Caso Chileno."

55. James Nelson Goodsell, "Chile Junta Stung by World Blasts," *Christian Science Monitor*, 13 June 1975.

56. Kamminga, *Violations of Human Rights*, 88–93.

57. Kamminga, *Violations of Human Rights*, 93–98.

58. Richard Burt, "Cutoff of Arms to Chile Sparks British Dispute," *Christian Science Monitor*, 12 April 1974.

59. Cassese, "Chile – A Case Study," 252–54.

60. Terri Shaw, "Chile Faces Problem on Debt Talks," *Washington Post*, 7 April 1975.

61. Muñoz, *Gobierno Militar Chileno*, 21.

62. Muñoz, *Gobierno Militar Chileno*, passim.

63. "Duplicidad de la NU," *Ercilla*, 26 November 1974, 11.

64. "Actas de la Junta," no. 122, May 13, 1974.

65. For a detailed look at some of Chile's failed lobbying attempts in the U.S. Congress, see Schoultz, *Human Rights and United States Policy*, 52–58.

66. "Actas de la Junta," no. 126, May 27, 1974.

67. Malú Sierra, *Ercilla*, August, 1975. Reprinted in Correa, Sierra, and Subercaseaux, *Generales del Régimen*, 7–21.

68. Raquel Correa, *Vea*, 1 August 1974. Reprinted in Correa, Sierra, and Subercaseaux, *Generales del Régimen*, 95–101.

69. Orellana, "Derechos Humanos en Chile," 14.

70. Lowden, *Moral Opposition*, 47–51.

71. Constable and Valenzuela, *Nation of Enemies*, 153.

72. "La Conjura Contra Chile," *Qué Pasa*, 21 November 1974; "Duplicidad," *Ercilla*, 21 November 1974.

73. "Duplicidad," *Ercilla*, 21 November 1974; also Muñoz, *Gobierno Militar Chileno*, 37–38.

74. "Actas de la Junta," no. 150, August 29, 1974.

75. "Actas de la Junta," no. 153, September 5, 1974.

76. The speech by Foreign Minister Ismael Huerta is reproduced in the government pamphlet *Realidad y Destino de Chile* (Santiago: Editora Nacional Gabriela Mistral, n.d.).

77. Arturo Valenzuela, "Origins, Consolidation, and Breakdown," 160.

78. Constable and Valenzuela, *Nation of Enemies*, 29–31.

79. Arturo Valenzuela and J. Samuel Valenzuela, "Party Oppositions," 208–9.

80. Brian Smith, "Old Allies, New Enemies," 274–75.

81. Barrera and Valenzuela, "Labor Movement Opposition to the Military Regime," 230–69.

82. Among moderate sectors, many Catholic bishops and prominent Christian Democrats initially believed that the military coup was necessary to end social chaos and restore order. See Loveman, "Military Dictatorship,"

16; Lowden, *Moral Opposition*, 71–72; and Smith, "Old Allies, New Enemies," 287–94.

83. Interview with a former cabinet official in the military government, April 1994. The essence of this quote was confirmed by other civilian elites and military officials.

84. Remmer, "Political Demobilization," 277–82.

85. Garretón, "Political Opposition and the Party System," 214.

86. Remmer, "Neopatrimonialism," 152–60.

87. Arturo Valenzuela, *Breakdown of Democratic Regimes: Chile*, 55–72; Foxley, "Neoconservative Economic Experiment," 13–50.

88. Silva, "Political Economy of Chile's Regime Transition," 102.

89. Foxley, "Neoconservative Economic Experiment," 16–17.

90. Oppenheim, *Politics in Chile*, 116–23.

91. O'Donnell and Schmitter, *Uncertain Democracies*, 15–17.

92. I base this assessment on a thorough review of the most important Chilean print media sources in these years, an examination of the minutes of the junta meetings, and an examination of some of the personal documents in the possession of the Fundación Jaime Guzmán.

93. Guzmán, *Escritos Personales*, 146–47.

94. Correa, Sierra, and Subercaseaux, *Generales del Régimen*, 11.

95. The commission's minutes and official documents may be found in the *Actas Oficiales de la Comisión Constituyente*. The commission met a few times before it was formally created by decree 1,064 on October 25, 1973 (published November 12, 1973 in the *Diario Oficial de la República de Chile*).

96. Found in the *Actas Oficiales de la Comisión Constituyente*.

97. See the speech by Enrique Ortúzar to mark the commission's one-year anniversary, published in *El Mercurio*, 9 November 1974.

98. "Enrique Ortúzar y Su Constitución," *Ercilla*, 14 July 1976.

99. Barnes, "Slaughterhouse in Santiago," 53–54.

100. "Actas de la Junta," no. 112, April 15, 1974.

101. Phil Gailey, "Kennedy Proposes 'No Hurry' To Aid New Chilean Regime," *Miami Herald*, 30 September 1973.

102. Schoultz, *Human Rights and United States Policy*, 200; Sigmund, *United States and Democracy in Chile*, 102–3.

103. Table 2; see also Letelier and Moffitt, "Supporting Repression."

104. Terri Shaw, "Chile Gets Disputed Loan from Inter-American Bank," *Washington Post*, 2 April 1974, and "Chile Gets Loans after Three-Year Ban," 26 April 1974.

105. See table 2.

106. Muñoz, *Gobierno Militar Chileno*, 21–33.

107. Stockholm International Peace Research Institute (SIPRI), *World Armaments and Disarmament, 1973–1980.*

108. McAdam, McCarthy, and Zald, "Perspective on Social Movements," 6.

3. CHANGING DISCOURSE

1. Fruhling, "Stages of Repression," 529.

2. Garretón, "Institutionalization and Opposition in Chile," 160.

3. Arturo Valenzuela, "Military in Power," 21–72.

4. Lowden, *Moral Opposition*, 53–69; Brian H. Smith, *Church and Politics in Chile*, 318–19.

5. Lowden, *Moral Opposition*, 56.

6. Hawkins, "Human Rights Norms and Networks."

7. Smith, *Church and Politics in Chile*, 325.

8. Smith, *Church and Politics in Chile*, 325–6.

9. Lowden, *Moral Opposition*, 133, 163.

10. Orellana, "Derechos Humanos en Chile," 40–41; Fruhling and Orellana, "Organismos No Gubernamentales de Derechos Humanos," 40–47.

11. Fruhling and Orellana, "Organismos No Gubernamentales de Derechos Humanos," 40–41.

12. Orellana, "Derechos Humanos en Chile," 26–31.

13. Fruhling and Orellana, "Organismos No Gubernamentales de Derechos Humanos," 45–47; Vidal, *Dar la Vida por la Vida*, 100–117.

14. Orellana, "Derechos Humanos en Chile," 26–29; Hutchison, "Movimiento de Derechos Humanos," 96–102.

15. Lowden, *Moral Opposition*, 80.

16. Angell, "International Support for the Chilean Opposition"; Montupil, ed., *Exilio, Derechos Humanos, y Democracia.*

17. Orellana, "Derechos Humanos en Chile," 40.

18. Angell, "International Support for the Chilean Opposition," 14–20.

19. Keck and Sikkink, *Activists beyond Borders*, 90–91.

20. Medina, *Battle of Human Rights.*

21. Vargas, "El Caso Chileno," 31–59.

22. Schoultz, *Human Rights and United States Policy*, 87–88.

23. Muñoz, *Gobierno Militar Chileno*, 26; Sigmund, *United States and Democracy in Chile*, 104; Cavallo, Salazar, and Sepúlveda, *Chile*, 149–50.

24. Lucy Kosimar, "Declassified Cable Shows Kissinger Abetted Pinochet," *London Observer*, 1 March 1999.

25. Schoultz, *Human Rights and United States Policy*, 75-83.

26. Schoultz, *Human Rights and United States Policy*, 201-2; Sigmund, *United States and Democracy in Chile*, 104; Salzberg and Young, "Parliamentary Role in Implementing International Human Rights," 265.

27. The best analyses of this incident are found in Dinges and Landau, *Assassination on Embassy Row*; and Branch and Propper, *Labyrinth*. My own research confirmed the details of these books with respect to the repercussions within the military government. A brief summary of the case may be found in Sigmund, *United States and Democracy in Chile*, 111-18.

28. Garretón, "Institutionalization and Opposition in Chile"; Arriagada, "Armed Forces in Chile," 117-43; Arriagada, *Pinochet*.

29. Useful overviews of nationalist thought may be found in Rodríguez, "Democracia Liberal o Democracia Orgánica?" 1-20; Rodríguez, "Poder Político y Poder Social," 17-26; Acuña, Willoughby, and Rodríguez, *Qué es el Nacionalismo Hoy?*

30. For a summary of their thought, see Guzmán, *Escritos Personales*. For an account of their rise in Chile, see Salazar, *Guzmán*. This split was only one of several fault lines running through the authoritarian government, and not all government officials fell into one camp or another. These factions were, however, the most important ones debating the political future of the government.

31. Vergara, *Auge y Caída del Neoliberalismo en Chile*.

32. See chapter 4 for a detailed discussion of the evolution of the constitution.

33. Interview with a former cabinet minister, March 1, 1994. See also Valenzuela, "Military in Power," 42-50, and Salazar, *Guzmán*, 210.

34. Interview with former cabinet minister, March 14, 1994. See also Cavallo, Salazar, and Sepúlveda, *Chile*, 192-93.

35. Valdés, *Pinochet's Economists*, 34.

36. Foxley, "Neoconservative Economic Experiment," 15-17.

37. Letelier and Moffitt, "Supporting Repression," 111-28; Somavía and Valdés, "Relaciones entre los Gobiernos de Estados Unidos y Chile," 255-77.

38. Chilean National Commission on Truth and Reconciliation, *Report of the Chilean National Commission*, 453, 620-21.

39. Cavallo, Salazar, and Sepúlveda, *Chile*, 52-60, 114-22.

40. Chilean National Commission on Truth and Reconciliation, *Report of the Chilean National Commission*, 620-21.

41. "Mensaje del Presidente Pinochet," El Mercurio, 12 September 1975.

42. "El Gobierno Se Presenta ante el País con la Frente en Alto," El Cronista, 12 September 1976.

43. The three acts are designated Two, Three, and Four because a previous Constitutional Act had been introduced in January with the purpose of setting up a Council of State in which distinguished Chileans could discuss matters of importance to the government.

44. Of 103 national constitutions from sixteen Spanish American nations in the 1800s, only two did not include provisions for governments of exception. See Loveman, Constitution of Tyranny, 378. Most Latin American constitutions in the mid- to late 1900s continued to carry such clauses.

45. Loveman, Constitution of Tyranny, 351–53.

46. See "Los Argumentos de Jaime Guzmán," Ercilla, 30 June 1976; and Enrique Ortúzar, "La Nueva Institucionalidad," Revista de Carabineros, May 1976.

47. Cavallo, Sepúlveda and Salazar, Chile, 165.

48. For an alternative account of the role of international pressures during the drafting of the Constitutional Acts, see Barros, "By Reason and Force," 197–209. Barros acknowledges the importance of international pressures, but emphasizes politics within the junta.

49. "Actas de la Junta," nos. 280-A and 281-A.

50. "Actas de la Junta," no. 280-A, 18–19.

51. "Actas de la Junta," no. 280-A, 36–46.

52. "Actas de la Junta," no. 280-A, 44.

53. "Actas de la Junta," no. 280-A, 199.

54. "Actas de la Junta," no. 281-A, 1.

55. "Actas de la Junta," no. 280-A, 180–200.

56. "Actas de la Junta," no. 280-A, 176. In this case, I have used the translation of Barros, "By Reason and Force," 205.

57. Portions of this section were first published in Hawkins, "Domestic Responses to International Pressures," 403–34.

58. Branch and Propper, Labyrinth, 303–27.

59. Constable and Valenzuela, Nation of Enemies, 56.

60. Cavallo, Salazar, and Sepúlveda, Chile, 42–50.

61. Marras, Confesiones, 29–30.

62. Valenzuela, "Military in Power," 48–49.

63. Cavallo, Salazar, and Sepúlveda, Chile, 138–39.

64. On the compatibility of neoliberal economic ideas and repression, see Pion-Berlin, Ideology of State Terror, 1–10.

65. Curry and Horowitz, *Subsidizing Pinochet*; Sigmund, *United States and Democracy in Chile*, 109.

66. Cohen, "Human Rights Diplomacy," 212–41; Somavía and Valdés, "Relaciones entre los Gobiernos de Estados Unidos y Chile," 256.

67. Dinges and Landau, *Assassination on Embassy Row*, 332.

68. Cavallo, Salazar, and Sepúlveda, *Chile*, 195–96.

69. Quoted in *Análisis*, 4 May 1987.

70. Interview, March 14, 1994. Guzmán himself also took some credit in 1989 for the end of the DINA when testifying before a judge at a related criminal investigation.

71. Interview, March 1, 1994.

72. Interview, March 15, 1994.

73. See Marras, *Confesiones*, 79. One of the most important changes in the CNI was its new place in the bureaucracy under the Interior Ministry. Previously, the law specified that the DINA answered to the junta, which in practice meant Pinochet.

74. Interview, March 30, 1994.

75. Interview, March 7, 1994.

76. Curry and Horowitz, *Subsidizing Pinochet*.

77. Curry and Horowitz, *Subsidizing Pinochet*.

78. Barrera and Valenzuela, "Labor Movement Opposition to the Military Regime," 243–48.

79. Barrera and Valenzuela, "Labor Movement Opposition to the Military Regime," 248–58.

80. Valenzuela and Valenzuela, "Party Oppositions," 207–12.

81. Valenzuela and Valenzuela, "Party Oppositions," 218–19.

82. Chilean National Commission on Truth and Reconciliation, *Report of the Chilean National Commission*, 636.

83. Fruhling, "Stages of Repression," 529.

84. Chilean National Commission on Truth and Reconciliation, *Report of the Chilean National Commission*, 636.

85. In the 1980s, state-sponsored violence came in waves, usually in response to open demonstrations of opposition strength. The CNI lost some of its new-found professionalism after 1981 as open opposition increased and reformers lost ground to hardliners. At the same time, the government was forced to liberalize its rule in the 1980s, tolerating opposition media, political parties, and labor activism to a degree not seen since the coup.

86. Garretón, "Institutionalization and Opposition in Chile."

87. See chapters 4 and 5.

88. Garretón, "Popular Mobilization and the Military Regime in Chile," 259–77; Garretón, "Political Opposition and the Party System," 211–50.

89. Cavallo, Salazar, and Sepúlveda, Chile, 212–20.

90. Valenzuela, "Military in Power," 42–49.

4. BUILDING NEW POLITICAL INSTITUTIONS

1. Garretón, "Political Opposition and the Party System," 211–50; Arturo Valenzuela, "Chile: Origins and Consolidation," 104–10.

2. A number of sources provide information on the history of the 1980 Constitution. The best basic legal sources – containing the 1980 Constitution, official drafts, concordances, annotations, related laws and jurisprudence, and the 1925 Constitution – are Blanc, Constitución Chilena; and Bulnes, Constitución Política de la República de Chile. A brief history of the drafting process is found in Carrasco, Textos Constitucionales Chilenos. The minutes from drafting committee meetings are recorded in "Actas del Consejo del Estado" (unpublished, located in Chile's National Library) and Actas Oficiales de la Comisión Constituyente. Other official documents related to the drafting process may be found in Revista Chilena de Derecho, 8, nos. 1–6 (January-December 1981).

3. Reprinted in the pamphlet Realidad y Destino de Chile, (Santiago: Editora Nacional Gabriela Mistral, n.d.).

4. "Actas de la Junta," no. 1, September 13, 1973.

5. Carrasco, Textos Constitucionales Chilenos, 86–87.

6. Carrasco, Alessandri, 117.

7. Francisco Bulnes, a distinguished and popular conservative politician who had a long career studying constitutional reform in the Senate, was an obvious choice for committee membership but was excluded. He and other former senators formed their own group to study constitutional reforms but never gained any influence in the junta. Interview, April 6 and 12, 1994.

8. "Metas Fundamentales para la Nueva Constitución," found in the Actas Oficiales de la Comisión Constituyente.

9. "Metas u Objetivos Fundamentales para la Nueva Constitución Política de la República," found in the Actas Oficiales de la Comisión Constituyente.

10. Carrasco, Textos Constitucionales Chilenos, 89–91.

11. Ortúzar made a public appearance to commemorate a year of work by the commission on November 8, 1974, but his comments showed few

if any advances in the commission's work. See "Nueva Constitución Será Moderna y Auténticamente Chilena," El Mercurio, 9 November 1974.

12. Carrasco, Textos Constitucionales Chilenos, 89–90.

13. Cavallo, Salazar, and Sepúlveda, Chile, 109.

14. See Ortúzar, "La Nueva Institucionalidad," Revista de Carabineros, May 1976 and "Enrique Ortúzar y Su Constitución," Ercilla, 14 July 1976.

15. "El Gobierno Se Presenta ante el País con la Frente en Alto," El Cronista, 12 September 1976.

16. The speech is reproduced in Contador, ed., Continuismo y Discontinuismo en Chile.

17. See "La Normalización Institucional," El Mercurio, 17 July 1977; "Etapas y Fechas en Vía Institucional," Hoy, 13 July 1977; "El Futuro Político de Chile," Hoy, 20 July 1977; and "Los Anuncios del Once," Hoy, 24 August 1977.

18. Interview, March 1, 1994.

19. Arturo Valenzuela, interview with Jaime Guzmán, December 3, 1985, Santiago, Chile; confirmed by author's interviews in April 1994 with other government officials close to Pinochet.

20. Arturo Valenzuela, interview with Jaime Guzmán.

21. See Cosas, July 1980; and Cavallo, Salazar, and Sepúlveda, Chile, 311–12.

22. "Las Críticas de Pablo Rodríguez," Ercilla, June 23, 1976; Rodríguez, "Democracia Liberal o Democracia Orgánica" and "Duros y Blandos Opinan," Qué Pasa, 17–23 July 1980. These individuals continued supporting corporatist solutions well into the 1980s. See Acuña, Willoughby, and Rodríguez, Qué Es el Nacionalismo Hoy?; and Rodríguez, "Poder Político y Poder Social," 17–26.

23. "Los Argumentos de Jaime Guzmán," Ercilla, 30 June 1976; Jorge Ovalle, "Sentido y Propósito de la Nueva Institucionalidad," Seguridad Nacional, no. 3, November-December 1976; Sergio Diez, "Las Elecciones Son el Final del Camino," Cosas, 14 April 1977; Ortúzar, "La Nueva Institucionalidad," Revista de Carabineros, May 1976; and "Enrique Ortúzar y Su Constitución," Ercilla, 14 July 1976.

24. Reprinted in Comisión de Estudio de la Nueva Constitución Política de la República de Chile (Constitutional Commission), Anteproyecto Constitucional y Sus Fundamentos.

25. Carrasco, Textos Constitucionales Chilenos, 92.

26. Cavallo, Salazar, and Sepúlveda, Chile, 161–66, 310–11.

27. Interview, March 1, 1994.

28. The memo was included as a separate document in the commission's

official version of its draft constitution, found in Constitutional Commission, *Anteproyecto Constitucional*, 1–12.

29. Carrasco, *Alessandri*, 119–20.

30. Carrasco, *Allesandri*.

31. Quoted in "Incógnita en la Generación de los Poderes Políticos," *Ercilla*, 18 May 1977,

32. See various articles in *El Mercurio*, 17 July 1977, and *Hoy*, 13 and 20 July 1977.

33. The commission's original deadline of May 21 was later extended to August 20.

34. Bulnes, *Constitución Política de la República de Chile*.

35. Fernández, *Mi Lucha por la Democracia*, 112–16.

36. Interview, March 1, 1994.

37. See the minutes of the Council of State, "Actas de Sesiones del Consejo del Estado," which are not published but are available in photocopy form in the National Library and in the law library of the Catholic University of Chile.

38. Interview, March 1, 1994.

39. Fernández, *Mi Lucha por la Democracia*, 114.

40. See Cavallo, Salazar, and Sepúlveda, *Chile*, 313–20; Fernández, *Mi Lucha por la Democracia*, 146–47; and "Transición: Una Historia Secreta," *Qué Pasa*, 26 March 1987. Interestingly, in the minutes of the Council of State, Alessandri reports that he met with Pinochet in March 1980 and offered to withdraw the council's discussion of a transition period in deference to Pinochet and the junta. Pinochet insisted that he was still interested in the council's opinion, and so the council continued to draft transition articles even though the junta later ignored them.

41. A comparison between the junta's transitional articles and those proposed by the Council of State may be found in Carrasco, *Alessandri*, 203–13.

42. Carrasco, *Alessandri*, 135–45.

43. I reach this conclusion based on an examination of the minutes of the drafting commissions and a variety of interviews with their members.

44. Interview, March 1, 1994.

45. In addition, an inter-American labor organization with strong support from the AFL-CIO threatened to boycott Chile due to its abuse of labor rights, but the threat dissipated when Chile implemented some half measures. See Barrera and Valenzuela, "Labor Movement Opposition to the Military Regime," 248–58. The boycott threat did not significantly affect

the content or timing of the constitution, the regime's future plans, or the broader scope of human rights abuses in Chile.

46. Lowden, *Moral Opposition*, 85.

47. Fruhling and Orellana, "Organismos No Gubernamentales de Derechos Humanos," 42.

48. Hutchison, "Movimiento de Derechos Humanos," 104–5; Pagnucco, "Transnational Strategies."

49. Cavallo, Salazar, and Sepúlveda, *Chile*, 256–64.

50. Cavallo, Salazar, and Sepúlveda, *Chile*, 260–64; Lowden, *Moral Opposition*, 81–84.

51. Lowden, *Moral Opposition*, 79–84.

52. Vidal, *Dar la Vida por la Vida*, 105–9, 154–92.

53. Barrera and Valenzuela, "Labor Movement Opposition to the Military Regime," 243–48.

54. Oxhorn, *Organizing Civil Society*, 106–42.

55. Interview, March 14, 1994.

56. Interview, March 30, 1994.

57. Interview, March 15, 1994.

58. Interview, March 1, 1994.

59. "El Once de Septiembre y el Nuevo Régimen Político-Institucional," undated speech filed in the Jaime Guzmán Foundation. Although undated, the content of the speech suggests it was given in mid- to late 1977, and the speech is filed in the 1977 folder at the foundation.

60. Interview, March 14, 1994.

61. Muñoz, *Gobierno Militar Chileno.*

62. Interview, March 15, 1994.

63. Interview, March 30, 1994.

64. Interview, March 7, 1994.

65. Interview, March 14, 1994.

66. Interview, March 14, 1994.

67. "Actas del Consejo del Estado," November 14, 1978.

68. "Actas del Consejo del Estado," November 21, 1978.

69. Leigh's history, including copies of his memos and speeches, may be found in Florencia Varas, *Gustavo Leigh*. An account of his sudden dismissal from the junta is in Cavallo, Salazar and Sepúlveda, *Chile*, 222–32.

70. Florencia Varas, *Gustavo Leigh*, 153–65.

71. "El Once de Septiembre y el Nuevo Régimen Político-Institucional," undated speech filed in the Jaime Guzmán Foundation.

72. Fernández, *Mi Lucha por la Democracia*, 23–24.

73. Cavallo, Salazar, and Sepúlveda, *Chile*, 212–14.

74. Interviews with former military officials and junta aides, March and April 1994.

75. This argument complements Forsythe's observation that many Latin American military regimes have faced difficulties justifying long-term rule in the face of their republics' long-standing declarations of allegiance to human rights principles. See Forsythe, "Human Rights, the United States and the Organization of American States."

76. Untitled memo, filed in the Jaime Guzmán Foundation, with a probable date of January 1979.

77. Interview, March 1, 1994.

78. José Piñera, "Dar un Golpe de Timón, Crear Esquemas Nuevos . . . ," *Qué Pasa*, 27 December 1979.

79. Cavallo, Salazar, and Sepúlveda, *Chile*, 207–10.

80. Cavallo, Salazar, and Sepúlveda, *Chile*, 244–54.

81. Barrera and Valenzuela, "Labor Movement Opposition to the Military Regime," 243–44.

82. Oxhorn, *Organizing Civil Society*, 96–99.

83. Garretón, "Political Opposition and the Party System," 214–16.

84. Garretón, "Institutionalization and Opposition in Chile," 144–83.

85. Arturo Valenzuela, "Military in Power," 21–72.

86. Munck, *Authoritarianism and Democratization*, 98.

87. Muñoz, "Chile: The Limits of Success," 43.

88. Portales, "External Factors and the Authoritarian Regime," 254.

89. J. Samuel Valenzuela and Arturo Valenzuela, introduction to *Military Rule in Chile*, 1–12.

90. Valenzuela, "Military in Power," 54.

91. Garretón, "Institutionalization and Opposition in Chile," 151.

5. LEGITIMACY AND ELECTIONS IN THE 1980S

1. For a summary of conditions in 1978 and 1980, see the Inter-American Commission on Human Rights, *Report on the Situation of Human Rights in Chile*.

2. International Commission of the Latin American Studies Association to Observe the Chilean Plebiscite, "Chilean Plebiscite," 25–29.

3. Cavallo, Salazar, and Sepúlveda, *Chile*, 566–88.

4. Silva, "Political Economy of Chile's Regime Transition," 107–9.

5. Garretón, "Popular Mobilization and the Military Regime in Chile," 259-77; Garretón, "Political Opposition and the Party System," 211-50.

6. "Posible Anticipación de Partidos y Parlamento," El Mercurio, 12 September 1983.

7. El Mercurio, "Posible Anticipación."

8. Vidal, Sebatián Acevedo.

9. Hutchison, "Movimiento de Derechos Humanos," 109-12.

10. Medina, Battle of Human Rights, 294-311.

11. Vargas, "El Caso Chileno."

12. Muñoz and Portales, Elusive Friendship, 63-82.

13. Muñoz and Portales, Elusive Friendship, 70-82; Sigmund, United States and Democracy in Chile, 154-78.

14. Sigmund, United States and Democracy in Chile, 168; Adams, "Generalized System of Preferences from Chile."

15. Garretón, "Political Opposition and the Party System," 223.

16. The full text was published in El Mercurio, 25-26 August 1985.

17. The language comes from American Convention on Human Rights, Article 23.

18. Whelan, Out of the Ashes, 859.

19. Keck and Sikkink, Activists beyond Borders, 2-10.

20. Angell, "International Support for the Chilean Opposition." Finding data on the international support for political groups is even more difficult than support for academic and human rights organizations. The range of potential donors is so large – from German and Italian political parties to the Ford Foundation – and the number of different recipients so vast – from individual leaders and small-scale community groups to grassroots voter registration movements and political parties – that compiling aggregate figures involves significant guesswork. Further, both international and domestic groups are understandably worried about releasing such figures. On the other hand, the funds were often appropriated by foreign governments and channeled through state-affiliated organizations and thus are matters of public record. Likewise, international funding of the Chilean opposition became such a salient issue in Chile that some scholars, journalists, and NGOs investigated and provided crucial information. A particularly comprehensive account may be found in an article titled "Money: Black, White . . . and Political," El Mercurio, 24 January 1988.

21. Pinto-Duschinsky, "Foreign Political Aid," 33-35.

22. Pinto-Duschinsky, "Foreign Political Aid," 38-40.

23. For example, Italian political groups apparently provided $20 million

to Chilean NGOs between 1987 and 1992, including $9 million that Chilean leftist parties allegedly spent directly on campaign expenses during the 1989 parliamentary and presidential elections in Chile. See "La Larga Mano Italiana," Qué Pasa, 14 May 1994.

24. Puryear, "Building Democracy."

25. Puryear, "Building Democracy," 6; Sigmund, United States and Democracy in Chile, 167–74.

26. International Human Rights Law Group, Chile: The Plebiscite and Beyond.

27. Cavallo, Salazar, and Sepúlveda, Chile, 566–88.

28. Fernández, Mi Lucha por la Democracia, 287.

29. Cavallo, Salazar, and Sepúlveda, Chile, 480–85.

30. "Informa sobre Ley Orgánica Constitucional del Tribunal Calificador de Elecciones (Boletín 548–06)," 26 November 1984, in "Transcripciones y Antecedentes de las Leyes."

31. "Actas de la Junta," no. 13/85, June 11, 1985.

32. Barros, "By Reason and Force," 317, n. 59.

33. Zapata, "Jurisprudencia," 295–97.

34. Eugenio Valenzuela, Repertorio, 185.

35. "Reglas para el Juego," Hoy, 30 September 1985.

36. "Actas de la Junta," no. 14/83-E, June 16, 1983.

37. "Actas de la Junta," no. 14/83-E, June 16, 1983, 4.

38. "Actas de la Junta," no. 14/83-E, June 16, 1983, 8.

39. "Actas de la Junta," no. 14/83-E, June 16, 1983, 12. I rely here on the translation provided by Barros, "By Reason and Force," 300.

40. See "Actas de la Junta," nos. 9/84-E, May 16, 1984; 22/84-E, August 30, 1984; and 31/84, November 6, 1984.

41. "Actas de la Junta," no. 38/86, December 2, 1986.

42. International Human Rights Law Group, Plebiscite, 34.

43. "El 'Primer Elector' del País," El Mercurio, 7 August 1988.

44. See the 1980 Constitution, Transitional Articles 15 and 24.

45. I make this claim based on a series of interviews with former officials in the Interior Ministry and the secretary general of the government, April-May, 1994.

46. Cea, "Plebiscito de 1988," 92–98.

47. International Human Rights Law Group, Plebiscite, 32.

48. Zapata, "Jurisprudencia," 308–12.

49. "Actas de la Junta," no. 22/88, August 2, 1988.

50. "La Política 'Clip,' " Hoy, 15 August 1988, 27.

51. Cea, "Plebiscito de 1988," 84–90.

52. "Estrategia Puesta a Prueba," *Hoy*, 9 November 1987.

53. "Entre el Drama y la Incertidumbre," *Hoy*, 6 July 1987.

54. Although Merino repeated this argument on several occasions, the Chilean constitution placed no clear limits on moving up the date of the plebiscite.

55. Cea, "Plebiscito de 1988," 89.

56. "El Plebiscito No Será Adelantado," *El Mercurio*, 8 November 1987.

57. "Plebiscito: Fin del Suspenso," *Hoy*, 11 July 1988.

58. Cavallo, Salazar, and Sepúlveda, *Chile*, 561–62.

59. Interviews, March 17 and 25, 1994.

60. This information is based on numerous interviews with former officials in the Interior Ministry and the secretary general of the government, April-May, 1994.

61. Arturo Valenzuela, "Chile: Origins and Consolidation," 108.

62. Although these editorials did not represent official military policy, they reflected the common beliefs of the institution's high command and were not published lightly.

63. *Memorial del Ejército*, no. 428, January-April 1988.

64. *Memorial del Ejército*, no. 430, September-December 1988.

65. Interview, March 7, 1994.

66. Angell, "Unions and Workers," 192–93.

67. María Elena Valenzuela, "Evolving Roles of Women," 161–87.

68. Oxhorn, *Organizing Civil Society*, 99.

69. "El Líder Que los Chilenos Buscan," *Hoy*, 15 July 1985.

70. Augusto Varas, "Crisis of Legitimacy," 84.

71. "La Caída de Mendoza," *Hoy*, 5 August 1985.

72. Larraín, "Economic Challenges," 287.

73. "Los Conceptos del Ministro Cuadra," *El Mercurio*, 17 November 1985.

74. For examples of hardline thought in the 1980s, see "En los Tribunales de la Política," *El Mercurio*, 17 July 1988; "Si Pinochet Es o No Demócrata, Lo Va a Decir la Historia," *Cosas*, November 1984; and the speech by Justice Minister Hugo Rosende on the fourth anniversary of the effective date of the constitution, *El Mercurio*, 12 March 1985.

75. Interview, November 24, 1993.

76. Numerous interviews and speeches offer insights into their ideas and strategies, of which I offer only a sampling. For Fernández, see "A Completar la Constitución," *El Mercurio*, 26 May 1985; for García, see the speeches

reprinted in *El Mercurio*, 13 March 1985 and 12 March 1986; for Jarpa, see the extensive interview published in *El Mercurio*, September 1983.

77. Cavallo, Salazar, and Sepúlveda, *Chile*, 405–6.

78. See the interview with General Jorge Ballerino, *Cosas*, 30 October 1986, and a variety of other interviews with military generals in *Cosas* from 1984 to 1988.

79. Interview with a former official in the Interior Ministry, March 9, 1994.

80. "Ganar Tiempo en Marcha Lenta," *Hoy*, 8 October 1984.

81. Cavallo, Salazar, and Sepúlveda, *Chile*, 480–83.

82. International Commission of the Latin American Studies Association, "Chilean Plebiscite," 20.

83. See, for example, Fernández, *Mi Lucha por la Democracia*, 254–77.

84. International Commission of the Latin American Studies Association, "Chilean Plebiscite"; Arturo Valenzuela, "Chile: Origins and Consolidation," 107–8.

6. CHILE IN INTERNATIONAL AND COMPARATIVE PERSPECTIVE

1. Krasner, "Sovereignty, Regimes, and Human Rights," 139–67; Mearsheimer, "False Promise."

2. I thank David Forsythe for suggesting this language.

3. King, Keohane, and Verba, *Designing Social Inquiry*, 137–42.

4. King, Keohane, and Verba, *Designing Social Inquiry*, 129–30.

5. King, Keohane, and Verba, *Designing Social Inquiry*, 217–28.

6. Garretón, "Institutionalization and Opposition in Chile," 144–83.

7. Hufbauer, Schott, and Elliott, *Economic Sanctions Reconsidered*, vol. 2, 194–204.

8. Eckstein, *Back from the Future*, 88–93.

9. Del Aguila, *Cuba*, 154–65.

10. Forment, "Political Practice"; Ackerman, "Strategic Calculation."

11. García, *Havana USA*, 146–56; Moreno, "The Cuban Model," 220–23.

12. Two of the most important groups include Cuba Independiente y Democrática and the Junta Patriótica Cubana, which is itself a coalition of dozens of organizations.

13. This information is based on a series of interviews with the leaders of several pro-embargo NGOs conducted in late 1998. See also García, *Havana USA*, 149–50.

14. Telephone interview with Adolfo Leyva, director of the Endowment for Cuban-American Studies of CANF, December 8, 1998.

15. Domínguez, "U.S.-Cuban Relations," 60–65.

16. Erisman, "U.S.-Cuban Relations," 58–59.

17. Erisman, "U.S.-Cuban Relations," 63–69.

18. "Anti-Castro Exiles Won Limit on Changes in U.S. policy," *New York Times*, 6 January 1999.

19. Ackerman, "Strategic Calculation," 8–9.

20. Moderate U.S.-based groups that were either founded or re-energized in the 1990s include Cambio Cubano, the Cuban Committee for Democracy, the Social Democrats, the Christian Democrats, and the Cuban Liberal Union. See García, *Havana USA*, 164–67; Castro, "Ideology of Exile," 98–101.

21. This observation is based on interviews with officials from several pro-engagement NGOs conducted in late 1998. See also Martínez, *Cuba Disidente*, 48–51, 60–63.

22. Amnesty International (AI), in particular, maintains lists of political prisoners and provides them to foreign dignitaries visiting Cuba. Author's telephone interview with Carlos Salinas, advocacy director for Latin America and the Caribbean for AI, United States, on December 1, 1998.

23. Domínguez, "Leadership Strategies," 1.

24. Del Aguila, "Process of Counterreform," 19–40.

25. Amnesty International, *Government Crackdown on Dissent*; Amnesty International, *Cuba*; Human Rights Watch, *Improvements without Reform*.

26. Eckstein, *Back from the Future*, 119–26.

27. Domínguez, "Cuba in the International Community," 298.

28. Del Aguila, "Process of Counterreform," 27–30.

29. Eckstein, *Back from the Future*, 18–19.

30. De la Fuente and Glasco, "Are Blacks 'Getting out of Control'?" 53–71; Domínguez, "Castro's Staying Power"; Pérez-Stable, "Vanguard Party Politics in Cuba," 67–85; Wayne S. Smith, "Cuba's Long Reform."

31. Del Aguila, "Process of Counterreform," 30–33. It is of course difficult – but not impossible – to diagnose the presence of rule-oriented officials in an authoritarian government because individual leaders are under strong pressure to preserve unanimity. Nevertheless, rule-oriented officials in other countries have floated reform ideas or quietly changed government policies within their area of responsibility in ways that make them identifiable.

32. I make this assessment based on a review of the Cuban press in re-

cent months and years. Although the Cuban media often fully reproduce the text of the speeches of the Castro brothers and other top leaders, observers search in vain for hints of reform ideas. The most important media sources are *Granma, Juventud Rebelde, Trabajadores,* and *Bohemia.*

33. Schulz, "Can Castro Survive?" 104–5.

34. Giuliano, *El Caso* CEA.

35. "Informe del Buró Político," printed in *Granma,* 27 March 1996.

36. Cardoso and Helwege, *Cuba after Communism.*

37. Carmelo Mesa-Lago, "Cambio de Régimen," 36–43; Pérez-López, "Cuban Economy."

38. Klotz, *Norms in International Relations.*

39. Klotz, "Norms and Sanctions," 184–88.

40. Grundy, *South Africa;* Geldenhuys, *Isolated States.*

41. Hufbauer, Schott, and Elliott, *Economic Sanctions Reconsidered,* vol. 2, 226–238.

42. O'Meara, *Forty Lost Years,* 150.

43. Price, *Apartheid State,* 39–40.

44. Black, "Long and Winding Road," 87.

45. Black, "Long and Winding Road," 87.

46. Mangaliso, "Disinvestment," 145–58.

47. Price, *Apartheid State,* 220–36.

48. Price, *Apartheid State,* 225.

49. O'Meara, *Forty Lost Years,* 188; Price, *Apartheid State,* 242–45.

50. Price, *Apartheid State,* 145–46.

51. Price, *Apartheid State,* 101.

52. Johnstone, "South Africa," 350.

53. Black, "Long and Winding Road," 92–93; Price, *Apartheid State,* 190–219.

54. Price, *Apartheid State,* 93.

55. Price, *Apartheid State,* 251–63.

56. Price, *Apartheid State,* 250.

57. Grundy, *South Africa,* 113–17; Price, *Apartheid State,* 276–78.

58. Price, *Apartheid State,* 278.

59. Price, *Apartheid State,* 275–78.

60. Sisk, *Democratization in South Africa,* 81–85.

61. Black, "Long and Winding Road," 98–99.

62. Lowden, *Moral Opposition,* 125–28.

63. Chilean National Commission on Truth and Reconciliation, *Report of the Chilean National Commission.*

64. A variety of journalistic and legal sources offer details on the ongoing pursuit of Pinochet. The most helpful, from which the information in the following paragraphs is drawn, include: Peter Kornbluh, "Prisoner Pinochet: The Dictator and the Quest for Justice," *The Nation*, 4 December 1998; Marguerite Feitlowitz, "Prosecuting Latin America's Dirty Wars," *Dissent*, spring 1999; Marc Cooper, "Chile and the End of Pinochet," *The Nation*, 26 February 2001; O'Shaughnessy, *Pinochet*, 1–5, 157–74; Wilson, "Prosecuting Pinochet"; and Oppenheim, *Politics in Chile*, 210–16.

65. Pape, "Why Economic Sanctions Do Not Work."

66. Hufbauer, Schott, and Elliott, *Economic Sanctions Reconsidered*, vol. 1, 91–115.

67. Hufbauer, Schott, and Elliott, *Economic Sanctions Reconsidered*, vol. 1, 102.

68. Drezner, "Conflict Expectations," 700–731.

69. Risse and Ropp also advocate this policy conclusion. See Risse and Ropp, "International Human Rights Norms," 276.

70. Evans, Jacobson, and Putnam, eds., *Double-Edged Diplomacy*; Putnam, "Diplomacy and Domestic Politics," 427–60.

71. Putnam, "Diplomacy and Domestic Politics," 454–56.

72. Risse-Kappen, "Ideas Do Not Float Freely," 208.

73. Moravcsik, "Explaining International Human Rights Regimes."

74. Cortell and Davis, "How Do International Institutions Matter?" 451–78.

Bibliography

GOVERNMENT DOCUMENTS

"Actas de la Comisión de Estudio de las Leyes Orgánicas Constitucionales," 1983–88.
"Actas de Sesiones de la Honorable Junta de Gobierno," 1973–89.
"Actas de Sesiones del Consejo del Estado," 1976–88.
Actas Oficiales de la Comisión Constituyente. Santiago: Talleres Gráficos de la Gendarmería de Chile, 1973–78.
Comisión de Estudio de la Nueva Constitución Política de la República de Chile. *Anteproyecto Constitucional y Sus Fundamentos.* Santiago: Editorial Jurídica de Chile, n.d.
Consejo del Estado. "Informe y Proyecto de la Nueva Constitución Política del Estado," 1980.
Constitution of Chile, 1980.
Declaración de Principios, 1974.
Realidad y Destino de Chile. Santiago: Editora Nacional Gabriela Mistral, n.d.
"Transcripciones y Antecedentes de los Decretos Leyes," 1973–80.
"Transcripciones y Antecedentes de las Leyes," 1981–89.

INTERVIEWS

This list is organized in alphabetical order. The interviews occurred from June to July 1992 and from September 1993 to May 1994 in Santiago, Chile.
Fernando Agüero, industrialist
Alvaro Bardón, economist who held various cabinet posts
Rosemarie Bornand, human rights lawyer in the Vicariate of Solidarity
Francisco Bulnes, conservative politician
Julio Canessa, army general who held various government posts, including junta member
Alberto Cardemil, conservative politician and under secretary to the interior minister
Juan de Dios Carmona, conservative politician and government advisor
Ascanio Cavallo, journalist
José Luis Cea, legal scholar

Malcolm Coad, journalist
Sergio Covarrubias, secretary general of the presidency
Francisco Javier Cuadra, secretary general of the government
Gustavo Cuevas, scholar and member of junta legislative committees
Manuel Délano, journalist
Mario Duvauchelle, navy admiral and junta legislative secretary
Sergio Fernández, interior minister
Ricardo García Rodríguez, interior minister
Ignacio González, journalist
Mónica González, journalist
Jorge Guerrero, industrialist
Francisco Herreros, journalist
Hernán Larraín, conservative politician
Rafael Larraín, secretary to various government organizations
Carlos López, secretary general of the Chilean Commission of Human
    Rights
Fernando Lyon, army general and legal advisor to Pinochet
Alfonso Márquez de la Plata, agriculturalist who held various cabinet posts
Sergio Marras, journalist
Fernando Matthei, air force general, junta member
Odlanier Mena, army general, head of the CNI
Jorge Olave, journalist
Juan Luis Ossa, conservative politician
María Eugenia Oyarzún, journalist
Roberto Palumbo, conservative politician
Hermógenes Pérez de Arce, journalist and member of junta legislative
    committees
Manuel Salazar, journalist
Abraham Santibáñez, journalist
Oscar Sepúlveda, journalist
Hernán Somerville, banker who held various government posts
Ernesto Videla, army general who held various government posts
Federico Willoughby, journalist and advisor to Pinochet   .
Cristián Zéjers, journalist

SECONDARY SOURCES

Ackerman, Holly. "Strategic Calculation and Democratic Society: The
    Cuban Democratic Resistance in the 1960s and 1990s." Paper presented

at the Twenty-first Congress of the Latin American Studies Association, Chicago, 1998.

Acuña, Gastón, Federico M. Willoughby, and Pablo Rodríguez. *Qué es el Nacionalismo Hoy? Síntesis de un Ideario.* Santiago: Artimpres, 1983.

Adams, Paul H. "Suspension of Generalized System of Preferences from Chile – The Proper Use of a Trade Provision?" *The George Washington Journal of International Law and Economics* 23, no. 2 (1989): 501-30.

Agency for International Development. *U.S. Overseas Loans and Grants and Assistance from International Organizations.* Washington DC: U.S. Government.

Ahumada, Eugenio, Rodrigo Atria, Javier Luis Egaña, Augusto Gógora, Carmen Quesney, Gustavo Saball, and Gustavo Villalobos. *Chile: La Memoria Prohibida.* Santiago: Pehuén, 1989.

Amnesty International. *Government Crackdown on Dissent.* New York: Amnesty International, 1996.

———. *Cuba: New Cases of Prisoners of Conscience and Possible Prisoners of Conscience.* New York: Amnesty International, 1998.

Angell, Alan. "Unions and Workers in Chile during the 1980s." In *The Struggle for Democracy in Chile, 1982-1990*, edited by Paul Drake and Ivan Jaksie, 188-210. Lincoln: University of Nebraska Press, 1991.

———. "International Support for the Chilean Opposition 1973-1989: Political Parties and the Role of Exiles." In *The International Dimensions of Democratization: Europe and the Americas*, edited by Laurence Whitehead, 175-200. New York: Oxford University Press, 1996.

Arms Control and Disarmament Agency. *World Military Expenditures and Arms Transfers.* Washington DC: U.S. Government.

Arriagada, Genaro. "The Legal and Institutional Framework of the Armed Forces in Chile." In *Military Rule in Chile: Dictatorship and Oppositions*, edited by J. Samuel Valenzuela and Arturo Valenzuela, 117-43. Baltimore: Johns Hopkins University Press, 1986.

———. *El Pensamiento Político de los Militares.* Santiago: Editorial Aconcagua, 1986.

———. *Pinochet: The Politics of Power.* Boston: Unwin Hyman, 1988.

Barkin, J. Samuel, and Bruce Cronin. "The State and the Nation: Changing Norms and the Rules of Sovereignty in International Relations." *International Organization* 48, no. 1 (1994): 107-30.

Barrera, Manuel, and J. Samuel Valenzuela. "The Development of Labor Movement Opposition to the Military Regime." In *Military Rule in Chile:*

Dictatorships and Oppositions, edited by J. Samuel Valenzuela and Arturo Valenzuela, 230–69. Baltimore: Johns Hopkins University Press, 1986.

Barros, Robert. "By Reason and Force: Military Constitutionalism in Chile, 1973–1989." Ph.D. diss., University of Chicago, 1996.

Black, David. "The Long and Winding Road: International Norms and Domestic Political Change in South Africa." In *The Power of Human Rights: International Norms and Domestic Change*, edited by Thomas Risse, Stephen C. Ropp, and Kathryn Sikkink, 78–108. New York: Cambridge University Press, 1999.

Blanc, Neville. *La Constitución Chilena*. 2 vols. Santiago: Centro de Estudios y Asistencia Legislativa, Universidad Católica de Valparaiso, 1990.

Branch, Taylor, and Eugene M. Propper. *Labyrinth*. New York: Viking Press, 1982.

Brysk, Alison. *The Politics of Human Rights in Argentina: Protest, Change and Democratization*. Stanford: Stanford University Press, 1994.

Bull, Hedley. *The Anarchical Society*. New York: Columbia University Press, 1977.

Bulnes, Luz. *Constitución Política de la República de Chile: Concordancias, Anotaciones y Fuentes*. Santiago: Editorial Jurídica de Chile, 1981.

Cardoso, Eliana, and Ann Helwege. *Cuba after Communism*. Cambridge: MIT Press, 1992.

Carleton, David, and Michael Stohl. "The Foreign Policy of Human Rights: Rhetoric and Reality from Jimmy Carter to Ronald Reagan." *Human Rights Quarterly* 7, no. 2 (1985): 205–31.

Carr, Edward Hallett. *Twenty Years Crisis, 1919–1939: An Introduction to the Study of International Relations*. New York: Harper and Row, 1964.

Carrasco, Sergio. *Génesis y Vigencia de los Textos Constitucionales Chilenos*. Santiago: Editorial Jurídica de Chile, 1983.

———. "Transición y Constitución Política: En el Consejo del Estado y en el Texto Aprobado." *Revista Chilena de Derecho* 11, nos. 2–3 (1984): 241–44.

———. *Alessandri: Su Pensamiento Constitucional — Reseña de Su Vida Pública*. Santiago: Editorial Jurídica de Chile, 1987.

Cassese, Antonio. "Foreign Economic Assistance and Respect for Civil and Political Rights: Chile – A Case Study." *Texas International Law Journal* 14 (1979): 251–63.

Castro, Max J. "Transition and the Ideology of Exile." In *Toward a New Cuba? Legacies of a Revolution*, edited by Miguel Angel Centeno and Mauricio Font, 91–105. Boulder CO: Lynne Rienner, 1997.

Cavallo, Ascanio, Manuel Salazar, and Oscar Sepúlveda. *Chile, 1973-1988: La Historia Oculta del Régimen Militar.* Santiago: Editorial Antártica, 1989.

Cea, José Luis. "Marco Jurídico-Político del Plebiscito de 1988." *Revista de Ciencia Política 9,* no. 2 (1988): 81-104.

Checkel, Jeffrey T. *Ideas and International Political Change: Soviet/Russian Behavior and the End of the Cold War.* New Haven CT: Yale University Press, 1997.

———. "International Norms and Domestic Politics: Bridging the Rationalist-Constructivist Divide." *European Journal of International Relations 3,* no. 4 (1997): 473-95.

———. "The Constructivist Turn in International Relations Theory." *World Politics 50,* no. 2 (1998): 324-48.

———. "Norms, Institutions, and National Identity in Contemporary Europe." *International Studies Quarterly 43,* no. 1 (1999): 83-114.

Chilean National Commission on Truth and Reconciliation. *Report of the Chilean National Commission on Truth and Reconciliation.* Santiago: Chilean National Commission on Truth and Reconciliation, 1993.

Claude, Inis L. "Collective Legitimization as a Political Function of the United Nations." *International Organization 20* (summer 1966): 367-79.

Cohen, Roberta. "Human Rights Diplomacy: The Carter Administration and the Southern Cone." *Human Rights Quarterly 4,* no. 2 (1982): 212-41.

Constable, Pamela, and Arturo Valenzuela. *A Nation of Enemies.* New York: W. W. Norton, 1991.

Contador, Ana María, ed., *Continuismo y Discontinuismo en Chile.* Santiago: Bravo y Allende Editores, 1989.

Correa, Enrique, and José Viera-Gallo. *Iglesia y Dictadura.* Santiago: Centro de Estudios Sociales, 1986.

Correa, Raquel, and Elizabeth Subercaseaux. *Ego Sum Pinochet.* Santiago: Zig-Zag, 1989.

Correa, Raquel, Malú Sierra, and Elizabeth Subercaseaux. *Los Generales del Régimen.* Santiago: Editorial Aconcagua, 1983.

Cortell, Andrew P., and James W. Davis Jr. "How Do International Institutions Matter? The Domestic Impact of International Rules and Norms." *International Studies Quarterly 40,* no. 4 (1996): 451-78.

———. "Understanding the Domestic Impact of International Norms: A Research Agenda." *International Studies Review 2,* no. 1 (2000): 65-87.

Crawford, Neta C., and Audie Klotz, eds., *How Sanctions Work: Lessons from South Africa.* New York: St. Martin's Press, 1999.

Curry, W. Frick, and Diana Horowitz. *Subsidizing Pinochet: Aid and Com-*

fort for the Chilean Dictatorship. Washington DC: Center for International Policy, 1985.

Davis, Nathaniel. *The Last Two Years of Allende*. Ithaca NY: Cornell University Press, 1985.

De la Fuente, Alejandro, and Laurence Glasco. "Are Blacks 'Getting Out of Control'? Racial Attitudes, Revolution, and Political Transition in Cuba." In *Toward a New Cuba? Legacies of a Revolution*, edited by Miguel Angel Centeno and Mauricio Font, 53–71. Boulder CO: Lynne Rienner, 1997.

De Vylder, Stefan. *Allende's Chile: The Political Economy of the Rise and Fall of the Unidad Popular*. Cambridge: Cambridge University Press, 1976.

Del Aguila, Juan M. *Cuba: Dilemmas of a Revolution*. Boulder CO: Westview Press, 1994.

———. "The Party, the Fourth Congress, and the Process of Counter-reform." In *Cuba at a Crossroads: Politics and Economics after the Fourth Party Congress*, edited by Jorge F. Pérez-López, 19–40. Gainesville: University Press of Florida, 1994.

Dessler, David. "What Is at Stake in the Agent-Structure Debate." *International Organization* 43, no. 3 (1989): 441–74.

Detzner, John A. "Utilización de Mecanismos Internacionales en la Protección de Derechos Humanos: El Caso Chileno." In *Derechos Humanos y Democracia: La Contribución de las Organizaciones No Gubernamentales*, edited by Hugo Frühling, 85–108. Santiago: Instituto Interamericano de Derechos Humanos, 1991.

Diamond, Larry. "Promoting Democracy in the 1990s: Actors, Instruments, and Issues." In *Democracy's Victory and Crisis*, edited by Axel Hadenius, 311–70. Cambridge: Cambridge University Press, 1997.

Diamond, Larry, Juan J. Linz, and Seymour Martin Lipset. "Introduction: What Makes for Democracy?" In *Politics in Developing Countries: Comparing Experiences with Democracy*, 2d ed., edited by Diamond, Linz, and Lipset, 1–66. Boulder CO: Lynne Rienner, 1995.

———, eds., *Politics in Developing Countries: Comparing Experiences with Democracy*, 2d ed. Boulder CO: Lynne Rienner, 1995.

Dinges, John, and Saul Landau. *Assassination on Embassy Row*. New York: Pantheon Books, 1980.

Domínguez, Jorge I. "The Secrets of Castro's Staying Power." *Foreign Affairs* 72, no. 2 (1993): 97–107.

———. "Leadership Strategies and Mass Support: Cuban Politics before and after the 1991 Communist Party Congress." In *Cuba at a Crossroads: Politics*

and Economics after the Fourth Party Congress, edited by Jorge F. Pérez-López, 1–18. Gainesville: University Press of Florida, 1994.
———. "Cuba in the International Community in the 1990s." In Beyond Sovereignty: Collectively Defending Democracy in the Americas, edited by Tom Farer, 297–315. Baltimore: Johns Hopkins University Press, 1996.
———. "U.S.-Cuban Relations: From the Cold War to the Colder War." Journal of Inter-American Studies and World Affairs 39, no. 3 (1997): 49–71.
Donnelly, Jack. Universal Human Rights in Theory and Practice. Ithaca NY: Cornell University Press, 1989.
———. "Progress in Human Rights." In Progress in Postwar International Relations, edited by Emanuel Adler and Beverly Crawford, 312–58. New York: Columbia University Press, 1991.
———. International Human Rights, 2d ed. Boulder CO: Westview Press, 1998.
Drezner, Daniel W. "Conflict Expectations and the Paradox of Economic Coercion," International Studies Quarterly 42, no. 4 (1998): 700–731.
Eckstein, Harry. "Case Study and Theory in Political Science." In Handbook of Political Science: Strategies of Inquiry, vol. 7, edited by Fred I. Greenstein and Nelson W. Polsby, 79–138. Reading MA: Addison-Wesley, 1975.
Eckstein, Susan Eva. Back from the Future: Cuba under Castro. Princeton NJ: Princeton University Press, 1994.
Ensalaco, Mark. Chile under Pinochet: Recovering the Truth. Philadelphia: University of Pennsylvania Press, 2000.
Erisman, H. Michael. "U.S.-Cuban Relations: Moving beyond the Cold War to the New International Order?" In The Repositioning of U.S.-Caribbean Relations in the New World Order, edited by Ransford W. Palmer, 51–81. Westport CT: Praeger, 1997.
Evangelista, Matthew. "Transnational Relations and Security Policy." International Organization 49, no. 1 (1995): 1–38.
Evans, Peter B., Harold K. Jacobson, and Robert D. Putnam, eds., Double-Edged Diplomacy: International Bargaining and Domestic Politics. Berkeley: University of California Press, 1993.
Evans, Tony. U.S. Hegemony and the Project of Universal Human Rights. New York: St. Martin's Press, 1996.
Falk, Richard A. "Theoretical Foundations of Human Rights." In Human Rights in the World Community: Issues and Action, edited by Richard Pierre Claude and Burns H. Weston, 31–42. Philadelphia: University of Pennsylvania Press, 1992.
Farer, Tom J. "The United Nations and Human Rights: More Than a Whimper, Less Than a Roar." Human Rights Quarterly 9, no. 4 (1987): 550–86.

——, ed. *Beyond Sovereignty: Collectively Defending Democracy in the Americas.* Baltimore: Johns Hopkins University Press, 1996.

——. "The Rise of the Inter-American Human Rights Regime: No Longer a Unicorn, Not Yet an Ox." *Human Rights Quarterly* 19, no. 3 (1997): 510–46.

Fernández, Sergio. *Mi Lucha por la Democracia.* Santiago: Editorial los Andes, 1994.

Finnemore, Martha. *National Interests in International Society.* Ithaca NY: Cornell University Press, 1996.

Finnemore, Martha, and Kathryn Sikkink. "International Norm Dynamics and Political Change." *International Organization* 52, no. 4 (1998): 887–917.

Fleet, Michael. *The Rise and Fall of Chilean Christian Democracy.* Princeton NJ: Princeton University Press, 1985.

Fontaine, Arturo. *La Historia No Contada de los Economistas y el Presidente Pinochet.* Santiago: Zig-Zag, 1988.

Forment, Carlos. "Political Practice and the Rise of an Ethnic Enclave: The Cuban American Case, 1959–1979." *Theory and Society* 18 (January 1989): 47–81.

Forsythe, David P. "Congress and Human Rights in U.S. Foreign Policy: The Fate of General Legislation." *Human Rights Quarterly* 9, no. 3 (1987): 382–404.

——. "Human Rights, the United States and the Organization of American States." *Human Rights Quarterly* 13, no. 1 (1991): 66–98.

——. *Human Rights and Peace.* Lincoln: University of Nebraska Press, 1993.

——. "Human Rights and U.S. Foreign Policy: Two Levels, Two Worlds." In *Politics and Human Rights,* edited by David Beetham, 111–30. Oxford: Blackwell Publishers, 1995.

——. *Human Rights in International Relations.* Cambridge: Cambridge University Press, 2000.

Foxley, Alejandro. "The Neoconservative Economic Experiment in Chile." In *Military Rule in Chile: Dictatorship and Oppositions,* edited by J. Samuel Valenzuela and Arturo Valenzuela, 13–50. Baltimore: Johns Hopkins University Press, 1986.

Franck, Thomas M. *The Power of Legitimacy among Nations.* New York: Oxford University Press, 1990.

Fraser, Arvonne. "Becoming Human: The Origins and Development of Women's Human Rights." *Human Rights Quarterly* 21, no. 4 (1999): 853–906.

Fruhling, Hugo. "Stages of Repression and the Legal Strategy for the Defense of Human Rights in Chile: 1973–1980." *Human Rights Quarterly* 5, no. 4 (1983): 510–33.

———. "Nonprofit Organizations as Opposition to Authoritarian Rule: The Case of Human Rights Organizations in Chile." In *The Nonprofit Sector in International Perspective*, edited by Estelle James, 358–76. New York: Oxford University Press, 1989.

Fruhling, Hugo, and Patricio Orellana. "Organismos No Gubernamentales de Derechos Humanos bajo Regímenes Autoritarios y en la Transición Democrática: El Caso Chileno desde una Perspectiva Comparada." In *Derechos Humanos y Democracia: La Contribución de las Organizaciones No Gubernamentales*, edited by Hugo Fruhling, 25–83. Santiago: Instituto Interamericano de Derechos Humanos, 1991.

García, María Cristina. *Havana USA: Cuban Exiles and Cuban Americans in South Florida, 1959–1994*. Berkeley: University of California Press, 1996.

Garretón, Manuel Antonio. "Political Processes in an Authoritarian Regime: The Dynamics of Institutionalization and Opposition in Chile, 1973–1979." In *Military Rule in Chile: Dictatorship and Oppositions*, edited by J. Samuel Valenzuela and Arturo Valenzuela, 144–83. Baltimore: Johns Hopkins University Press, 1986.

———. "Popular Mobilization and the Military Regime in Chile: The Complexities of the Invisible Transition." In *Power and Popular Protest: Latin American Social Movements*, edited by Susan Eckstein, 259–77. Berkeley: University of California Press, 1989.

———. "The Political Opposition and the Party System under the Military Regime." In *The Struggle for Democracy in Chile, 1982–1990*, edited by Paul Drake and Iván Jaksic, 211–50. Lincoln: University of Nebraska Press, 1991.

Garretón, Manuel Antonio, and Tomás Moulián. *Análisis Coyuntural y Proceso Político: Las Fases del Conflicto en Chile (1970–73)*. San José, Costa Rica: Editorial Universitaria Centro-Americana, 1978.

Geldenhuys, Deon. *Isolated States: A Comparative Analysis*. Cambridge: Cambridge University Press, 1992.

George, Alexander, and Timothy J. McKeown. "Case Studies and Theories of Organizational Decision Making." In *Advances in Information Processing in Organizations*, vol. 2, edited by Robert F. Coulam and Richard A. Smith, 21–58. Greenwich CT: Jai Press, 1985.

Giuliano, Maurizio. *El Caso CEA: Intelectuales e Inquisidores en Cuba*. Miami: Ediciones Universal, 1998.

Gourevitch, Peter. *Politics in Hard Times: Comparative Responses to International Economic Crises*. Ithaca NY: Cornell University Press, 1986.

Grundy, Kenneth W. *South Africa: Domestic Crisis and Global Challenge.* Boulder CO: Westview Press, 1991.

Gunn, Gillian. "Cuba's NGOs: Government Puppets or Seeds of Civil Society?" Cuban Briefing Paper Number 7. Washington DC: Georgetown University, 1995.

Guzmán, Jaime. *Escritos Personales.* Santiago: Zig-Zag, 1992.

Hawkins, Darren. "Domestic Responses to International Pressure: Human Rights in Authoritarian Chile." *European Journal of International Relations* 3, no. 4 (1997): 403–34.

———. "Human Rights Norms and Networks in Authoritarian Chile." In *Restructuring World Politics: Transnational Social Movements, Networks, and Norms,* edited by Sanjeev Khagram, James Riker, and Kathryn Sikkink. Minneapolis: University of Minnesota Press, 2002.

Hufbauer, Gary Clyde, Jeffrey J. Schott, and Kimberly Ann Elliott. *Economic Sanctions Reconsidered,* 2d ed. Vol. 1, *History and Current Policy.* Vol. 2, *Supplemental Case Histories.* Washington DC: Institute for International Economics, 1990.

Human Rights Watch. *Improvements without Reform.* New York: Human Rights Watch, 1995.

Huntington, Samuel. *The Third Wave: Democratization in the Late Twentieth Century.* Norman: University of Oklahoma Press, 1991.

Hurd, Ian. "Legitimacy and Authority in International Politics." *International Organization* 53, no. 2 (1999): 379–408.

Hutchison, Elizabeth Q. "El Movimiento de Derechos Humanos bajo el Régimen Autoritario, 1973–1988." In *El Movimiento de Derechos Humanos en Chile, 1973–1990,* edited by Patricio Orellana and Elizabeth Q. Hutchison, 70–142. Santiago: Centro de Estudios Políticos Latinoamericanos Simón Bolívar, 1991.

Inter-American Commission on Human Rights. Organization of American States. *Report on the Situation of Human Rights in Chile.* Washington DC: Organization of American States, 1985.

International Commission of the Latin American Studies Association to Observe the Chilean Plebiscite. "The Chilean Plebiscite: A First Step toward Redemocratization." *LASA Forum* 19, no. 4 (1989): 18–36.

International Human Rights Law Group. *Report on the Chilean Electoral Process.* Washington DC: International Human Rights Law Group, 1987.

———. *Chile: The Plebiscite and Beyond.* Washington DC: International Human Rights Law Group, 1989.

Johnstone, Frederick. "South Africa." In *International Handbook of Human*

Rights, edited by Jack Donnelly and Rhoda Howard, 339-57. Westport CT: Greenwood Press, 1987.

Kamminga, Menno T. *Inter-State Accountability for Violations of Human Rights*. Philadelphia: University of Pennsylvania Press, 1992.

Keck, Margaret, and Kathryn Sikkink. *Activists beyond Borders: Advocacy Networks in International Politics*. Ithaca NY: Cornell University Press, 1998.

Keeler, John T. S. "Opening the Window for Reform: Mandates, Crises, and Extraordinary Policy-Making." *Comparative Political Studies* 25, no. 4 (1993): 433-86.

Keohane, Robert. *After Hegemony: Cooperation and Discord in the World Political Economy*. Princeton NJ: Princeton University Press, 1984.

———. "Neoliberal Institutionalism: A Perspective on World Politics." In *International Institutions and State Power*, edited by Robert Keohane. Boulder CO: Westview Press, 1989.

King, Gary, Robert Keohane, and Sidney Verba. *Designing Social Inquiry: Scientific Inference in Qualitative Research*. Princeton NJ: Princeton University Press, 1994.

Klotz, Audie. "Norms and Sanctions: Lessons from the Socialization of South Africa." *Review of International Studies* 22, no. 2 (1996): 173-90.

———. *Norms in International Relations: The Struggle against Apartheid*. Ithaca NY: Cornell University Press, 1996.

Krasner, Stephen D. "Sovereignty, Regimes, and Human Rights." In *Regime Theory and International Relations*, edited by Volker Rittberger, 139-67. Oxford: Clarendon Press, 1993.

Larraín, Felipe. "The Economic Challenges of Democratic Development." In *The Struggle for Democracy in Chile, 1982-1990*, edited by Paul W. Drake and Iván Jaksic, 276-301. Lincoln: University of Nebraska, 1991.

Lauren, Paul Gordon. *The Evolution of International Human Rights: Visions Seen*. Philadelphia: University of Pennsylvania Press, 1998.

Legro, Jeffrey W. "Which Norms Matter? Revisiting the 'Failure' of Internationalism." *International Organization* 51, no. 1 (1997): 31-63.

Letelier, Isabel, and Michael Moffitt. "Supporting Repression: Multinational Banks in Chile." *Race and Class: A Journal for Black and Third World Liberation* 20, no. 2 (1978): 111-28.

Linz, Juan. *The Breakdown of Democratic Regimes: Crisis, Breakdown, and Reequilibration*. Vol. 1 of *The Breakdown of Democratic Regimes*, edited by Juan Linz and Alfred Stepan. Baltimore: Johns Hopkins University Press, 1978.

Linz, Juan, and Alfred Stepan. *Problems of Democratic Transition and Consolidation*. Baltimore: Johns Hopkins University Press, 1996.

Loveman, Brian. "Military Dictatorship and Political Opposition in Chile, 1973–1986." *Journal of Interamerican Studies and World Affairs* 28, no. 4 (1986–87): 1–38.

————. *The Constitution of Tyranny: Regimes of Exception in Spanish America.* Pittsburgh: University of Pittsburgh Press, 1993.

Loveman, Brian, and Thomas M. Davies Jr. *The Politics of Antipolitics: The Military in Latin America.* Wilmington DE: Scholarly Resources, 1997.

Lowden, Pamela. *Moral Opposition to Authoritarian Rule in Chile, 1973–90.* New York: St. Martin's Press, 1996.

Mainwaring, Scott. "Transitions to Democracy and Democratic Consolidation: Theoretical and Comparative Issues." In *Issues in Democratic Consolidation: The New South American Democracies in Comparative Perspective,* edited by Scott Mainwaring, Guillermo O'Donnell, and J. Samuel Valenzuela, 294–341. Notre Dame: University of Notre Dame Press, 1992.

Mangaliso, Mzamo. "Disinvestment by Multinational Corporations." In *How Sanctions Work: Lessons from South Africa,* edited by Neta C. Crawford and Audie Klotz, 145–58. New York: St. Martin's Press, 1999.

Marras, Sergio. *Palabra de Soldado.* Santiago: Las Ediciones de Ornitorrinco, 1989.

————. *Confesiones: Entrevistas de Sergio Marras.* Santiago: Las Ediciones de Ornitorrinco, 1990.

Martin, Lisa L., and Kathryn Sikkink. "U.S. Policy toward Human Rights in Argentina and Guatemala, 1973–1980." In *Double-Edged Diplomacy: International Bargaining and Domestic Politics,* edited by Peter Evans, Harold Jacobson, and Robert Putnam. Berkeley: University of California Press, 1993.

Martin, Lisa L., and Beth Simmons. "Theories and Empirical Studies of International Institutions." *International Organization* 52, no. 4 (1998): 729–57.

Martínez, José Luis. *La Cuba Disidente.* Montevideo: Editorial Fin de Siglo, 1996.

Mastanduno, Michael, David A. Lake, and G. John Ikenberry. "Toward a Realist Theory of State Action." *International Studies Quarterly* 33, no. 4 (1989): 457–74.

McAdam, Doug, John D. McCarthy, and Mayer Zald. "Introduction: Opportunities, Mobilizing Structures, and Framing Processes – Toward a Synthetic, Comparative Perspective on Social Movements." In *Comparative Perspectives on Social Movements: Political Opportunities, Mobilizing Struc-*

tures, and Cultural Framings, edited by Doug McAdam, John D. McCarthy, and Mayer Zald, 1–22. New York: Cambridge University Press, 1996.

McCormick, James M., and Neil J. Mitchell. "Human Rights Violations, Umbrella Concepts, and Empirical Analysis." World Politics 49, no. 4 (1997): 510–25.

Mearsheimer, John J. "The False Promise of International Institutions." International Security 19, no. 3 (1994): 5–49.

Medina, Cecilia. The Battle of Human Rights: Gross, Systematic Violations and the Inter-American System. Dordrecht, Netherlands: Martinus Nijhoff Publishers, 1988.

Mercer, Jonathan. Reputation and International Politics. Ithaca NY: Cornell University Press, 1996.

Mesa-Lago, Carmelo. "Cambio de Régimen o Cambios en el Régimen? Aspectos Políticos y Económicos." Encuentro de la Cultura Cubana, nos. 6–7 (1997): 36–43.

Meyer, John W., David John Frank, Ann Hironaka, Evan Schofer, and Nancy Brandon Tuma. "The Structuring of a World Environmental Regime, 1870–1990." International Organization 51, no. 4 (1997): 623–51.

Montealegre, Hernán. La Seguridad del Estado y los Derechos Humanos. Santiago: Academia de Humanismo Cristiano, 1979.

Montupil, Fernando, ed., Exilio, Derechos Humanos, y Democracia. Santiago: Servicios Gráficos Caupolicán, 1993.

Moravcsik, Andrew. "Explaining International Human Rights Regimes: Liberal Theory and Western Europe." European Journal of International Relations 1, no. 2 (1995): 157–89.

———. "Taking Preferences Seriously: A Liberal Theory of International Politics." International Organization 51, no. 4 (1997): 513–53.

Moreno, David. "The Cuban Model: Political Empowerment in Miami." In Pursuing Power: Latinos and the Political System, edited by F. Chris Garcia, 208–26. Notre Dame: University of Notre Dame Press, 1997.

Morgan, T. Clifton, and Valerie L. Schwebach. "Fools Suffer Gladly: The Use of Economic Sanctions in International Crises." International Studies Quarterly 41, no. 1 (1997): 27–50.

Morgenthau, Hans. Politics among Nations: The Struggle for Power and Peace, 2d ed. New York: Alfred A. Knopf, 1959.

Moulián, Tomás, and Isabel Torres. "La Derecha Política en Chile." In Muerte y Resurrección: Los Partidos Políticos en el Autoritarianismo y Las Transiciones del Cono Sur, edited by Marcelo Cavarozzi and Manuel Antonio Garretón. Santiago: FLACSO, 1989.

Munck, Gerardo. *Authoritarianism and Democratization: Soldiers and Workers in Argentina, 1976–1983.* University Park PA: Pennsylvania State University Press, 1998.

Muñoz, Heraldo. "La Inserción Internacional de los Partidos de Izquierda Chilenos: Un Análysis en la Perspectiva de la Redemocratización." *Alternativas* no. 3 (1984): 41–87.

———. *Las Relaciones Exteriores del Gobierno Militar Chileno.* Santiago: PROSPEL-CERC, 1986.

———. "Chile: The Limits of Success." In *Exporting Democracy*, edited by Abraham Lowenthal, 39–52. Baltimore: Johns Hopkins University Press, 1991.

Muñoz, Heraldo, and Carlos Portales. *Elusive Friendship: A Survey of U.S.-Chilean Relations.* Boulder CO: Lynne Rienner, 1991.

Nye, Joseph S., Jr. *Bound to Lead: The Changing Nature of American Power.* New York: Basic Books, 1990.

O'Donnell, Guillermo, and Philippe C. Schmitter. *Transitions from Authoritarian Rule: Tentative Conclusions about Uncertain Democracies.* Baltimore: Johns Hopkins University Press, 1986.

O'Meara, Dan. *Forty Lost Years: The Apartheid State and the Politics of the National Party, 1948–1994.* Athens: Ohio University Press, 1996.

O'Shaughnessy, Hugh. *Pinochet: The Politics of Torture.* Washington Square: New York University Press, 2000.

Oppenheim, Lois Hecht. *Politics in Chile: Democracy, Authoritarianism, and the Search for Development,* 2d ed. Boulder: Westview Press, 1998.

Orellana, Patricio. "Los Organismos de Derechos Humanos en Chile hacia 1985." In *El Movimiento de Derechos Humanos en Chile, 1973–1990*, edited by Patricio Orellana and Elizabeth Q. Hutchison, 9–68. Santiago: Centro de Estudios Políticos Latinoamericanos Simón Bolívar, 1991.

Orellana, Patricio, and Elizabeth Q. Hutchison, eds., *El Movimiento de Derechos Humanos en Chile, 1973–1990.* Santiago: Centro de Estudios Políticos Latinoamericanos Simón Bolívar, 1991.

Oxhorn, Philip D. *Organizing Civil Society: The Popular Sectors and the Struggle for Democracy in Chile.* University Park PA: Pennsylvania State University Press, 1995.

Pagnucco, Ron. "The Transnational Strategies of the Service of Peace and Justice in Latin America." In *Transnational Social Movements and Global Politics: Solidarity beyond the State*, edited by Jackie Smith, Charles Chatfield, and Ron Pagnucco, 123–38. Syracuse NY: Syracuse University Press, 1997.

Pape, Robert A. "Why Economic Sanctions Do Not Work." *International Security* 22, no. 2 (1997): 90–136.

Pérez-López, Jorge F. "The Cuban Economy in the Age of Hemispheric Integration." *Journal of Interamerican Studies and World Affairs* 39, no. 3 (1997): 3–48.

Pérez-Stable, Marifeli. " 'We Are the Only Ones and There Is No Alternative': Vanguard Party Politics in Cuba, 1975–1991." In *Conflict and Change in Cuba*, edited by Enrique A. Baloyra and James A. Morris, 67–85. Albuquerque: University of New Mexico Press, 1993.

Pinto-Duschinsky, Michael. "Foreign Political Aid: The German Political Foundations and Their U.S. Counterparts." *International Affairs* 67, no. 1 (1991): 33–63.

Pion-Berlin, David. *The Ideology of State Terror: Economic Doctrine and Political Repression in Argentina and Peru.* Boulder CO: Lynne Rienner, 1989.

Poe, Steven C. "Human Rights and U.S. Foreign Aid: A Review of Quantitative Studies and Suggestions for Future Research." *Human Rights Quarterly* 12, no. 4 (1990): 499–512.

Poe, Steven C., and C. Neal Tate. "Repression of Human Rights to Personal Integrity in the 1980s: A Global Analysis." *American Political Science Review* 88, no. 4 (1994): 853–72.

Portales, Carlos. "External Factors and the Authoritarian Regime." In *The Struggle for Democracy in Chile, 1982–1990*, edited by Paul Drake and Iván Jaksic, 251–75. Lincoln: University of Nebraska Press, 1991.

Price, Richard. "A Genealogy of the Chemical Weapons Taboo." *International Organization* 49, no. 1 (1995): 73–103.

Price, Robert M. *The Apartheid State in Crisis: Political Transformation in South Africa, 1975–1990.* New York: Oxford University Press, 1991.

Puryear, Jeffrey M. "Building Democracy: Foreign Donors and Chile." Conference Paper no. 57. The Columbia University–New York University Consortium, 1991.

———. *Thinking Politics.* Baltimore: Johns Hopkins University Press, 1994.

Putnam, Harold. "Diplomacy and Domestic Politics: The Logic of Two-Level Games." *International Organization* 42, no. 3 (1988): 427–60.

Remmer, Karen. "Political Demobilization in Chile, 1973–1978." *Comparative Politics* 12, no. 3 (1980): 275–301.

———. "Neopatrimonialism: The Politics of Military Rule in Chile, 1973–1987." *Comparative Politics* 21, no. 2 (1989): 149–70.

Risse, Thomas. " 'Let's argue!' Communicative Action in World Politics," *International Organization* 54, no. 1 (2000): 1–39.

Risse, Thomas, and Stephen C. Ropp. "International Human Rights Norms and Domestic Change: Conclusions." In *The Power of Human Rights: International Norms and Domestic Change*, edited by Thomas Risse, Stephen C. Ropp, and Kathryn Sikkink, 234–78. Cambridge: Cambridge University Press.

Risse, Thomas, and Kathryn Sikkink. "The Socialization of International Human Rights Norms into Domestic Practices." In *The Power of Human Rights: International Norms and Domestic Change*, edited by Thomas Risse, Stephen C. Ropp, and Kathryn Sikkink, 1–38. Cambridge: Cambridge University Press, 1999.

Risse-Kappen, Thomas. "Ideas Do Not Float Freely: Transnational Coalitions, Domestic Structures, and the End of the Cold War." *International Organization* 48, no. 2 (1994): 185–214.

———. "Bringing Transnational Relations Back In: Introduction." In *Bringing Transnational Relations Back In: Non-State Actors, Domestic Structures and International Institutions*, edited by Thomas Risse-Kappen, 3–33. Cambridge: Cambridge University Press, 1995.

Rodríguez, Pablo. "Democracia Liberal o Democracia Orgánica?" *Cuadernos del Instituto de Ciencia Política*, no. 12 (January 1977): 1–34.

———. "Poder Político y Poder Social." *Política y Geoestrategia*, no. 41 (1987): 17–26.

Ron, James. "Varying Methods of State Violence." *International Organization* 51, no. 2 (1997): 275–300.

Salazar, Manuel. *Guzmán: Quién, Cómo, y Por Qué*. Santiago: Ediciones BAT, 1994.

———. *Contreras: Historia de un Intocable*. Santiago: Grijalbo, 1995.

Salzberg, John, and Donald D. Young. "The Parliamentary Role in Implementing International Human Rights: A U.S. Example." *Texas International Law Journal* 12 (1977): 251–78.

Sánchez, Domingo. "Las Resoluciones Internacionales sobre Chile: Un Desafío para la Futura Democracia." *Revista Chilena de Derechos Humanos*, no. 12 (1990): 61–97.

Schoultz, Lars. *Human Rights and United States Policy toward Latin America*. Princeton NJ: Princeton University Press, 1981.

Schulz, Donald E. "Can Castro Survive?" *Journal of Interamerican Studies and World Affairs* 35, no. 1 (1993): 89–117.

Shin, Doh Chull. "On the Third Wave of Democratization: A Synthesis and Evaluation of Recent Theory and Research." *World Politics* 47, no. 1 (1994): 135–70.

Sigmund, Paul. *The Overthrow of Allende and the Politics of Chile*. Pittsburgh: University of Pittsburgh Press, 1977.

———. *The United States and Democracy in Chile*. Baltimore: Johns Hopkins University Press, 1993.

Sikkink, Kathryn. "Human Rights, Principled Issue Networks, and Sovereignty in Latin America." *International Organization* 47, no. 3 (1993): 411–41.

———. "The Power of Principled Ideas: Human Rights Policies in the United States and Western Europe." In *Ideas and Foreign Policy: Beliefs, Institutions, and Political Change*, edited by Judith Goldstein and Robert Keohane, 139–70. Ithaca NY: Cornell University Press, 1993.

———. "The Emergence, Evolution, and Effectiveness of the Latin American Human Rights Network." In *Constructing Democracy: Human Rights, Citizenship, and Society in Latin America*, edited by Elizabeth Jelin and Eric Hershberg, 59–84. Boulder CO: Westview Press, 1996.

Silva, Eduardo. "The Political Economy of Chile's Regime Transition: From Radical to 'Pragmatic' Neo-liberal Policies." In *The Struggle for Democracy in Chile, 1982–1990*, edited by Paul W. Drake and Iván Jaksic, 98–127. Lincoln: University of Nebraska Press, 1991.

Sisk, Timothy D. *Democratization in South Africa*. Princeton NJ: Princeton University Press, 1995.

Smith, Brian H. *The Church and Politics in Chile: Challenges to Modern Catholicism*. Princeton NJ: Princeton University Press, 1982.

———. "Old Allies, New Enemies: The Catholic Church as Opposition to Military Rule in Chile, 1973–1979." In *Military Rule in Chile: Dictatorships and Oppositions*, edited by J. Samuel Valenzuela and Arturo Valenzuela, 270–303. Baltimore: Johns Hopkins University Press, 1986.

Smith, Wayne S. "Cuba's Long Reform." *Foreign Affairs* 75, no. 2 (1996): 99–112.

Somavía, Juan, and Juan Gabriel Valdés. "Las Relaciones entre los Gobiernos de Estados Unidos y Chile en el Marco de la Política de Derechos Humanos." *Cuadernos Semestrales — Estados Unidos: Perspectiva Latinoamericana* 6 (1979): 255–77.

Stockholm International Peace Research Institute. *World Armaments and Disarmament: SIPRI Yearbook*. Cambridge: MIT Press, various years.

Suchman, Mark C. "Managing Legitimacy: Strategic and Institutional Approaches." *Academy of Management Review* 20, no. 3 (1995): 571–610.

Thomas, Daniel C. *The Helsinki Effect*. Princeton NJ: Princeton University Press, 2001.

U.S. Congress. Senate. Select Committee on Intelligence Activities. *Covert Action in Chile, 1963–1973*. 94th Congress, 1st session, 1975.

248   Bibliography

Valdés, Juan Gabriel. *Pinochet's Economists: The Chicago School in Chile*. Cambridge: Cambridge University Press, 1995.

Valenzuela, Arturo. *The Breakdown of Democratic Regimes: Chile*. Vol. 3 of *The Breakdown of Democratic Regimes*, edited by Juan Linz and Alfred Stepan. Baltimore: Johns Hopkins University Press, 1978.

———. "Chile: Origins, Consolidation, and Breakdown of a Democratic Regime." In *Democracy in Developing Countries: Latin America*, edited by Larry Diamond, Juan J. Linz, and Seymour Martin Lipset. Boulder CO: Lynn Rienner, 1989.

———. "The Military in Power: The Consolidation of One-Man Rule." In *The Struggle for Democracy in Chile, 1982–1990*, edited by Paul Drake and Iván Jaksic, 21–77. Lincoln: University of Nebraska Press, 1991.

———. "Chile: Origins and Consolidation of a Latin American Democracy." In *Politics in Developing Countries: Comparing Experiences with Democracy*, edited by Larry Diamond, Juan Linz, and Seymour Martin Lipset, 67–118. 2d ed. Boulder CO: Lynne Rienner, 1995.

Valenzuela, Arturo, and J. Samuel Valenzuela. "Party Oppositions under the Chilean Authoritarian Regime." In *Military Rule in Chile: Dictatorships and Oppositions*, edited by J. Samuel Valenzuela and Arturo Valenzuela, 184–229. Baltimore: Johns Hopkins University Press, 1986.

Valenzuela, Eugenio. *Repertorio de Jurisprudencia del Tribunal Constitucional*. Santiago: Editorial Jurídica de Chile, 1989.

Valenzuela, J. Samuel, and Arturo Valenzuela. Introduction to *Military Rule in Chile: Dictatorship and Oppositions*, edited by J. Samuel Valenzuela and Arturo Valenzuela. Baltimore: Johns Hopkins University Press, 1986.

Valenzuela, María Elena. "The Evolving Roles of Women under Military Rule." In *The Struggle for Democracy in Chile, 1982–1990*, edited by Paul Drake and Iván Jaksic, 161–87. Lincoln: University of Nebraska Press, 1991.

Varas, Augusto. "The Crisis of Legitimacy of Military Rule in the 1980s." In *The Struggle for Democracy in Chile, 1982–1990*, edited by Paul Drake and Iván Jaksic, 73–97. Lincoln: University of Nebraska Press, 1991.

Varas, Augusto and Felipe Agüero. *El Proyecto Político Militar*. Santiago: FLACSO, 1984.

Varas, Florencia. *Gustavo Leigh: El General Disidente*. Santiago: Editorial Aconcagua, 1979.

Vargas, María Carolina. "El Caso Chileno en la Asamblea General y la Comisión de Derechos Humanos de la Organización de las Naciones Unidas." *Revista Chilena de Derechos Humanos*, no. 12 (1990): 31–59.

Vergara, Pilar. *Auge y Caída del Neoliberalismo en Chile.* Santiago: FLACSO, 1985.

Vidal, Hernán. *El Movimiento contra Tortura Sebatián Acevedo.* Minneapolis: Institute for the Study of Ideologies and Literature, 1986.

———. *Dar la Vida por la Vida: Agrupación Chilena de Familiares de Detenidos Desaparecidos.* 2d ed. Santiago: Mosquito Editores, 1996.

Weber, Max. *Economy and Society: An Outline of Interpretive Sociology.* Berkeley: University of California Press, 1978.

Wendt, Alexander. "The Agent-Structure Problem in International Relations Theory." *International Organization* 41, no. 3 (1987): 335–70.

———. "Anarchy Is What States Make of It: The Social Construction of Power Politics." *International Organization* 46, no. 2 (1992): 391–425.

———. *Social Theory of International Politics.* Cambridge: Cambridge University Press, 1999.

Whelan, James R. *Out of the Ashes: Life, Death, and Transfiguration of Democracy in Chile, 1833–1988.* Washington DC: Regnery Gateway, 1989.

Wilson, Richard. "Prosecuting Pinochet: International Crimes in Spanish Domestic Law." *Human Rights Quarterly* 21, no. 4 (1999): 927–79.

Zapata, Patricio. "Jurisprudencia del Tribunal Constitucional." *Revista Chilena de Derecho* 18, no. 2 (1991): 261–330.

Index